What Kind

of

Nation

Thomas Jefferson, John Marshall,
and the Epic Struggle
to Create a United States

James F. Simon

SIMON & SCHUSTER
New York   London   Toronto   Sydney   Singapore

SIMON & SCHUSTER
Rockefeller Center
1230 Avenue of the Americas
New York, NY 10020

Title page illustrations:
Portrait of President Thomas Jefferson (detail) by Rembrandt Peale, © Bettmann/Corbis;
Portrait of John Marshall (detail) by Edward F. Peticolas,
Kirby Collection of Historical Paintings, Lafayette College, Easton, PA

For information regarding special discounts for bulk purchases, please contact
Simon & Schuster Special Sales at 1-800-456-6798 or
business@simonandschuster.com

Designed by Deirdre Amthor

Manufactured in the United States of America

5 7 9 10 8 6 4

Library of Congress Cataloging-in-Publication Data

Simon, James F.
What kind of nation : Thomas Jefferson, John Marshall, and the epic struggle
to create a United States / James F. Simon
p. cm.
Includes bibliographical references and index.
1. Constitutional history—United States. 2. Political questions and judicial power—
United States—History. 3. Executive power—United States—History. 4. United States.
Supreme Court—History. 5. Jefferson, Thomas, 1743–1826. 6. Marshall, John,
1755–1835. 7. United States—Politics and government—1783–1809. I. Title.
KF4541 .S53 2002
342.73'029—dc21   2001055027
ISBN 0-684-84870-8

For Ethan, Lindsay, and Natalie

"He [Jefferson] is among the most ambitious &, I suspect, among the most unforgiving of men. His great power is over the mass of the people & this power is chiefly acquired by professions of democracy. Every check on the wild impulse of the moment is a check on his own power, & he is unfriendly to the source from which it flows. He looks, of course, with ill will at an independent judiciary."

John Marshall

"The great object of my fear is the federal judiciary. That body, like gravity, ever acting with noiseless foot & unalarming advance, [is] gaining ground step by step. . . . Let the eye of vigilance never be closed."

Thomas Jefferson

Contents

WHAT KIND

of

NATION

Prologue

THE AMERICAN MINISTER to France, Thomas Jefferson, had loathed George III from afar for years. Almost a full decade earlier, the thirty-three-year-old Jefferson had denounced the British monarch: *usurper, plunderer, oppressor.* Had his draft of the Declaration of Independence not been edited by the Continental Congress, it would have added that the king of England "waged cruel war against human nature itself."

On March 17, 1786, Jefferson waited at the Court of St. James's to meet the English king. He was accompanied by another hero of the American Revolution, his close friend John Adams, the American minister to Great Britain. They hoped to negotiate a commercial treaty between Great Britain and her former colonies. Jefferson was no longer a young American revolutionary, but a prominent member of an independent government's diplomatic corps. And though the United States was a struggling young confederation, no match in political, economic, or military might for Great Britain, Jefferson expected to be treated with the respect due a representative of a sovereign nation.

At noon on that March day, George III entered the palatial chamber where Jefferson and Adams waited with other foreign envoys to be formally presented. Neither Jefferson nor Adams recorded the event in letters or journals at the time. But as an old man, Jefferson recalled with bitterness the moment that he was introduced to the British king.

Nothing could have been more ungracious, Jefferson remembered, than his introduction to King George and Queen Charlotte. The king barely acknowledged Jefferson's presence, which may have had something to do with the monarch's low regard for the author of the Declaration of Independence.

Adams's grandson, the historian Charles Francis Adams, later provided a vivid explanation for Jefferson's reaction. Upon his grandfather's presentation of Jefferson to the king and queen, they rose from their chairs and turned around so that the two American ministers were faced with their royal posteriors.

Jefferson's sour memory of the event is more important than the fact that modern historians have poked large holes in both Jefferson's and Charles Francis Adams's versions of the event. It is improbable that Queen Charlotte was present in court that day, since, by tradition, George III presided alone at the twice-weekly levees such as the one attended by Jefferson and Adams. The king's practice, moreover, was to greet visitors during a "walkabout" of the room, much as contemporary leaders of state customarily do at official ceremonies. If that was the case, it would have been virtually impossible for King George to turn his back on Jefferson without performing an abrupt about-face, an exercise that no one claimed to have witnessed.

Details aside, Jefferson's antipathy for Great Britain's monarch was real enough, and enduring, as was his abiding mistrust of the motives and policies of His Majesty's government. Those feelings were reinforced when he and Adams met with the marquis of Carmarthen, the English secretary of state for foreign affairs, to work out the terms of a commercial treaty.

Before their meeting with Lord Carmarthen, Adams and Jefferson had discussed the terms that might be included in an agreement. At the instruction of Congress, Adams had already proposed that the resolution of political issues be a part of any commercial treaty. Specifically, Adams requested that any settlement of outstanding claims of British creditors against Americans be combined with an agreement that the British relinquish their military outposts in the old Northwest Territory (as yet, an unfulfilled promise of the 1783 Peace Treaty). Adams had also asked that Great Britain provide financial compensation for slaves and other property expropriated by British troops during the Revolutionary War, a demand of more than diplomatic concern to Jefferson.

While governor of Virginia in 1781, Jefferson was not only forced to retreat from the temporary state capital of Charlottesville by invading British troops, but later discovered that General Cornwallis's soldiers had overrun his Monticello estate, absconded with thirty of his slaves, and burned his entire year's crop of tobacco. Jefferson did not dwell on those past grievances in his strategy session with Adams, or, for that matter, on his steadily mounting debts to British creditors. He focused on general negotiating points, insisting that any treaty include not only absolute commercial reciprocity between the two nations but the exchange of citizenship rights, so that Americans and the British would each enjoy the same protections on the other's soil.

Adams and Jefferson made the oddest of diplomatic couples, both in physical stature and temperament. Adams was short (five feet seven inches), plump, and naturally combative; Jefferson stood over six feet two inches, was lean and long-limbed, and projected an air of cool detachment. Once the American ministers began their discussions with Lord Carmarthen, it became immediately apparent that neither their diplomatic skills nor their careful preparations would be rewarded. The British secretary of state wasted no time in informing the Americans of the cold facts of life between two such unequal nations. He made clear that His Majesty's government would dictate the terms of any treaty, and quickly ruled out any discussion of political issues. The British secretary's tepid attempts to respond to Adams and Jefferson's trade proposals were so vague and evasive, Jefferson observed, that he could not have been serious about an agreement.

In the weeks that followed, Jefferson's initial pessimism deepened. After he and Adams received word that the British Foreign Office would entertain a redrafted proposal from the Americans limited to commercial subjects, Adams and Jefferson worked furiously overnight to rewrite their previously submitted treaty terms. Lord Carmarthen did not respond, though he knew that Adams's and Jefferson's congressional commissions to reach agreement on a treaty were to expire by the end of May.

Later, Jefferson concluded that the British government had never intended to sign a trade treaty with the United States. This was made obvious from the dismissive treatment that he and Adams had received at Whitehall, which, Jefferson surmised, was rooted in British arrogance and the conviction that the British had nothing to gain from a treaty with the fledgling nation.

Lord Carmarthen's attitude toward the American ministers reflected the British assessment of the international status of the new nation they represented. The United States had signed a peace treaty with Great Britain three years earlier, but the end of hostilities had not brought Americans power, prosperity, or, in truth, genuine independence. The mother country still dominated her former colonies, not so much by the sword as by the purse. With Americans' appetite for British manufactured goods, the balance of trade tilted overwhelmingly eastward. And Great Britain did not hesitate to press her advantage. She continued to seal off American goods from the lucrative British West Indies market, while her superior navy patrolled the commercial corridors of the Atlantic and the Caribbean.

Jefferson suspected that there was more to the rough British treatment that he and Adams received than diplomatic calculation. "That nation hates us," Jefferson wrote, "their ministers hate us, and their king, more than all other men."

That harsh assessment was more than reciprocated. Jefferson detested the hauteur that permeated the high echelons of British government and society, and speculated that perhaps it had something to do with their unbalanced, meat-heavy diet. Nor did he like the cold, damp British climate. And he found London's architecture positively "wretched."

Jefferson could not deny, of course, that the British had made significant contributions to Western civilization, and during his seven-week visit, he took full advantage of what the nation had to offer. John and Abigail Adams escorted him to the British Museum and to Covent Garden, where he attended performances of *Macbeth* and *The Merchant of Venice*. He made the requisite tourist's pilgrimage to Shakespeare's birthplace at Stratford-upon-Avon (and recorded the price of admission: one shilling). Adams organized for his guest an extended tour of British estates and gardens, which Jefferson judged superior to any that he had seen in France or the United States. With notebook in hand and a copy of Thomas Whateley's *Observations on Modern Gardening* in his pocket, he took copious notes on his own observations, and later appropriated some of the best ideas for his home and gardens in the Virginia mountains.

No nation, Jefferson admitted, could compete with the British for ingenious mechanical innovations. He was awed by the steam-powered grist mill at Blackfriars on the Thames and predicted that the newly discovered source of energy would soon propel ships. He marveled at a portable copying press that could instantly replicate a letter and bought one for himself, as well as several other gadgets, including a solar microscope, a globe telescope, a protractor, and a thermometer. And, with Abigail Adams, he shopped and shopped, purchasing a new suit, a carriage and plated harness, and a harpsichord for his fourteen-year-old-daughter, Patsy.

For all of the private pleasures that London and the English countryside had provided him, Jefferson was delighted to return to Paris. Among the nations of the world, France had occupied a special place in Jefferson's head and heart since the Revolution, when she gave critical support to the Americans against the British. France offered true heroes to match America's own, such as the brave young nobleman the General Marquis de Lafayette. Jefferson and Lafayette were the best of friends in Paris, where the Frenchman proudly displayed a framed copy of the Declaration of Independence in his study. As Jefferson's most valued political adviser, Lafayette helped the American minister navigate the labyrinthine French governmental bureaucracy. And Jefferson needed all the help he could get as he attempted, with only modest success, to persuade the government to lower the high tariffs on American goods.

By 1786, there were faint rumblings that the French government faced impending bankruptcy and that Louis XVI was incapable of managing a financial crisis or the rising public unrest. Jefferson remained confident that crisis could be averted and that peaceful accommodation could be reached among the king, the nobles and clergy, and the commoners.

In general, Jefferson's attitude toward life and politics had become noticeably more sanguine in Paris, where the gaiety and sophistication of the French had provided the perfect elixir for his low spirits when he arrived in 1784 as minister plenipotentiary to France. At that time, Jefferson's suffering was due to excruciating disappointment and loss that had beset him in Virginia. In 1781, the state legislature had called for an official investigation into his behavior as wartime governor. His detractors charged that he had acted both irresponsibly and cowardly, first, in not making necessary preparations to defend the state, and then in fleeing from invading British troops. Although no investigation ever occurred, Jefferson felt compelled to justify his actions in a powerful speech on the floor of the House of Delegates. But the bad taste of the accusations lingered. And the next year, Jefferson's wife, Martha, died following the birth of their sixth child. Her death left him grief-stricken and responsible for the care of their three surviving children.

Once he had settled into his residence at the Hôtel de Langeac, a spacious three-story villa near the Champs-Élysées, Jefferson's spirits demonstrably brightened. In contrast to his decidedly negative views of the British, Jefferson admired the polite manners and contagious conviviality of the French. He loved their cuisine and fine wines, their stimulating salons and plentiful evening concerts. And he was so impressed by the classical Roman architecture in France, particularly the Maison-Carrée at Nîmes, that he successfully implored Virginia's directors of public buildings to change the design of the state capitol, after the foundation had been laid, to emulate the Nîmes model.

Jefferson had promised his wife on her deathbed that he would never remarry. We now know that he later engaged in a lasting relationship with his beautiful young slave, Sally Hemings, who joined his staff of servants in Paris. And while in the French capital, Jefferson courted Maria Cosway, the enchanting wife of the British miniaturist Richard Cosway. For six weeks in the late summer and fall of 1786, Jefferson and Maria were virtually inseparable, touring galleries, attending concerts in the Tuileries, and strolling in the Bois de Boulogne. Later, Jefferson's ardor for Maria cooled, though they remained friends and long-distance correspondents for decades.

As enamored as Jefferson was with his life in Paris, he kept close tabs on political developments in the United States, primarily through regular correspondence with his Virginia ally, James Madison, who in the summer of 1787 was a delegate to the Constitutional Convention in Philadelphia. Jefferson and Madison had served together in Virginia's legislature. Both men had understood their collaborative roles: Jefferson was the visionary whose ideas and lilting phrases breathed life into the abstract demands for individual rights and liberties. He valued Madison for his extraordinary intellect and shrewd judgment. A subtle, sophisticated political thinker, Madison knew how to translate Jefferson's grand concepts into law. An early example of their successful joint efforts was the passage of the Virginia Statute for Religious Freedom, which called for a strict separation between church and state. Jefferson had contributed the eloquent draft; Madison had devised the winning legislative strategy and, in the process, offered his own brilliant defense of religious liberty.

Madison had much to report to Jefferson after the convention in Philadelphia. The document reflected Madison's and the other framers' commitment to representative democracy under a tripartite federal system. But throughout the document, there were compromises, both among the three branches of the federal government and between the federal government and the states. After the struggle for passage at the Constitutional Convention, Madison and other Federalists knew that they faced formidable opposition to ratification by the states. It would be led by Anti-Federalists, who continued to object to the substantial power given to the federal government at the expense of the states, as well as the absence of a Bill of Rights.

Madison could not have been happy, then, that Jefferson's initial reaction to the document he had worked so mightily to create was unenthusiastic. At first, Jefferson expressed disappointment that a few provisions had not been added to the old Articles of Confederation, which gave the dominant government power to the states, rather than replacing the entire document. With memories of the British monarchy still fresh, Jefferson worried that the renewable four-year term for the U.S. president invited monarchy by another name. Once a president was elected to office, Jefferson feared, he could control the levers of power so that he effectively could hold office for life. Jefferson also shared the Anti-Federalists' concern that the Constitution did not include a Bill of Rights to protect individual citizens from the potential tyranny of a powerful central government. To make matters worse for Madison, reports of Jefferson's reservations about the document circulated publicly and were eagerly repeated by Anti-Federalist leaders, such as Virginia's great orator Patrick Henry, who urged his state's delegates to vote "no" on the Constitution.

By the time Virginia's delegates convened in Richmond on June 2, 1788, to vote on the Constitution, eight states had already approved the document, one short of the number needed for ratification. But the numbers were deceptive and did not guarantee ultimate success. In fact, the Constitution had stirred fierce opposition, even in states that, like Pennsylvania, the Federalists had considered safely in their column. And now came the battle for Virginia, the nation's most populous and prosperous state. The most influential native son, George Washington, was fully supportive of the Constitution. But he was not in Richmond and could only offer his encouragement by letter to Madison, who directed the Federalist forces. That Jefferson was also absent was not necessarily detrimental to the Constitution's cause, given his stated ambivalence about the document. There was, to be sure, talent enough to make the case for the Constitution. Besides Madison, the Federalists could call upon leaders of the Virginia bar, including Governor Edmund Randolph, the venerable advocate Edmund Pendleton, and a thirty-two-year-old Richmond lawyer named John Marshall.

The Virginia Anti-Federalists were well equipped to challenge the formidable Madison and his allies. They were led by Patrick Henry, the more cerebral member of the Virginia establishment, George Mason, and Jefferson's protégé, James Monroe, who provided multiple reasons for the delegates to reject the Constitution. The debate raged over three weeks in a two-year-old wooden building known as the New Academy, where the cramped, sweltering delegates traded barbs and arguments in the sultry June heat. Throughout the sessions, Madison remained apprehensive about the Federalists' chances of success. The main reason for his trepidation was the opposition of Henry, whose impassioned arguments continually captivated the convention. If Henry's rhetorical spell over wavering delegates was sustained, the powerful and influential state of Virginia would reject the Constitution, and the ninth and crucial vote for ratification might never be cast.

Once he had the floor, Henry, stooped, bespectacled, and looking much older than his fifty-two years, wasted no time in striking the most fearful chord of the Anti-Federalists. "The question turns," he said, "on that poor little thing—the expression, 'We, the *people;* instead of the *states*.'" With that sly elusion, Henry suggested, the Federalists had imperiled everything that the colonists had fought for, not just the sovereignty of the states but also individual liberties. The confederation of the states, he reminded his opponents, had won the War of Independence. And for what? To be replaced by an all-powerful central government that "will oppress and ruin the people." The Constitution "squints toward monarchy," Henry declared. "Your President may easily become a king," he continued, raising the issue that had alarmed Jefferson. Henry accused the framers of eviscerating the executive and legislative powers of the states. And with the creation of a federal judiciary, "the scales of justice are to be given away." Do not abandon the Articles of Confederation, he pleaded, claiming that no less a patriot than Thomas Jefferson agreed with him. "It [the Confederation] rendered us victorious in that bloody conflict with a powerful nation. It has secured us a territory greater than any European monarch possesses. And shall a government which has been this strong and vigorous be accused of imbecility and abandoned for want of energy?"

Madison was no orator and wisely decided not to try to compete with Henry's pyrotechnics. Small, pale, and with a weak, reedy voice, he addressed the delegates in a conversational, diffident manner, holding his hat (which contained his notes) in his hand. Madison never overwhelmed an audience. But no one knew the intricacies of the Constitution better than he. Over the course of the three-week debate, Madison methodically laid out the case for a constitution, delivering, in effect, a comprehensive treatise on the document.

Slowly, Madison proceeded to undercut Henry's argument that the framers had created a federal engine for oppression. The overriding purpose of the Constitution was to provide an effective governing structure for a representative democracy. The people were protected through the system of checks and balances among the three branches of the federal government. Taking the Constitution as a whole, Madison insisted that there was ample protection against monarchy in the office of the presidency or the accumulation of imperious powers by Congress or the federal judiciary. And the states remained sovereign, he reminded the delegates, on issues that did not concern the federal government.

As to the need for a Bill of Rights, Madison argued before the convention, as he did privately to Jefferson, that the Constitution did not give the federal government authority to intrude on the individual liberties of citizens, and that therefore explicit guarantees were unnecessary. He rejected Henry's suggestion that the Constitution should be amended to include a Bill of Rights before ratification. Ratify first, said Madison, adjust for imperfections in the document later.

Madison noted to the delegates that Henry had invoked Jefferson's name. Mr. Jefferson endorsed many of the Constitution's provisions that Anti-Federalists claimed he opposed, Madison said, an assurance that was backed by Jefferson's statements in his private correspondence with Madison. Despite his reservations, Jefferson had ultimately agreed with Madison on the need for ratification. And Madison accepted Jefferson's argument that there must be a Bill of Rights, which Madison later drafted.

Pendleton and Randolph also hammered away at the Anti-Federalists' arguments against ratification. But the outcome was still in doubt when the Federalists called upon the services of young John Marshall. Marshall had only been practicing law for five years and did not enjoy the stature in the legal community of Randolph or Pendleton. But he was a Revolutionary War hero, having served with Washington at Valley Forge, and had already begun to build a reputation as an outstanding state legislator and lawyer.

Marshall and Jefferson were second cousins, both descendants of the prominent Randolph family of Virginia, and, on the surface, they appeared to have much in common. Both revered their fathers, who had supervised educations that led them to study law with George Wythe at the College of William and Mary. But Marshall and Jefferson's shared bloodline did not make them friends or political allies. Unlike Jefferson, Marshall believed in a strong federal government, his Federalist convictions permanently formed during the Revolutionary War, when, as he later wrote, he considered "America as my country and Congress as my government."

Like Jefferson, Marshall was a big man, over six feet tall. He had piercing black eyes and dark, unkempt hair. His clothes appeared to be rumpled even when he had hardly worn them. He was immensely popular in Richmond, a hearty, gregarious fellow who liked to drink with his friends in the local taverns. When he addressed the convention in Richmond, his forensic skills had not fully developed; but he was already an accomplished lawyer who knew how to make an effective argument.

Marshall chose to meet Henry's core argument, that the Constitution was an invitation to monarchy, head-on. His opponent misread the document, he asserted. The Constitution provided for "a well regulated democracy" where no king, or president, could undermine representative government. His most sustained argument was saved for the defense of a federal judiciary. The future chief justice of the United States told the delegates that an independent federal judiciary was a necessary bulwark against an overreaching Congress. If Congress were to exceed its powers, said Marshall, it would be the duty of the judiciary to declare the action void.

Marshall's tone was conciliatory. He did not speak apocalyptically of dire results that would inevitably follow if the delegates rejected the Constitution. There might be "small defects," he conceded, but if the other delegates were convinced, as he was, "that the good greatly preponderates," then they should vote for ratification. And if the Constitution proved to be less than the framers hoped or the people deserved, there was ample provision for amendment.

Henry responded ruefully that Marshall was wrong in every particular of his argument. But the older man spoke of his antagonist without rancor. His opposition to Marshall's position, said Henry, did not diminish his "highest veneration and respect for the honorable gentleman." Henry's compliment underscored one of Marshall's greatest talents, his ability to earn the respect of his adversaries. Except, as we shall see, for Thomas Jefferson.

By the time Jefferson received the news that the Virginia delegates had voted, by a margin of eighty-nine to seventy-nine, to ratify the Constitution, he was fully supportive of Madison's successful efforts. But he was less satisfied with developments in Paris, where efforts for a peaceful resolution of the grievances against Louis XVI were foundering. By the winter of 1789, it was clear that the nobles and clergy were exercising no moderating influence on the king, nor were they genuinely interested in pressing for financial and political reforms. In the spring, bread lines lengthened, tempers exploded, and the streets became ready incubators for violence. Jefferson did his part to accommodate the growing demands of the masses, collaborating with Lafayette to draft a declaration of rights that Lafayette introduced in the National Assembly. Even after the storming of the Bastille, Jefferson did not abandon his hope that governmental reforms could avoid the worst excesses of revolution.

In September, when Jefferson and his two daughters, Martha (nicknamed Patsy) and Mary (called Maria or Polly), packed for a six-month home visit, the National Assembly was still in session trying to draft a constitution, and the French Revolution was far from running its course. But the massive social and political upheaval, only dimly perceived a year earlier, was closer than Jefferson was yet prepared to concede. He remained optimistic that the recent chaos would ultimately redound to the lasting benefit of France and the world. More than ever, he was an unabashed Francophile. To the list of reasons for his affection, Jefferson could now add his admiration for the ideals of the incipient revolution. He believed that France's first halting steps toward republican government would spread from Paris to other parts of the European continent. And he was more convinced than ever that France was the United States' most important ally, perfectly positioned to serve as the necessary wedge to break the British stranglehold on U.S. trade.

Expecting to return to Paris in the spring, Jefferson had renewed his lease at the Hôtel de Langeac and had left all of his furnishings in place. When he and his daughters sailed on the *Clermont* for Norfolk, they nonetheless transported thirty-eight boxes and several trunks of possessions, as well as the carriage and harpsichord Jefferson had purchased in London. Jefferson's intention was to settle Martha and Maria permanently at Monticello, take care of important financial matters, and then return for the remaining two years of his ministerial term. But shortly after he arrived in Virginia, he was confronted with an unwelcome alternative. He received a letter from President George Washington inviting him to join the Cabinet as secretary of state. Jefferson much preferred to complete his tour in France, but he felt a loyalty to the nation's first president that he could not ignore. Soon after

Jefferson received Washington's offer, Madison came calling, urging him to accept the Cabinet post. Before long, he was serenaded with praise from a committee of the local citizenry, an outpouring surely orchestrated by his friend Madison. Despite the subtle pressure, Jefferson kept his own counsel and waited until January to inform Washington that he would accept his offer.

The first Cabinet in American history was small in size, but not in intellectual firepower, thanks to the dominating presence of Jefferson and Secretary of the Treasury Alexander Hamilton. They were joined by Henry Knox, Washington's secretary of war; and his part-time attorney general, Edmund Randolph. Vice President John Adams was not considered a member of the Cabinet and did not attend their policy sessions.

Jefferson first met the thirty-five-year-old Hamilton in New York in the spring of 1790, when both were newly appointed Cabinet members. Undoubtedly, Jefferson had learned something about Hamilton from Madison, who had collaborated with Hamilton (and to a lesser extent with John Jay, who would become the first chief justice of the United States) in writing *The Federalist,* the classic defense of the Constitution that was published after the Constitutional Convention. But nothing Madison could have told Jefferson would have prepared him for the tightly wound human dynamo whom Washington chose as secretary of the treasury.

Jefferson's and Hamilton's backgrounds could not have been more different. Jefferson's first memory was of being carried on horseback on a pillow by one of the family slaves. His father, Peter, a land surveyor and leader in his Albemarle County community, had left his son more than fourteen hundred acres of land. Hamilton was, literally, a poor bastard, born on the British West Indies island of Nevis to an unhappily married woman, Rachel Lavien, and a wandering, financially inept Scottish merchant, James Hamilton. He eventually emigrated to New York, where he distinguished himself as a brilliant special student at King's College (now Columbia University) and, later, as a practicing attorney in Manhattan. As compensation for his humble, illegitimate beginnings, it was later said, Hamilton was fueled by inexhaustible energy and ambition. He never seemed satisfied merely to accomplish a difficult task; he attacked it in the most dramatic fashion possible. That was the case when the five-foot-seven, slight Hamilton, as General Washington's field commander at Yorktown in 1781, leapt over a parapet ahead of his troops to assault a British regiment.

Hamilton's and Jefferson's political philosophies were as different as their personalities and backgrounds. Jefferson's primary loyalties were to states' rights, popular (if limited) sovereignty, and individual liberty. Hamilton was committed to a strong federal government. His convictions had been laid out in elaborate detail in the articles he wrote for *The Federalist*. As secretary of the treasury, he was determined to put his philosophical arguments into practice, consolidating the power of the newly constituted national government.

In his first month in office, Hamilton sent the First Congress his "Report on the Public Credit," a sweeping proposal for the federal government to assume over $75 million in public debt. He recommended that the federal government accept responsibility not only for the United States' domestic and foreign debts under the old Articles of Confederation, but for an additional $25 million of debt incurred by the states in prosecuting the Revolutionary War against Great Britain.

At first glance, Hamilton's proposal appeared to make the new federal government weaker, not stronger, because it would be saddled with an enormous public debt. But his ingenious vision looked beyond the short-term debt to the long-term gains that would accrue to the federal government. By drawing all financial obligations to the national government, Hamilton immediately stanched the centrifugal economic forces that had, in large part, doomed the Articles of Confederation. He also offered Congress an urgent reason to collect taxes for the federal treasury—namely, to help pay off the gigantic national debt.

Hamilton's proposal challenged some of the most cherished tenets of Jefferson's philosophy. Jefferson believed that America's destiny depended upon a traditional agrarian economy that was based on the hard work and democratic ideals of yeoman farmers. He deplored public indebtedness and paper currencies, and the Northern speculators who profited from both. Most of all, he feared the consolidation of power in the federal government. That had been his primary reservation about the Constitution and remained so after its adoption. He conceded broad power to the federal government only in the sphere of foreign affairs. Domestically, he believed that the states represented the most efficacious governmental unit, in large part because they were closest to the people.

Although Jefferson viewed Hamilton's debt proposal warily, he was not prepared to oppose it. He did not want to appear negative toward his Cabinet colleague before they had yet had the opportunity to work together. There was opposition enough to Hamilton's plan, and it came most significantly from Madison, who had already made himself the most influential leader in the House of Representatives. Besides his general suspicion about the pull of Hamilton's program toward the federal government, Madison was particularly concerned that it would unfairly reward speculators who had bought government securities from poor farmers, tradesmen, and Revolutionary War veterans at a fraction of their par value, which, under Hamilton's plan, the federal government would pay off.

When his proposal bogged down in Congress, Hamilton approached Jefferson for help, asserting that the failure of the bill to pass would imperil the union. Despite his anxiety about Hamilton's proposal, Jefferson agreed to serve as a political power broker between the secretary of the treasury and Madison, arranging for them to meet at his residence on Maiden Lane in lower Manhattan to resolve their differences. By evening's end, the three men had struck a deal. Jefferson and Madison accepted Hamilton's plan for the federal government to assume the states' debts. In return, Hamilton agreed to work on their behalf to relocate the nation's capital to the Potomac after a ten-year interim period in Philadelphia. At the time, Jefferson was pleased with the agreement, thinking that it would ultimately benefit the agrarian Southern states, and particularly Virginia, which bordered on the Potomac. But Jefferson later admitted that it was the worst political decision he ever made, providing Hamilton with the first important victory in his drive to increase the power of the federal government.

Hamilton hardly paused after his initial success before proposing a second, equally bold financial innovation: the creation of a national bank of the United States. Great Britain was his economic model. Hamilton was impressed by the ambitious policies of the powerful

British financial ministers and the essential role that the Bank of England played in providing credit to the national government. He anticipated that a national bank of the United States would serve the nation much as the Bank of England functioned in Great Britain. Responding to Hamilton's initiative, Congress passed a bill chartering the Bank of the United States.

This time, Secretary of State Jefferson did not pledge his cooperation with Hamilton but instead urged Washington to veto the legislation. Now fully alert to the treasury secretary's centralizing agenda, Jefferson contended that Congress could only do what was explicitly authorized by the text of the Constitution. And nowhere in that document, he maintained, was Congress given the authority to establish a national bank—not even under the seemingly open-ended "necessary and proper clause."* The bank was not *absolutely* necessary for Congress to exercise its constitutional authority. If the term "necessary" could be so loosely interpreted as to permit Congress to charter a national bank, Jefferson maintained, there would be almost no end to which ingenious minds might not torture the constitutional language. Under such a broad interpretation, Jefferson insisted, the federal government "would swallow up" all of the delegated powers of the states. And the framers surely did not intend to authorize Congress "to break down the most ancient and fundamental laws" of the states.

In his response, Hamilton made the argument that convinced President Washington. Hamilton maintained that the whole purpose of the "necessary and proper" clause was to give "a liberal latitude to the exercise of the specified powers." The phrase did not grant Congress independent powers, Hamilton conceded, but it did sanction the exercise of authority implied by their express constitutional powers. The relevant inquiry was whether the means selected by Congress was related to an end explicitly given to the legislature in the Constitution. And a national bank satisfied that constitutional standard, because it would facilitate Congress's ability to collect taxes, borrow money, regulate commerce, and raise and support armies, all powers explicitly

---

*Under Article I, section 8, of the Constitution, Congress is given the authority to tax, regulate commerce, borrow money, and raise and support armies, among other powers, and "to make all Laws which shall be necessary and proper" to implement those powers.

granted to Congress. "If the end be clearly comprehended with any of the specified powers, and if the measure have an obvious relation to that end, and is not forbidden by any particular provision of the Constitution," Hamilton declared, "it may safely be deemed to come within the compass of the national authority."

After Hamilton bested Jefferson in the debate over the constitutionality of the national bank, the secretary of state viewed him as a dangerous enemy, not just of his philosophy but of the future of the republic. The two Cabinet members' breach widened further when Hamilton invaded Jefferson's official foreign-policy turf and, Jefferson believed, systematically undermined the secretary of state's initiatives. Their disagreements centered on U.S. relations with Great Britain. Hamilton considered Great Britain to be the United States' most valued trade partner, and the key to the future prosperity of the American economy. Jefferson's distrust of the British and disgust with their discriminatory trading policies were well known. As secretary of state, he was determined to do all in his power to shift the United States' trade away from Great Britain and toward his favorite foreign nation, France.

But at every turn, it seemed, Jefferson was frustrated by Hamilton in his design to end Great Britain's dominating presence in U.S. trade relations. The secretary of state prepared a report for Congress recommending that the U.S. give preferential treatment to nations that did not discriminate against American trade. France had made modest concessions to American imports; Great Britain had not. As a result, Jefferson concluded, there should be an adjustment in the tonnage duties imposed on foreign carriers to reduce the duties on friendly, nondiscriminatory nations like France. But the policy was never implemented—in large part, Jefferson suspected, because Hamilton had lobbied his allies in Congress to oppose it.

The final insult for Jefferson came in 1792, after he had begun negotiations with the British minister, George Hammond, to settle the outstanding differences of the two nations under the Peace Treaty of 1783. No progress had been made since Jefferson and Adams met with Lord Carmarthen in 1786. British creditors continued to demand payment from Americans for outstanding debts. The U.S. countered that British troops must relinquish their military posts in the old Northwest Territory, and that there should be reimbursement for British troops' confiscation of slaves and other property during the war.

Hammond had taken the initiative in the negotiation, submitting a paper blaming the United States for every infraction of the treaty. Jefferson responded with a state paper of gigantic and elegant proportions. In 250 manuscript pages, a product of eight weeks of interviews with officials and research into the public record, the American secretary of state aggressively met each British charge with an explanation and a countercharge. It was an astounding diplomatic *tour de force* that stunned Hammond. Over dinner with Jefferson, the British minister said that the secretary of state's paper put matters in a different light, and that he would need further instructions from London. But before Jefferson could apply additional pressure on the British minister, Hamilton intervened, assuring Hammond that Jefferson did not speak for the administration and that his paper was an ill-conceived, regrettably anti-British attack. Given that critical knowledge of dissension within the Washington Cabinet, Hammond and his superiors at Whitehall felt no urgent need to respond to Jefferson's demands. Nothing came of the secretary of state's work; every outstanding issue from the peace treaty remained unresolved during the remainder of Jefferson's Cabinet term.

In 1792, Jefferson began to speak of "the heats and tumults of conflicting parties," dividing the Cabinet and Congress into the categorical "we" and "them." The "we" included Jefferson, Madison, and like-minded republicans who were committed to an agrarian-based economy that favored state sovereignty, popular democracy, and a closer trade relationship with France. The "monarchial federalist" opposition was led by Hamilton and, in Jefferson's eyes, was catapulting the nation toward economic and political disaster, consolidating political power in the federal government, building a huge national debt that primarily benefited Northern speculators, and binding the nation to the arrogant and discriminatory trade policies of Great Britain.

Relations between Jefferson and Hamilton spiraled downward, as the rhetoric of their partisans in the press escalated. The *National Gazette,* founded by Philip Freneau with the encouragement of both Madison and Jefferson, began to publish regular attacks on Hamilton as a dangerous consolidationist. Those attacks were answered by the

Gazette of the United States, which openly assailed Jefferson's philosophy and his character.

The two antagonists eagerly joined the fray. Hamilton privately referred to Jefferson's foreign policy as "a womanish attachment to France and a womanish resentment against Great Britain." And in the pages of the *Gazette of the United States,* an article signed "An American" and written in the distinctive style of the treasury secretary accused Jefferson of secretly working to undermine public confidence in the government. Jefferson countered by telling the president that Hamilton's policies had poisoned public trust in the government and had led the people "to occupy themselves and their capital in a species of gambling" that was "destructive of morality." Later, he enlisted a young republican supporter, Virginia Congressman William Branch Giles, to introduce a series of resolutions on the floor of the House of Representatives condemning Hamilton's economic policies.

The president counseled moderation and understanding between his two most valued Cabinet members, but even the revered Washington was helpless to tamp down the raging controversy. When the armies of revolutionary France declared war on Great Britain in 1793, only ten days after King Louis XVI had been executed, Jefferson and Hamilton's arguments over foreign policy suddenly posed immediate dangers for the nation. Jefferson sided with France and urged the president to adopt a policy that recognized U.S. obligations to France under the treaty signed between the two nations during the Revolutionary War. Hamilton countered that preferential treatment of France would lead to war with Great Britain, a result to be avoided at all costs. Washington's answer to both men was an official proclamation of neutrality; this effectively favored Great Britain, Jefferson believed, since it took no notice of the U.S.'s 1778 treaty with France.

For more than a year, Jefferson had been telling President Washington that he wanted to retire from public service. He had long expressed his desire to return to private life. And after three years in the Cabinet, it was quite obvious to Jefferson that Hamilton had the president's ear and that his own advice was of decreasing importance. Jefferson's warnings of the dangers of Hamilton's economic policies had largely gone unheeded. To Jefferson, Washington's pattern was maddeningly familiar. The president patiently listened to the arguments of both

Hamilton and Jefferson and then—invariably, it seemed—sided with his treasury secretary. That had been the case with the bank controversy, as well as most of Hamilton's other economic initiatives. And in Jefferson's mind, Washington held true to form in the debate over the U.S.'s neutrality policy.

Despite pleas from the president that Jefferson remain in the Cabinet, Jefferson announced in December 1793 that he was retiring from public life to attend to his farm and family at Monticello. Few believed him. Hamilton had already predicted that Jefferson would run for president.

With the indispensable organizational talents of Madison, Jefferson's republican message spread from Monticello through county organizations and a growing network of sympathetic newspapers. The president was spared criticism, but the policies of his dominant Cabinet member were not. It was time for the nation to return to the republican principles on which it had been founded. Domestically, that meant the rejection of Hamilton's monarchial economic policies. In foreign policy, the U.S. must stop mortgaging its future to the imperious British.

The Jay Treaty of 1794 provided Jefferson and his republican supporters with a ready campaign issue for the anticipated contested presidential election in 1796. Washington had sent Chief Justice John Jay to London to come to terms with a restive and not altogether friendly British government. The president's declaration of neutrality had momentarily placated Great Britain, but the increasingly debilitating war with France had made the British navy bolder in confiscating the cargoes on U.S. ships and impressing young American sailors into His Majesty's service.

Jay negotiated as if his diplomatic choices were extremely narrow: either sign a treaty with Great Britain that subordinated U.S. interests to those of His Majesty's government or risk open warfare. Jay chose the peaceful alternative, and Congress ratified the terms of the treaty. When Washington signed the Jay Treaty, Jefferson denounced the agreement as "nothing more than a treaty of alliance between England and the Anglomen of this country against . . . the people of the United States." The French government was just as angry, accusing the U.S. of violating the terms of their 1778 treaty. Soon enough, France retaliated by seizing cargoes on American ships with the same abandon as the British appeared to be exercising under cover of the treaty.

The Jay Treaty became the political fault line between Federalists and supporters of Jefferson's newly formed Democratic-Republican party (known as Republicans).* In Virginia, the treaty was greeted with widespread Republican condemnation, though there were pockets of support from outnumbered Federalists. The most prominent defender of the treaty in Virginia was John Marshall, now one of Richmond's most respected attorneys as well as a prosperous landowner. President Washington had been so impressed with Marshall's talents that he had offered him the position of attorney general, but Marshall had declined.

Although Jefferson began to take notice of Marshall, it was not the kind that could have pleased either man. After Marshall was reelected to the Virginia legislature in 1795, Jefferson wrote Madison that Marshall's hypocrisy ("acting under the mask of Republicanism") and his "lax lounging manners" had made him popular in Richmond. But Jefferson was confident that Marshall could not continue to fool the people once his true politics forced him to "come forth in the plenitude of his English principles."

Jefferson's old friend John Adams was his Federalist opponent in the 1796 presidential election. Though the two men were not as close as they had been during their diplomatic days in Europe, they still respected each other. And they agreed on at least one important subject: each despised Hamilton. Hamilton had retired from Washington's Cabinet in 1795 to return to the private practice of law in New York City but, nonetheless, retained great political influence. Adams represented the moderate Federalists, a fact that thoroughly alienated Hamilton, who wanted the Federalists to act more aggressively in consolidating federal power and openly supporting Great Britain in her war with France. Ironically, Jefferson treated his opponent, Adams,

---

*The concept of political parties in 1796 was a far cry from modern political organizations. Rather than rigidly disciplined organizations, Federalists and Republicans were loosely formed political alliances.

more honorably than did Hamilton. The treasury secretary worked behind the scenes in support of Adams's running mate, Thomas Pinckney, with the hope that Pinckney might receive more electoral votes than Adams. In contrast, Jefferson let it be known that if, by chance, the election ended in a tie he would defer to Adams in the interest of a harmonious transition of power.

When Adams eked out a victory over Jefferson by three electoral votes, the defeated Republican candidate did not seem distraught or hostile to the new president. Having accumulated the second-highest number of electoral votes, Jefferson became the nation's vice president and pledged to cooperate with Adams, an attitude that was reciprocated by Adams.* One of President Adams's first gestures of reconciliation toward Jefferson was to ask the vice president to represent the United States on a diplomatic mission to France. Jefferson declined this appointment on the advice of Madison, who disapproved of such a cozy relationship between rival political leaders.

Undeterred by Jefferson's rejection, Adams was determined to encourage bipartisanship in his diplomatic approach to the settlement of the nation's differences with France. The president next proposed a bipartisan three-member commission to negotiate a treaty in Paris. Adams named Charles Cotesworth Pinckney, who was already in Paris, to the commission, as well as Elbridge Gerry, a moderate Federalist from Massachusetts and a close friend of Adams. As the third member of the delegation, the president wanted Madison (who had retired from the House of Representatives) to serve, but he refused. Adams's replacement for Madison was John Marshall, an appointment that would have momentous historic implications.

Two events in the late spring of 1797 changed the tenor of the political discourse between the controlling Federalists and Jefferson's Republicans. Adams, in response to what he considered France's hostile actions toward the U.S., called Congress into special session in May and

---

*The original version of the electoral college required two candidates, both theoretically standing for the presidency, though one candidate was generally acknowledged to be the preferred candidate for president. The candidate receiving the most electoral votes was elected president; the candidate with the second-highest number of votes became vice president. In 1796, when Federalists and Republicans each offered two candidates, the system allowed for the election of a president (Adams) and vice president (Jefferson) from different political alliances.

delivered what Republicans termed a "war message" aimed at France's ruling Directory. For the first time since Adams's inauguration, Jefferson openly criticized the president, accusing him of unwarranted partisanship in his foreign policy. During the same month, a letter that Jefferson had written in 1796 to his old friend and Virginia neighbor Philip Mazzei was published. In the letter Jefferson made an apparent reference to Washington as one of the "men who were Samsons in the field and Solomons in the council, but who have had their heads shorn by the harlot England." The Federalists, Marshall included, never forgave Jefferson for defaming the great Washington.

Battle lines between the Adams administration and Jefferson's Republicans were now irrevocably drawn. The vice president viewed every Adams initiative with suspicion, particularly in the field of foreign affairs, convinced that the Federalists were intent on a permanent alliance with monarchial Great Britain. At just this time, Marshall and Gerry embarked on their diplomatic mission to Paris. The Richmond lawyer's leadership role in the negotiation with the French government marked the beginning of a conflict between Marshall and Jefferson that would profoundly affect American politics and constitutional law.

[1]

"Swindling Propositions"

WEEKDAY MORNINGS DURING the month of February 1798, Vice President Thomas Jefferson walked three blocks from his rooms at Francis's Hotel in Philadelphia to Congress Hall, where he presided at the formal sessions of the Senate. When he had agreed to accept the nation's second-highest elective office, Jefferson had thought that his duties would be modest and not unpleasant. That expectation had dissolved in the welter of fierce feuding between the ruling Federalists and his Republicans. By the winter of 1798, after nearly a year in office, neither house of Congress was engaged in serious legislative business. Instead, the members were reduced to partisan bickering.

Federalist Congressman Roger Griswold of Connecticut had taunted Matthew Lyon, a Republican from Vermont, that he had used a wooden sword in his military service during the Revolutionary War. Lyon replied by spitting in Griswold's face. Griswold retaliated on the floor of the House by beating Lyon with a cane. The Federalists in the House then solemnly took up the business of whether to expel "the spitting beast" Lyon from the chamber. The motion fell short of the required two-thirds needed for expulsion.

Jefferson wrote James Madison, who had returned to private life in Virginia, that such a spectacle could only degrade the federal government in the public's view. He was also infuriated by the Federalists' attempt to rob the Republicans of a precious vote in the House, where the Federalists held a narrow majority.

One floor above the House chamber, Jefferson presided over the Senate from a high-backed red leather chair behind a mahogany table covered with a silk cloth. He was by now fifty-four years old. The vice president usually appeared calm as he sat expressionless at the front of the room. But that February of 1798, he, like everyone else in the chamber, was anxiously awaiting word from the three American envoys in Paris—Elbridge Gerry, John Marshall, and Charles Cotesworth Pinckney—whom President Adams had appointed eight months earlier to attempt to negotiate a peace settlement with the French government.

No news, Jefferson wrote General Horatio Gates, was good news. As if to reassure himself as well as Gates, Jefferson offered reasons for his optimism: "If the dispositions at Paris threatened war, it is impossible that our envoys should not find some means of putting us on our guard." Since there had been no such warnings from Paris, Jefferson concluded, "peace, then, must be probable."

The long war between France and Great Britain continued to pose serious problems for the United States, particularly on the high seas, where both belligerents were freely plundering unarmed American merchant ships. Great Britain could claim that she was acting within the terms of the Jay Treaty of 1794, which did not recognize the principles of neutral commerce and, in general, acquiesced in British maritime rule and practice.

Jefferson had condemned the Jay Treaty, charging that it gave unfair advantage to Great Britain. As the war between the two great powers continued, Jefferson reluctantly conceded in the letter to General Gates that France could pillage American commercial ships with the same abandon permitted Great Britain under Jay's Treaty: "In fact I apprehend that those two great nations will think it in their interests for us not to be navigators."

Madison was not sanguine about the prospects for a peace treaty with France, primarily because of the obstacles posed by the Jay Treaty. To the pragmatic Madison, France appeared to have no reason to make peace with the United States except on the same terms that the U.S. had offered Great Britain. Our envoys in Paris could either agree to dissolve the Jay Treaty or permit France to "plunder us as we have stipulated that Great Britain may plunder us." Neither alternative seemed likely. Madison did not interpret the silence from Paris as a sign of good news.

In early March, Jefferson's optimism was shattered when reports from the American envoys in Paris were received. President Adams announced that the envoys held out no hope for successful negotiations with the French. He reported, further, that the governing French Directory had issued a decree ordering the seizure of British goods on neutral ships. Ten days later, Adams declared that the U.S. would take aggressive defensive measures, including the creation of a formidable navy and the arming of merchant ships to protect her interests on the high seas.

Jefferson's response was disbelief and anger. He labeled Adams's speech "insane" and began to refer to the Federalists as "the war party." He proposed that Congress adjourn and that the representatives return to their home districts, where, he was confident, they would learn that the American voters did not share the Federalists' exuberance for military measures. The Republicans demanded that the Adams administration disclose fully the correspondence from the American envoys; Jefferson and Madison believed the president had distorted the communications for his party's advantage.

The president quickly obliged. When the envoys' reports were made public, the French were placed in a more negative light than Jefferson could have imagined. John Marshall, who wrote the reports on behalf of the three envoys, told of the delaying tactics of French Foreign Minister Charles-Maurice de Talleyrand-Périgord, who had kept the American envoys waiting for three months and, ultimately, refused to engage in official negotiations. Even more shocking, Marshall reported that three French intermediaries, identified in public accounts as Messrs. X, Y, and Z, had demanded an apology from President Adams for his unfriendly address to Congress the previous spring, a large loan from the U.S. government, and a bribe of £50,000 before any peace settlement could be concluded. The sordid diplomatic episode, labeled the XYZ Affair, infuriated the American public and gave the defiant President Adams a much-needed boost in popularity. It also prompted the High Federalists—the conservative wing of Adams's party, led by Alexander Hamilton—to demand a declaration of war against France.

The dispatches from the American envoys in Paris placed Jefferson's Republicans in a political bind. If they defended the French government, they would appear naïve and unpatriotic. If they echoed the Federalists' outrage, they would hand the Federalists a potent issue for the next presidential election. The Republicans chose a middle ground, expressing indignation at the XYZ Affair but drawing a distinction between the outrageous behavior of Messrs. X, Y, and Z and that of the governing Directory, who, they maintained, was not party to the scandal. Since the ruling Directory was not clearly implicated in the scandal, the Republicans argued, the United States should continue to seek a peace treaty with the French government.

Jefferson made his case to, among others, his son-in-law, John Eppes (Maria's husband), shortly after the XYZ Affair was made public. Enclosing a copy of the envoys' reports, Jefferson insisted, "The communications do not offer a single motive . . . for going to war." He did not deny the scandal, but only that the Directory should be held responsible for the "swindling propositions."

Jefferson noted that there had been a similar scandal involving the Portuguese minister to France. When the Directory had discovered that "similar propositions were made," it had immediately imprisoned the swindler. If only President Adams would apologize for the speech that had so offended the French government, Jefferson was convinced that there could be a peaceful settlement of all differences between the two nations, including restitution by France for her "spoliation" of American commerce on the high seas.

A month later, Jefferson again wrote Eppes, noting that additional correspondence from the American envoys had not altered his views except to raise doubts about the objectivity of the envoys, especially Marshall and Pinckney. Although the reports continued to create excitement, particularly in the nation's coastal trading centers, Jefferson was satisfied that "the country, in general, seems not moved." Jefferson believed that the majority of voters had already begun to adopt his view that the whole affair was a sensational tempest that would soon pass. He pointed to recent state elections in New York, in which the Republicans had done well, to show "the small effect these communications had on the people who were called to the elections fresh from reading them."

In that same letter, Jefferson's optimism about the eventual outcome of the XYZ Affair was tempered by his general sense of malaise and fervent wish for a quick congressional adjournment. "I was never more homesick or heart sick," he wrote. "The life of this place is peculiarly

hateful to me, and nothing but a sense of duty and respect for the public could keep me here a moment."

In early June, Jefferson was still waiting for adjournment so that he
could return to his family and his beloved Monticello. But the political
fires ignited by the XYZ Affair continued to burn, and adjournment
was not in sight. Like other members of the national government, he
listened anxiously for further news from France. He learned that Marshall and Pinckney had left Paris, and that only Gerry remained in the
French capital. More important, he wrote his daughter Maria, "They
have no idea of war between the two countries, and, much less, that we
have authorized the commencement of it."

Jefferson also heard a rumor that there was a split in opinion among
the envoys. "It is even whispered that Gerry is in opposition to his colleagues," Jefferson wrote his college chum John Page. "This may produce accommodation with the Directory. At any rate it gives a chance
that we will have the facts and opinions on both sides."

The rumor that there was a significant difference of opinion about
French intentions between Elbridge Gerry and the other two American
envoys proved to be accurate. Gerry accepted the good intentions of
the French government and remained hopeful that an honorable peace
settlement could be negotiated. His position, of course, was compatible
with Jefferson's and that of the Republican party (even though Gerry
was a moderate Federalist). Not surprisingly, Jefferson and the Republican press were soon supporting Gerry.

Jefferson's position placed him directly at odds with John Marshall.
Their disagreement over French intentions and the consequences of
the XYZ Affair deepened a mutual distrust that had been building for
several years.

After his delegation's failure to negotiate a peace treaty with France,
John Marshall left Paris on April 15, 1798, for Bordeaux and passage
on the *Alexander Hamilton* to return to the United States. With his fellow
envoys, Gerry and Pinckney, Marshall had endured eight months of
delay, frustration, and insult in his dealings with the French government. He could, therefore, view the minor inconveniences of a six-day
carriage ride to Bordeaux with characteristic good humor. "The journey was in nothing remarkable," Marshall wrote Pinckney, "since, as

usual, two wheels broke down on the road." Alluding to his letters to the Adams administration cataloguing the perfidious behavior of the French toward the American delegation, he added wryly, "I do not, however, think this must of necessity be communicated to the Secretary of State, and, consequently, my broken wheels will be saved the circuit of the United States."

The mission to Paris had been a diplomatic fiasco for the United States, but for Marshall the experience proved beneficial. After his letters were made public, his political stature in the Federalist party was greatly enhanced. Perhaps more important to Marshall, the mission produced a financial windfall that allowed him to make the substantial payments necessary for his purchase of more than 160,000 acres of prime Virginia land that had been the estate of Lord Fairfax. He was paid the astonishing sum of $19,963 for his service as an envoy to France (compared with the $5,000 annual salary of Vice President Jefferson). Marshall was reported to have considered the diplomatic appointment "the greatest God-send that could ever have befallen a man."

Fifty-three days after leaving Bordeaux, Marshall's ship docked in New York Harbor. As the first of the three American envoys to return to the United States, he was welcomed as a national hero. The Federalist newspaper the *New York Commercial Advertiser* published a special edition announcing the arrival of "the Hon. J. MARSHALL, one of our envoys Extraordinary to the French Republic." The newspaper noted that Marshall and Pinckney had received their passports on April 14, "which, though not a formal dismissal, was, nevertheless, considered tantamount to the same." The *Commercial Advertiser* did not disguise its disdain for Gerry, who, at Talleyrand's written request, had remained in Paris to continue negotiations. The implication of Talleyrand's invitation was that Gerry was the only envoy who could be impartial. "This infamous insinuation ought to have aroused the immediate indignation of Mr. Gerry," complained the *Commercial Advertiser,* "and we believe he will acquire few laurels by yielding to a proposition calculated and doubtless intended not only to insult his two colleagues, but to add fresh indignities to our government."

Marshall chose to forgo a gala New York reception in his honor to report immediately to President Adams in Philadelphia. But Federalist leaders refused to allow their returning hero to slip into the capital unnoticed. They prepared a celebration that exceeded anything Americans had witnessed since the first presidential inauguration of George Washington in 1789.

At Frankfort, Pennsylvania, six miles north of the nation's capital, Marshall's carriage was met by an official delegation led by Hamilton's High Federalist ally Secretary of State Timothy Pickering, an array of dignitaries, and three corps of armed cavalry in full-dress military uniform. When the entourage arrived in Philadelphia on an oppressively hot day, June 18, huge crowds lined the city's streets and peered from windows and the tops of buildings along the parade route. Cannons fired their welcome, and church bells rang out late into the night.

Behind the giddy swirl of celebration, there was intense jockeying for political advantage between the conservative and moderate Federalist factions, as the leader of the rival Republicans, Thomas Jefferson, looked on warily. The High Federalists hoped to enlist Marshall for their cause: a full-fledged declaration of war on France. But President Adams and other more moderate Federalists vacillated between peace and war and did not, in any case, wish Marshall to limit their options. Marshall himself signaled both privately and publicly that he was no war hawk, though he was disgusted with representatives of the French government whom he had encountered in Paris. He indicated to Edward Livingston, a Republican member of the House of Representatives from New York who accompanied him on the carriage ride from New York to Philadelphia, that he did not share the High Federalists' enthusiasm for war with France.

That carriage conversation was related by Livingston to Jefferson, who greeted the news with relief, tinged with edgy distrust of all Federalists. Commenting on Marshall's arrival in New York and conversations he presumed him to have had with Alexander Hamilton, Jefferson wrote Madison: "No doubt he [Marshall] there received more than hints from Hamilton as to the tone required to be assumed. Yet I apprehend he is not hot enough for his friends. Livingston came with him from New York. M. [Marshall] told him they had no idea in France of a war with us."

Jefferson was relieved that his worst fear—that Marshall would openly join the High Federalists' demand for war with France—had not come to pass. But he viewed the festivities in Marshall's honor as little more than the High Federalists' extravagant attempt to continue to woo Marshall. Jefferson reported to Madison that the High Federalists were spreading rumors of Marshall's approval of their position. "Since his [Marshall's] arrival," Jefferson wrote, "I can hear of nothing directly from him, while they are disseminating through the town things, as from him, diametrically opposite to what he said to Livingston."

To Jefferson, the future of his party and of the republic itself might well hinge on whether the U.S. stayed out of war with France. His sympathy for revolutionary France and his antipathy for monarchial Great Britain were well known. He had opposed the Jay Treaty, which tilted U.S. foreign policy toward Great Britain, and continued to believe, even after the XYZ Affair, that peace with France was both possible and desirable. The American delegation in Paris had not tried hard enough to consummate a peace treaty, he suspected, and he still held out hope that Gerry could succeed where Marshall and Pinckney had failed. He was not prepared to accept Marshall's version of events that put representatives of the French government in the unflattering roles of bullies and extortionists. He later referred scathingly to Marshall's role in the XYZ Affair: "You know what a wicked use has been made of the French negotiation," Jefferson wrote Edmund Pendleton, "and particularly the X.Y.Z. dish cooked up by Marshall, where the swindlers are made to appear as the French government."

Philadelphia's partisan Republican newspaper, the *Aurora,* echoed Jefferson's suspicions of Marshall and the Federalists. "What an occasion for rejoicing!" the *Aurora* sardonically observed. "Mr. Marshall was sent to France for the *ostensible* purpose, at least, of effecting an amicable accommodation of differences. He returns without having accomplished that object, and on his return the tories [Federalists] rejoice." The *Aurora* applauded the continued efforts of "the patriotic Gerry" but held out little hope for his success as long as the policies of the Adams administration persisted.

Jefferson had planned to leave Philadelphia for Virginia before Marshall's arrival, but had postponed his journey so that he might receive a firsthand report from the returning envoy. He twice called on Marshall at his hotel, only to be told that Marshall was out. Jefferson then wrote him a note of regret: "Th: Jefferson presents his compliments to General Marshall. He had the honor of calling at his lodgings twice this morning, but was so un-lucky as to find that he was out on both occasions."* In Jefferson's original note to Marshall, he had written that he was "so *lucky* as to find him out," but corrected it by inserting "un-" in the final version.

Years later, Marshall is reported to have said that Jefferson's telling slip in his original note was the rare occasion in which Jefferson came close to speaking the truth. Marshall returned Jefferson's polite note with one of his own: "J. Marshall begs leave to accompany his respectful compliments to Mr. Jefferson with assurances of the regret he feels at being absent when Mr. Jefferson did him the honor to call on him."

During a six-day stay in Philadelphia, Marshall met with President Adams and Secretary of State Pickering to discuss his Paris mission and future U.S. policy toward France. Although Marshall left no written record of his conversations with Adams and Pickering, his views were laid out in a letter to Pickering shortly after he returned to Virginia later that summer. He wrote that he worried that Elbridge Gerry would be manipulated by French representatives who would hint at the possibility of peace, "not with real pacific views, but for the purpose of dividing the people of this country and separating them from their government. I shall therefore continue to feel considerable anxieties on this subject until I hear of his [Gerry's] arrival and that he has brought with him either real peace, which I am sure is impossible, or no seductive intimations. The people of this country generally, so far as I can judge in the very short time I have been here, are pretty right as it respects France. Few are desperate enough to defend her conduct or to censure that of our government with respect to her."

Marshall dismissed as inconsequential, and wrong, the opinions of "some leading characters" who had faulted the American envoys for failing to succumb to France's demands, and others who continued to believe that Gerry, negotiating alone with the French government, held out the best hope for a fair, peaceful settlement, a position taken by Jefferson as well as the Republican press.

After meeting with the president and secretary of state, Marshall received various delegations of well-wishers. Members of the grand

---

*"General Marshall" referred to Marshall's rank in the Virginia militia; he was elected brigadier general of militia in 1793.

jury of Gloucester County, New Jersey, came to Marshall's hotel to congratulate him for being "unawed by power and uncorrupted by seduction" and praised him for his refusal to "surrender to vindictive and profligate men." Representatives of Gloucester's militia acknowledged Marshall's valiant service to his country and pledged "to enforce by the sword" American rights that "the milder means of negotiation have failed to secure."

Marshall responded to the accolades with stilted modesty, gratified that his service "receives your matured approbation." He also delivered a subtle message of support for the Adams administration and the moderates in his party, telling the Gloucester militia that the nation's true interests "require at all times that all honorable means of avoiding war should be essayed before the sword be appealed to."

On Saturday evening, June 24, the day before his departure for Winchester, Virginia, and reunion with his ailing wife, Polly, Marshall was fêted at an elaborate banquet at Oeller's Hotel attended by 120 Federalist luminaries, including members of the Adams Cabinet, leaders of Congress, and justices of the Supreme Court. As the wine flowed, guests offered no fewer than sixteen toasts, ranging from tributes to General George Washington and President Adams to the American eagle and, naturally, to Marshall himself. By far the most memorable toast was given by Congressman Robert Goodloe Harper of South Carolina, a High Federalist and bitter enemy of Jefferson, who issued a defiant challenge to France: "Millions for defense but not a cent for tribute."

President Adams did not need to be reminded of the bellicose mood of Harper and other Federalist leaders. That same week, in a message to Congress, he had warned France that the U.S. would not tolerate further humiliation in her diplomatic relations. "The negotiations [with France] may be considered at an end," he said. "I will never send another minister to France without assurances that he will be received, respected, and honored as the representative of a great, free, powerful, and independent nation."

[2]

"The Reign of Witches"

THE POLITICAL FRENZY created by the XYZ Affair provided a needed lift to Adams's standing inside his party as well as among the general electorate. Almost immediately upon entering office in March 1797, Adams had been faced with a bitter split between moderate and conservative Federalists. Hamilton and other High Federalists, such as Secretary of State Timothy Pickering, had begun to plot behind Adams's back, attempting to push the party toward a more radically conservative domestic and foreign policy. At the same time, Adams felt pressure from the increasingly powerful Republicans led by Jefferson.

Adams had narrowly won the presidency, but the man who placed second, Jefferson, was not unduly disturbed by his defeat. The only reason he had wanted the presidency in 1796, Jefferson told Madison, was "to put our vessel on her republican tack before she should be thrown too much to leeward of her true principles." He was so pessimistic about any president's ability to steer a safe and successful course in foreign affairs that he concluded, "This is certainly no time to covet the helm."

In addition to the difficulties that Adams would face in the realm of foreign affairs, it could not have escaped Jefferson that any president succeeding Washington would suffer by comparison. In contrast to the tall, regal Washington, the short, stout Adams was the butt of an unending flow of unflattering speculations and jokes by his detractors.

It was reported, for example, that he favored monarchy and preferred the title of "His Highness, the President of the United States and Protector of the Rights of the Same." Benjamin Franklin Bache, the editor of the Republican *Aurora* (and Benjamin Franklin's grandson), conferred on the president the title of "His Rotundity."

Once Marshall's dispatches from Paris had stirred Americans' patriotism, Adams suddenly became the defender of the nation's honor, the resolute commander-in-chief. The president embraced his new role with enthusiasm, delivering bombastic speeches (most often in response to pledges of allegiance by volunteer militia groups) that preached vigilance in the face of a menacing foreign enemy. He dressed in full military regalia to receive twelve hundred young men who had paraded to martial music along Philadelphia's Market Street to offer their lives for their country in the anticipated war with France. And he solemnly proclaimed a national day of prayer and fasting to ask the Almighty's guidance at that moment when the nation was imperiled by the belligerent actions and unreasonable demands of a foreign power.

The result of Adams's speeches and activities, at least from his perspective, were gratifying. "We are wonderfully popular," the President's wife, Abigail, exclaimed, "except with Bache & Co. who in his paper calls the President old, querulous, bald, blind, crippled, toothless Adams."

Jefferson, who was a friend and supporter of Bache, did not indulge in such personal attacks, but his appraisal of the president's performance was no more flattering. He believed that Adams was participating in a dangerous game in boosting his popularity on a contrived crisis of the Federalists' own making. In time, Jefferson thought, Adams and the Federalists would take advantage of the spreading martial spirit to punish and silence the political opposition. Adams did nothing to assuage Jefferson's fears when he publicly condemned "a spirit of party which scruples not to go all lengths of profligacy, falsehood, and malignity in defaming our government." It did not take long for Jefferson's prophecy to become law.

In fact, four laws that focused on patriotism, and the stifling of political dissent, were passed by the Federalist majority in Congress in the summer of 1798. The first, the Naturalization Act, raised from five to fourteen years the period of residence required for citizenship; the fact that the majority of new citizens, primarily immigrants from France and Ireland, were joining Jefferson's party was not lost on the Federalists. Then the Alien Enemies Act gave the president the authority to confine or deport aliens of an enemy country during a state of war. (This legislation, alone among the four measures, received support from many Republicans as well as Federalists.) The third piece of legislation, the Alien Act, like the Naturalization Act, was the product of raw political partisanship: it authorized the president to deport summarily any aliens—of whatever country—that he deemed dangerous "to the peace and safety" of the United States. Such aliens, moreover, would be denied a jury trial, and the president would not have to explain or justify his decision. Jefferson considered the Alien Act "worthy of the eighth or ninth century."

The fourth, the most controversial, was the Sedition Act, which provided for a fine of up to $2,000 and a sentence of up to two years in prison for "false, scandalous and malicious" accusations against the president, the Congress, or the government (the vice president was excepted from the act's protection). Early in June, before the final draft had taken form, Jefferson wrote Madison: "They have brought into the lower house a sedition bill which, among other enormities, undertakes to make printing certain matters criminal, though one of the amendments to the Constitution has so expressly taken . . . printing presses . . . out of their coercion. Indeed, this bill and the alien bill both are so palpably in the teeth of the Constitution as to show they mean to pay no respect to it."

The Federalists' leader in the House, Robert Goodloe Harper, made no secret of the purpose of the Sedition Act: to protect the country from the enemy within, namely the Republican party. The law would prevent the United States from "being driven into a war with a nation which openly boasts of its party among us," Harper claimed. Without offering proof, Harper announced from the House floor that France was "not without a party in this country, engaged in a most criminal correspondence with her agents, devoted to her service, and aiding . . . the efforts of her 'diplomatic skill.'" The Sedition Act, Harper said, was a necessary response to the treacherous tendencies of the French faction in the country—Jefferson's Republicans.

After the Senate passed the Sedition Act on July 4, 1798, Federalist leaders toasted Adams (who signed the bill into law ten days later):

"May he, like Samson, slay thousands of Frenchmen with the jawbone of Jefferson."

Federalists defended the legislation as more liberal than the prevailing common law of seditious libel—under which the *Aurora*'s editor, Benjamin Bache, had been arrested less than three weeks before passage of the Sedition Act. Why, asked Republicans, if the courts already had the authority to punish sedition, was a statute needed? Unlike common-law sedition, the Federalists pointed out, the Sedition Act required proof of "malice and intent," making truth a defense.

But no one was fooled, least of all the Republicans. In their view, the Sedition Act was designed as a weapon of repression to be wielded by partisan Federalist prosecutors and judges against the party's political opponents. In fact, the procedural safeguards against repression would be largely ignored by the federal judges, exclusively Federalists, who were charged with interpreting the law. Under the Sedition Act, twenty-five persons were arrested, fourteen indicted, and ten tried and convicted, all of them supporters of the Republicans and critics of the governing Federalists.

Even before the Sedition Act was passed, Jefferson had challenged the unbridled power of the Federalist-dominated executive and judicial branches to punish political opponents for seditious libel. In his native Virginia a year earlier, a grand jury of the federal circuit court at Richmond brought in a presentment against Congressman Samuel J. Cabell, the representative of Jefferson's own district, condemning him for the spreading of "unfounded calumnies against the happy government of the United States . . . [in order] to separate the people therefrom, and to increase or produce a foreign influence ruinous to the peace, happiness, and independence of the United States."

Jefferson charged that the grand jury, with the notable assistance of a biased instruction from the presiding Federalist judge, Associate Justice James Iredell of the U.S. Supreme Court, had transformed the proceeding "from a legal to a political engine." He was so outraged by Iredell's conduct that he drafted a petition to the Virginia General Assembly that asserted not only the right of an elected representative to communicate freely with his constituents, but also the right of a state to interpose its authority against that of the federal judiciary as a necessary safeguard of the freedom of expression. Jefferson's theory—that a state had the right to interject itself between individual citizens and the federal government—would become a cornerstone of the constitutional philosophy that would be formalized in the original draft of his Kentucky Resolutions shortly after the Adams administration began, in the fall of 1798, to enforce the Sedition Act.

Before passage of the Sedition Act, the Cabell case was an isolated incident of a Federalist judge actively participating in the federal government's suppression of political dissent. Once the Sedition Act was passed, however, Federalist judges at the highest level—members of the Supreme Court of the United States on circuit duty, like Justice Iredell—became actively engaged in the official process of stifling criticism of the Adams administration. Their blatantly partisan actions in pursuit of convictions under the Sedition Act reinforced Jefferson's profound distrust of the federal judiciary, a distrust that would develop into outright hostility after he was elected president. Then, confronted with a Federalist-dominated federal judiciary led by a brilliant new chief justice, John Marshall, Jefferson would again insist that states, under the Tenth Amendment of the U.S. Constitution,* possessed independent constitutional authority and were not bound by what he considered overreaching constitutional interpretations by the federal judiciary.

In one of the earliest prosecutions under the Sedition Act, Associate Justice of the U.S. Supreme Court William Paterson, serving as federal circuit-court judge in Rutland, Vermont, presided at the trial of Republican Congressman Matthew Lyon of Vermont, who was accused of various calumnies aimed at members of the Federalist opposition. Congressman Lyon, who earlier that year had been involved in the infamous spitting-and-caning incident with Federalist Congressman Roger Griswold, was an immigrant who had arrived in America as an indentured servant and rose to prominence and wealth as a businessman in Vermont. He himself had been the subject of particularly vicious attacks by Federalists, for both his rough manners and his outspoken Republican views.

After the XYZ dispatches were made public, Lyon was singled out by Federalists as a "wild Irishman" with traitorous sympathies for France.

---

*The Tenth Amendment provides: "The powers not delegated to the United States by the Constitution, nor prohibited by it to the States are reserved to the States respectively, or to the people."

The specific charges against Lyon under the Sedition Act centered on his published responses to his Federalist critics. In his spirited rejoinders, Lyon not only defended his Republican politics, but also attacked prominent Federalists, including the president of the United States, who he charged were consumed with their own importance and power.

When a grand jury was convened in October 1798 to consider the charges of sedition against Lyon, Justice Paterson discussed the yet-untried Sedition Act with the jurors and recommended that careful attention be paid "to the seditious attempts of disaffected persons to disturb the government." The grand jury agreed with the views that "the honorable judge has so powerfully expressed, that licentiousness more endangers the liberties and independence of a free government than hosts of invading foes." Lyon was indicted, and at his trial, Justice Paterson prepared to give his charge to the jury without even hearing Lyon's defense. Before he could do so, Lyon interrupted to request permission to address the jury on his own behalf (his lawyers did not arrive in time for the trial). Lyon asserted that the jury had no jurisdiction because the Sedition Act was unconstitutional, that some of the charges against him were for writings made before the Sedition Act was passed, and that, finally, what he said was true.

In his charge to the jury, Justice Paterson first dismissed the claim that the act was unconstitutional; the legislation was valid until a competent tribunal declared it null and void. Whether Lyon was guilty under the law, Paterson advised the jurors, depended on their answers to two questions. First, had Lyon published the writings listed in the indictment? Lyon admitted that he had. All that remained to render a guilty verdict, the judge instructed, was to ask if Congressman Lyon's writings were done with seditious or "bad intent." In his instruction to the jury, Justice Paterson did not mention the value of political opposition in a constitutional democracy, or that truth was a defense under the Sedition Act, or that acquittal was a possible outcome. The jury returned a guilty verdict in an hour. Justice Paterson then fined Lyon $1,000 and sentenced him to four months in jail, where he campaigned successfully for another term in Congress.

Shortly after Congressman Lyon's conviction, the Federalists began prosecution under the Sedition Act of the editor of the leading Republican journal in New England, Boston's *Independent Chronicle,* with a circulation second only to Philadelphia's *Aurora*. The *Chronicle,* like the *Aurora,* had maintained a steady drumbeat of criticism of the Adams administration, which reached a crescendo after passage of the Alien and Sedition Acts. The *Chronicle*'s editor, Thomas Adams, attacked the Sedition Act as the enemy of constitutional freedom and alerted his readers of the Federalists' attempt to "screen from scrutiny the conduct of your own government and to silence by an argument of force the remonstrances of reason."

On October 23, 1798, Thomas Adams was brought before the federal circuit court in Boston, presided over jointly by U.S. Supreme Court Justice Paterson and U.S. District Judge John Lowell, where he was indicted on charges of "sundry libelous and seditious publications . . . tending to defame the government of the United States." Seriously ill, Adams was not brought to trial, and died soon thereafter.

Justice Paterson's colleague Supreme Court Justice Samuel Chase was even more deeply involved in prosecutions under the Sedition Act. In one instance, Chase not only charged the grand jury to bring an indictment against a Republican journalist and pamphleteer named James T. Callender, but he furnished it with a copy of the writing in which the offensive passages had been marked. Shortly after presiding at the Callender trial, Chase held court in New Castle, Delaware, where he detained the grand jury an extra day in his attempt to secure an indictment against a "seditious printer" in Wilmington. And it was Justice Chase who condemned David Brown, an itinerant, poorly educated critic of Federalist policy, for "sowing sedition in the interior country" of Massachusetts. In Brown's case, Chase meted out the most severe punishment imposed under the Sedition Act—eighteen months in prison and a fine of $480—for the defendant's "vicious industry" in circulating "his disorganizing doctrines and impudent falsehoods."

Justice Chase's prominent role in Sedition Act prosecutions would be publicly investigated during the first term of the Jefferson administration. The result of the investigation would be the only impeachment of a Supreme Court justice in the Court's history.

One prominent Federalist, John Marshall, questioned the wisdom of the Sedition Act. Marshall wrote a letter to Secretary of State Pickering less than a month after passage of the law, reporting the widespread criticism in Virginia of both the Alien and the Sedition Acts. The Sedition Act especially, Marshall wrote, was "viewed by a great many well meaning men as unwarranted by the Constitution." Marshall added, "I am entirely persuaded that with many the hate of the government of our country is implacable, and that if these bills did not exist, the same clamor would be made by them on some other account, but there are also many who are guided by very different motives and who, though less noisy in their complaints, are seriously uneasy on this subject."

Much has been made of Marshall's concern about the Sedition Act. It has been suggested by historians and Marshall's biographers alike that he had revealed his libertarian principles (Marshall had been on the committee at the Virginia convention that had initially drafted the First Amendment). But Marshall's words to Pickering hardly represented a thundering endorsement of freedom of the press—nor did they contain even a suggestion that criticism of the Adams administration might be a healthy development in a constitutional democracy. Marshall appeared to be saying only that the Federalists were suffering unnecessary political damage as a result of the Sedition Act, and that even men of good will and objectivity questioned the constitutionality of the measure. Marshall, a lawyer who had argued constitutional issues before the Supreme Court, did not include himself among those who challenged the Sedition Act as a violation of the First Amendment.

Perhaps Marshall did not want to offend Secretary of State Pickering, who zealously advocated prosecutions under the Sedition Act of Federalist critics. Certainly he was candid about other issues in his letter. He told Pickering that he continued to fear that Gerry would be duped by Talleyrand and other members of the French government into thinking that a peace treaty with France on honorable terms was still achievable. (For his part, Pickering was so disgusted with Gerry's apparent sympathies for the French government that he had called for his impeachment.) Marshall also pleaded with Pickering to send the money the government owed him for his service in Paris. Unless he received the payments, Marshall wrote Pickering, he would have to sell some of his property holdings or delay making interest payments on the lands that he had purchased shortly before going to Paris.

Two months after writing that letter to Pickering, Marshall publicly questioned the wisdom—but not the constitutionality—of the Sedition

Act. His public pronouncement drew angry criticism from some of the most partisan High Federalists in New England, but by then Marshall was fighting for a seat in Congress held by an incumbent Republican in a state where criticism of the Sedition Act was widespread and politically advantageous. Nonetheless, compared with the stunning silence of virtually every other prominent Federalist, Marshall's concern about the Sedition Act is noteworthy.

By the late summer of 1798, Jefferson was at Monticello attending to long-neglected affairs of his estate, including supervision of his nail business and the construction of a new roof for his house. Though he was disappointed that his younger daughter, Maria, could not make a visit, he was pleased to welcome his older daughter, Martha, and her children (Martha had married Thomas Mann Randolph).

Far from the fractious political atmosphere of Philadelphia, Jefferson prepared a Republican response to the Alien and Sedition Acts. The laws, he believed, posed a basic threat to the republican form of government and, more immediately, to the existence of the Republican party. He considered the laws an integral part of the Federalists' plan to consolidate the power of the executive and judicial branches of the federal government, inevitably weakening Congress and the state governments, which he believed were most responsive to the will of the people.*

He also believed that the laws threatened the civil liberties guaranteed in the Bill of Rights for which both Jefferson and Madison had fought. If the Federalists succeeded in stifling dissent, then the First Amendment's protection of expression was worthless. The enforcement of the Sedition Act, in particular, posed the gravest danger to the free flow of ideas in America's struggling constitutional democracy. As Jefferson later wrote a William and Mary College student: "To preserve the human mind . . . and freedom of the press, every spirit should be ready to devote itself to martyrdom; for as long as we may think as we will, and speak as we think, the condition of man will proceed in improvement."

---

*Jefferson primarily opposed the Alien and Sedition Acts on grounds of federalism; he believed that the legislation gave too much power to the federal government to suppress political dissent. After he was elected president, Jefferson did not object to selective prosecutions of his political critics under state seditious libel laws.

In his private correspondence, Jefferson revealed the passion and ide-
alism of a purist who would selflessly defend his political principles
without compromise. But as the leader of the Republicans—and his
party's almost certain candidate for president in the election of 1800—he
was also thinking in strategic terms. If the Federalists' Sedition Act prosecutions of Republican critics of the Adams administration proceeded
unchallenged, no effective Republican campaign could be mounted to
defeat Adams in 1800. The law, therefore, must be openly attacked.

In considering the mode of attack, Jefferson faced a difficult, and
dangerous, dilemma. If the vice president of the United States publicly
condemned the legislation as unconstitutional, the Federalists might
well train their prosecutorial sights on him. Federalist prosecutors
could argue that a vice president who attacked duly enacted legislation
as unconstitutional was guilty of malicious and false accusations
against the government—which were prohibited by the Sedition Act.
But the threat of prosecution, not to mention the vice president's possible impeachment, was not necessarily the worst outcome. For Jefferson
and other Republican leaders to do nothing and allow the Federalists
to wreak political havoc with the Sedition Act would mean the party's
certain defeat in 1800—and its possible extinction.

With his ally Madison, Jefferson developed a Republican strategy. As
a rule, the two men wrote each other several times a month when both
were in Virginia, as they were in the late summer and autumn of 1798.
Between July 21 and October 26, however, not a single letter was exchanged between them, possibly reflecting their growing suspicion that
the privacy of their letters was not protected by federal postal officials.
It was during this time that Jefferson drafted resolutions boldly claiming
the constitutional authority of the individual states to declare the Alien
and Sedition Acts not only unconstitutional but null and void.*

In his original draft of what became the Kentucky Resolutions, Jefferson began with the unexceptional proposition that the states in the
union were not obligated to give blind obeisance to the federal govern-

*When the correspondence between Jefferson and Madison was resumed in the late
autumn of 1798, it was clear that Madison was completely aware of what Jefferson had
done. It was inconceivable, scholars have concluded, that Jefferson would have acted
without consulting Madison on a matter of such monumental importance to the future
of the Republican party.

ment. He followed that initial statement with the critical constitutional premise that the union was a compact among the individual states. Under that compact, the federal government was assigned certain explicit powers; all other governmental authority necessarily remained with the states. Because the Constitution was derived from the compact among the states, Jefferson concluded that each state retained the right to judge for itself whether an act of Congress was unconstitutional. When an act of Congress was unconstitutional, as Jefferson believed the Alien and Sedition Acts were, redress was left to the states.

The states, through their elected representatives in Congress, could, of course, fight for the repeal of unconstitutional legislation. But, as Jefferson well knew, repeal of the Alien and Sedition Acts was unlikely in the Federalist-controlled Congress. As an alternative to congressional repeal, Jefferson claimed that the individual states could declare the Alien and Sedition Acts unconstitutional—and null and void. Jefferson wrote that, "where powers are assumed which have not been delegated, a nullification of the act is the rightful remedy; . . . every state has a natural right in cases not within the compact . . . to nullify of their own authority all assumptions of powers by others within their limits." Although his resolutions were drafted for a single state legislature, Jefferson invited other states to "concur in declaring these acts void and of no force" and to prohibit the application of any other legislation "not plainly and intentionally authorized by the Constitution" within their respective states.

Jefferson gave the draft to his neighbor and confidant, Wilson Cary Nicholas, who passed it on to John Breckinridge, a Kentucky legislator and loyal Republican. Both men were sworn to strict secrecy in protecting the identity of the author of the resolutions. Breckinridge introduced the resolutions in his state assembly without disclosing that Jefferson was the author. By the time the Kentucky legislature passed the resolutions in revised form on November 10, Jefferson's most controversial proposal—that Kentucky *act* upon the declaration that the alien and sedition laws were null and void—was eliminated. Significantly, the Kentucky legislature's relatively moderate remedy was to work with other state assemblies for the repeal of the Alien and Sedition Acts.

Madison's companion resolutions passed by the Virginia legislature in December did not contain Jefferson's provisions justifying a declaration by the state that the federal legislation was null and void. Madison, in fact, disagreed with Jefferson on that critical point, as well as the exact nature of the constitutional compact. He conceded that states joined together to form the union, but he was not convinced, as Jefferson was, that the Constitution allowed a state to declare an act of Congress null and void. He was not even certain that a state was the ultimate judge of the constitutionality of a congressional act, nor did he demand that the states redress what he considered an unconstitutional act. Madison's Virginia Resolutions called for congressional repeal of the Alien and Sedition Acts.

In preparing the Republican response to the Alien and Sedition Acts, Jefferson had, characteristically, worked simultaneously on two distinct levels: the philosophical and the pragmatic. At the theoretical level, Jefferson could proclaim the most radical constitutional position, as he did in his original resolutions. Taken literally, such a states'-rights position justified the most extreme political measures, even secession. But Jefferson strongly opposed any secessionist movement, calming distraught colleagues such as another states'-rights advocate, Virginia's John Taylor, who had raised the possibility of Virginia's and North Carolina's withdrawing from the union in 1798.

Admitting that the crisis was serious, Jefferson nonetheless told Taylor, "In every free and deliberating society, there must, from the nature of man, be opposite parties and violent dissensions and discords; and one of these, for the most part, must prevail over the other for a longer or shorter time. Perhaps this party division is necessary to induce each to watch and relate to the people the proceedings of the others." Jefferson concluded his letter to Taylor optimistically: "A little patience, and we shall see the reign of witches pass over, their spells dissolved, and the people recovering their true sight, restoring their government to its true principles."*

---

*In 1799, after his fears intensified that the Adams administration would, in the name of national union, destroy self-government, Jefferson proposed to Madison that the Republicans make a public declaration that secession was the democratic option of last resort, a proposal that Madison tactfully rejected, with Jefferson's acquiescence (see discussion in chapter 5).

Jefferson's resolutions also gave credence to a constitutional claim, highly controversial in 1798 *and* two centuries later, that the states, through their legislatures, possessed a sovereignty under the Constitution comparable in scope and authority to that of the federal government.

Despite his pronouncements in 1798, Jefferson was rarely consumed with abstract constitutional theory. Besides fulfilling the role of his party's ideologue, Jefferson also skillfully served the Republicans at the practical level as partisan political leader. Otherwise, he could not have worked so effectively with the more pragmatic Madison to forge a realistic strategy for his party. Indeed, Jefferson revealed this more pragmatic side shortly after he had drafted his resolutions in the fall of 1798 and sent a copy to Madison. "I think we should distinctly affirm all the important principles they contain," he wrote Madison, who was then preparing the Virginia Resolutions, "so as to hold to that ground in future, and leave the matter in such a train as that we may not be committed absolutely to push the matter to extremities, and yet be free to push as far as events will render prudent."

If Jefferson had operated on a purely philosophical level, he undoubtedly would have been deeply disappointed in the ultimate resolutions passed by the Kentucky and Virginia legislatures. His most radical idea for correcting the abuses of the Alien and Sedition Acts—state nullification—had been omitted by Madison in his Virginia Resolutions and diluted in the resolutions passed by the Kentucky legislature. There is good reason to believe, however, that Jefferson was not entirely unhappy with the legislation. The resolutions satisfied his most immediate political goal—to create the focus for an official protest movement against the Alien and Sedition Acts.

Had Jefferson's original demand for state nullification of an unconstitutional act of Congress been enacted into law by the Kentucky legislature, it would have offered the Republicans a dramatic document to rally political support. But it also would have carried considerable risk, by giving credence to the Federalists' charge that the Republicans were attempting to break up the union. Madison's more moderate approach proved to be an effective political strategy. Madison called for repeal of the hated legislation and, simultaneously, pilloried the Federalists for their sustained threats to democracy.

As it turned out, no other state followed the lead of Kentucky and Virginia in calling for the repeal of the alien and sedition laws. Still, Jefferson and Madison had effectively transformed their private repugnance over the laws into official denunciations by the legislatures of two powerful states. For the Republicans, the Kentucky and Virginia Resolutions had the additional desirable effect of frightening the Federalists in power and, at the same time, establishing what would become a winning issue in the presidential election campaign of 1800.

[3]

A Sense of Duty

JOHN MARSHALL ROSE early in his Philadelphia hotel room on June 25, 1798, the morning after the Federalists' lavish banquet in his honor. He had made arrangements to travel by public coach for most of his journey to northern Virginia, where he was to be reunited with his wife, Polly, who had been staying with relatives since the birth of their seven-month-old son, John. Her husband's absence had been painfully difficult for Polly, who had strongly opposed his Paris mission. During the time that he was in Paris, Marshall regularly wrote Polly affectionate letters; she did not write a single letter in return. In fact, she had become physically weak and increasingly reclusive, suffering from a deep depression that would plague her for the rest of her life.

When Marshall arrived to board the public coach for his return to Virginia, he realized that there were no vacant seats inside the carriage. Unfazed, the nation's reigning hero promptly climbed on top of the coach, next to the driver, to begin the three-day ride.

If Marshall was satisfied to return to Virginia without privilege or fanfare, the citizens of Pennsylvania, Maryland, and Virginia who enthusiastically greeted him along his route were decidedly of a different opinion. From the moment the coach left Philadelphia, accompanied by a detachment of cavalry, until he reached his final destination of Richmond, Marshall was proudly welcomed and celebrated. Uniformed local cavalry units escorted Marshall's coach into the towns of York and

Lancaster, Pennsylvania, and Frederick, Maryland. He received military salutes, church bells of welcome, and banquet toasts of appreciation throughout the journey.

Marshall mounted a horse in Frederick for the last leg of his trip to Winchester. There he found Polly in bed and under a physician's care. Her condition improved slightly during the five weeks Marshall stayed with her. But Marshall continued to worry about Polly, and on August 18, soon after he had left her to return to their home in Richmond, he wrote her a letter of concern and encouragement:

"I have been a little indisposed by the hot and disagreeable ride but am now perfectly well and, if I could only learn that you were entirely restored, I should be happy," Marshall wrote. He reported that their three-year-old daughter, Mary, "is the most coquettish little prude and the most prudish little coquet I ever saw. I wish she was with you, as I think she would entertain you more than all the rest of your children put together." He concluded: "I hear nothing from you, my dearest Polly, but I will cherish the hope that you are getting better and will indulge myself with expecting the happiness of seeing you in October quite yourself. Remember, my love, to give me this pleasure, you have only to take the cold bath, to use a great deal of exercise, to sleep tranquilly, and to stay in cheerful company."

In his letter Marshall did not tell Polly about the extraordinary welcome he had received upon reaching the outskirts of Richmond on August 8. Met by the Richmond Troop of Horse, the Light Infantry Blues, Virginia's Governor James Wood, as well as other high state officials and Revolutionary War veterans, Marshall entered the city to the accompaniment of an eleven-gun salute (appropriate for his rank of brigadier general) by the Richmond artillery company. That evening, two hundred guests attended a banquet in his honor.

In his responses to the accolades, Marshall defended his Paris mission. He described France as "a haughty and victorious government, holding in perfect contempt the rights of others," and insisted that to have accepted peace on France's terms would have resulted in a peace that "would be purchased at too high a price by bending beneath a foreign yoke." Nonetheless, Marshall continued to oppose the High Federalists' call for war with France, preaching wary vigilance. He suggested to his fellow Virginians that the United States could remain free and independent without going to war, in part because of "an immense ocean placed by a gracious providence," which posed a substantial natural obstacle "to invading ambition." Finally, he urged support for the Adams administration. A lack of confidence in the government, he warned, "must impair the means of self defense, must increase a danger already but too great, and furnish, or at least give the appearance of furnishing, to a foreign enemy those weapons which have so often been so successfully used."

In retirement, George Washington followed the startling political events of 1798 from his home in Mount Vernon with growing concern. The public disclosure of the XYZ Affair had convinced him of the infamy and thorough corruption of the French government. Washington had also received a private briefing from Marshall. "Before this reaches you," Marshall had written Washington from Paris on March 8, 1798, "it will be known universally in America that scarcely a hope remains of accommodating on principles consistent with justice, or even with the independence of our country, the differences subsisting between France and the United States."

The Republicans' refusal to acknowledge the dishonorable behavior of the French representatives had infuriated Washington almost as much as the reports of the affair themselves. The dispatches should have opened "the eyes of the blindest," Washington had written Secretary of State Pickering soon after the scandal was made public. "And yet I am persuaded that those communications will produce no change in the leaders of the opposition unless there should appear a manifest desertion of their followers." Washington did not refer to Jefferson by name, but certainly did by implication. And he spoke with disdain of the treatment of the XYZ Affair in the Republican press, most notably the *Aurora,* which, according to Washington, turned the dispatches from Paris "into harmless chit-chat and trifles."

Washington strongly supported the Alien and Sedition Acts, convinced that the Republican leaders and their followers in the press and among the alien communities were primarily responsible for dividing the country. If unchecked, their attacks on the government, he feared, would lead to civil war. Washington approved of the Sedition Act prosecution of William Duane, who had succeeded Bache as the editor of the Republican *Aurora,* for example, because "there seems to be no bounds to his attempts to destroy all confidence that the people might and (without sufficient proof of its demerits) ought to have in their government, thereby dissolving it, and producing a disunion of the states." As to the deportation of aliens, Washington advocated that extreme measure against those "who acknowledge no allegiance to this country and in many cases are sent among us . . . for the express purpose of poisoning the minds of our people and to sow dissensions among them, in order to alienate their affections from the government of their choice, thereby endeavoring to dissolve the union."

Washington was so concerned about the security—indeed, the survival—of the nation that he reluctantly agreed to accept President Adams's invitation to return to public service on July 4, 1798, to assume command of a greatly enlarged standing army (authorized and paid for by legislation passed by the Federalist Congress). In accepting the appointment, he denounced "the domineering spirit and boundless ambition of a nation [France] whose turpitude has set all objections, divine and human, at naught." Rhetoric aside, the Washington appointment was largely symbolic; he remained at Mount Vernon, insisting that Alexander Hamilton serve as his second-in-command and take over day-to-day military responsibilities.

The external threat posed by France was, for Washington, not the only danger to the United States. The rising anti-Federalist sentiment, particularly in his native Virginia, was also of profound concern. The Federalists' advantage reaped from the XYZ Affair had all but disappeared by the late summer, as a result of the Alien and Sedition Acts. In spite of Washington's approval of the legislation, the reaction to the laws was overwhelmingly negative in the nation's most populous state of Virginia, where the Republicans, led by Jefferson and Madison, were dominant.

Even the state's newest hero, the Federalist stalwart John Marshall, experienced a taste of the anti-Federalist feeling when, shortly after his return to Richmond, he traveled on legal business to Fredericksburg, north of Richmond. At an evening's theater performance that Marshall attended, a visiting Federalist from Philadelphia ordered the local military band to play "The President's March," a patriotic anthem that had recently enjoyed popularity in the nation's capital. Republicans in the audience were offended by the anthem as well as by Marshall's presence. An insulted Marshall left, shortly before "a considerable riot took place."

The growing hostility to the Federalist cause in Virginia, Washington concluded, demanded his immediate attention. The most effective response, he decided, was to recruit outstanding Federalists to challenge incumbent Republicans in the state's congressional delegation. At the time, only four members of Virginia's nineteen-member delegation in the House of Representatives were Federalists (and only one of those four Federalists had voted in favor of the Alien and Sedition Acts).

In late August, with the congressional elections only eight months away, Washington responded enthusiastically to word that John Marshall, the most prominent Federalist in the state (except for the former president himself), would like to pay him a visit.

Marshall admired Washington above all other mortals. Then and for the rest of his life, Washington symbolized to him all that was exemplary in the American character: courage, patriotism, vision. Yet, when Marshall prepared for his visit to Mount Vernon on September 3, 1798, he must have known that the two men would disagree about the subject uppermost in Washington's mind—the proposed candidacy of Marshall for the congressional district that included the state capital of Richmond.

Marshall remained heavily in debt as a result of his Fairfax land purchases and considered it his most urgent business to pay off that debt by returning to his thriving law practice in Richmond. During the same month that he visited Mount Vernon, he rejected an appointment by President Adams to the U.S. Supreme Court. Marshall wrote Secretary of State Pickering, who had extended the president's offer, that "considerations which are insurmountable oblige me to decline the offer." Marshall would find it more difficult to reject Washington's overtures than President Adams's.

The story of the visit made by Marshall and Bushrod Washington (George's nephew) to Mount Vernon was recounted in an early biography of the nation's first president. The two men began their trip on horseback, with their clothing packed into a single pair of saddle bags.

After stopping to rest at a tavern between Richmond and Mount Vernon, they continued their journey in a torrential rain, arriving at Washington's palatial estate thoroughly soaked and exhausted. When they unpacked, they discovered that their saddle bags had been mistakenly exchanged for those of wagoners at the tavern. Marshall and Washington were left with the wagon drivers' gear, which included a twist of chewing tobacco, a chunk of cornbread, and a meager supply of worn britches and shirts. As they unpacked, they also found a large bottle of whiskey–which each laughingly accused the other of secretly packing for the trip. Washington delighted at the sight of his nephew and Marshall in such disheveled condition and jokingly suggested that the poor wagoners would not be happy with their end of the forced bargain with the two lawyers. Then Washington offered his guests a more fashionable change of clothing.

Over the next four days, Washington flattered, cajoled, and entreated both men to agree to become candidates for Congress. Bushrod could not, and did not, refuse his esteemed uncle. But Marshall balked, even when Washington arranged for yet another festive banquet in his honor in nearby Alexandria. He must make good on his debt, Marshall told Washington, and a seat in Congress would not allow him to do so. Finally, on the fourth day, Marshall decided to leave before sunrise to avoid another confrontation with his mentor. But Washington, anticipating his guest's early departure, greeted him on the piazza–in full military uniform–and made a last plea to Marshall.

Marshall later recalled Washington's argument that at last persuaded him to become a candidate. The first president offered himself as an example of a patriot who had already served his country and did not want to enter public life again. And yet, when President Adams asked him to suspend his retirement to serve as lieutenant general in charge of the newly forming standing army, he could not refuse.

"He [Washington] had withdrawn from office with a declaration of his determination never again, under any circumstances, to enter public life," Marshall wrote, recalling their conversation at Mount Vernon. "Yet I saw him in opposition to his public declaration, in opposition to his private feelings, consenting, under a sense of duty, to surrender the sweets of retirement and again to enter the most arduous and perilous station which an individual could fill. My resolution yielded to this representation, and I became a candidate for Congress."

Marshall faced a daunting challenge in his congressional campaign. His Republican opponent, John Clopton, had represented his congressional district for four years in a state that strongly favored incumbents. Like Marshall, Clopton had served honorably as an officer in the Revolutionary War, and later in the state assembly. He was also a successful Richmond lawyer whose family was well known and respected in the district. Add to Clopton's résumé his congressional record as a moderate Republican in an overwhelmingly Republican state, and Marshall's chances in the April election appeared slim indeed.

Marshall knew that his only chance to succeed depended on his ability to attract independent and moderate Republican voters in the district. Demonstrating a shrewdness that was often camouflaged by his conviviality, Marshall tacked to the district's political center, distancing himself from unpopular Federalist policies. By the end of the campaign, there was little discernible difference between Marshall's positions on the major issues and those of Clopton. Shorn of Federalist policies, so unpopular in Virginia, Marshall and his supporters could emphasize the candidate's universally acclaimed role in Paris in preserving the nation's integrity and independence. Marshall could also take advantage of his natural warmth and gregariousness to meet the voters wherever he found them—on the Richmond green, in taverns, at barbecues where he was seen "dancing around bonfires."

The first order of campaign business was to declare that he did not differ significantly from the general policies favored by the majority of the district's voters. Toward that end, several broad questions were addressed to the candidate in the Federalist newspaper the *Virginia Gazette and General Advertiser* by a pseudonymous reader identified as "A Freeholder." Both the timing, only two weeks after Marshall had announced his candidacy, and the sympathetic nature of the questions suggested that Marshall had either drafted the questions himself or been consulted. The questions covered five general areas: the candidate's allegiance to the Constitution; his general view of U.S. alliances with foreign powers; his specific position on an alliance with Great Britain beyond that called for in the controversial Jay Treaty; his view of U.S. policy toward France; and, finally, his position on the Alien and

Sedition Acts. Significantly, the most sensitive question—Marshall's position on the Alien and Sedition Acts—did not ask him whether he thought the laws were constitutional or not.

Marshall's first answer, on the authority of the Constitution, was both simple and deceptively profound. "In heart and sentiment, as well as by birth and interest," he wrote, "I am an American, attached to the genuine principles of the Constitution, as sanctioned by the will of the people, for their general liberty, prosperity, and happiness." The key Marshall phrase was that the Constitution was "sanctioned by the will of the people." At the time, Jefferson was challenging that fundamental premise as wrong and destructive: in his Kentucky Resolutions, he contended that the Constitution's authority derived from the states, not from the people.

Marshall responded easily to the next question posed by "A Freeholder," embracing the neutrality principle in foreign affairs that had first been articulated by President George Washington in his second inaugural address, in 1793. The third question was slightly trickier, since Marshall had been widely criticized in Virginia for his staunch defense of the Jay Treaty. "I am not in favor of an alliance offensive and defensive with Great Britain, or for any closer connection with that nation, *than already exists,*" he wrote (italics added). "We ought to have commercial intercourse with all, but political ties with none." In that response, Marshall subtly distanced himself from his earlier position of endorsing a broad alliance with Great Britain.

The last question on foreign affairs allowed Marshall to reiterate the position that he had taken consistently since returning from the Paris negotiations. Neither the Adams administration nor his American delegation in Paris could have avoided a rupture of relations with France, without sacrificing the nation's independence.

Finally, Marshall addressed the potentially most damaging question: "Are you an advocate for the alien and sedition bills? or, in the event of your election, will you use your influence to obtain a repeal of those laws?"

In his answer, Marshall found a middle ground that appealed to the district's independent and moderate Republican voters and infuriated High Federalists as well as his most outspoken Republican critics. Had he been a member of Congress when the legislation was proposed,

Marshall wrote, he would have opposed the bills. "Yet, I do not think them fraught with all those mischiefs which many gentlemen ascribe to them," he added. "I should have opposed them, because I think them useless; and because they are calculated to create, unnecessarily, discontents and jealousies at a time when our very existence as a nation may depend on our union." If elected, Marshall promised that he would "obey the voice of my constituents" on the issue of repeal. Should the laws survive until 1801, the year they were due to expire, he would oppose their renewal. He took no position on the constitutionality of the laws.

Marshall's published answers circulated far beyond Virginia, since his success or failure was perceived to have serious implications for the future of his party and the nation. His lack of support for the Alien and Sedition Acts—a litmus test for Federalist party loyalty—received scathing criticism from High Federalists in New England.

Massachusetts's Fisher Ames was outraged: "John Marshall, with all his honors in blossom and bearing fruit, answers some newspaper queries unfavorably to these laws. . . . No correct man—no incorrect man, even—whose affections and feelings are wedded to the government, would give his name to the base opposers of the law—This he has done. Excuses may palliate, future zeal in the cause may partially atone, but his character is done for. . . . The moderates [like Marshall] are the meanest of cowards, the falsest of hypocrites."

A second Massachusetts High Federalist, Theodore Sedgwick, who would soon become the Speaker of the House of Representatives, charged that Marshall's "mysterious and unpardonable" conduct aided "French villainy"; Marshall had "degraded himself by a mean and paltry electioneering trick."

George Cabot, also of Massachusetts and Marshall's lone defender among the New England High Federalists, could do no better than note that Marshall needed to moderate his views to win in hostile (for Federalists) Virginia, not sensible New England. At least, Marshall had not claimed that the Alien and Sedition Acts were unconstitutional. Cabot's point was made by a friend writing as a "Yankee Freeholder" in the *Columbian Centinel:* "If General Marshall thought them unconstitutional or dangerous to liberty, would he be satisfied merely to say they were unnecessary?" the writer asked. "Would a man of General

Marshall's force of reasoning simply denominate laws useless," if he thought them unconstitutional? "No—the idea is too absurd to be indulged."

What Cabot and the "Yankee Freeholder" defended as Marshall's subtle reasoning, his Republican critics attacked as the work of a hypocritical politician. "Notwithstanding the magnitude of your talents, you are ridiculously awkward in the arts of dissimulation and hypocrisy," wrote John Thompson, a young Virginia lawyer, in a series of essays published in the *Aurora* under the heading "The Letters of Curtius." The author, with mock reluctance, scolded Marshall for his equivocal stand on the Alien and Sedition Acts: "It is painful to attack . . . a man whose talents are splendid and whose private character is amiable, but sacred duties . . . to the cause of truth and liberty require it."

Thompson's attack on Marshall was not the worst he endured during the campaign. Marshall was labeled an "enemy of free speech," a "monarchist," and a "British agent," decried for profligacy in his social habits, and accused of an adulterous affair with the glamorous widow of a wealthy French nobleman while serving as an envoy in Paris.

Marshall did not publicly respond to the assaults on his character and opinions. But in private he seethed. His decision to run for Congress, he wrote Pickering, was "a punishment for some unknown sins." Convinced that anything he put in writing would be hopelessly distorted by his political enemies, Marshall declined Pickering's request that he publish a fresh account of his Paris negotiations.

Though Marshall refused to reply publicly to any of the attacks, his advocates were more than happy to trade incendiary charges with the opposition. Clopton was called "anarchist," "Frenchman," "traitor," and "foe of law and order." The most vicious, and false, of all charges against Clopton accused him of libeling President Adams. The rumor, reported by a writer identified as "Buckskin" in the Virginia Federalist *Gazette,* had Clopton calling the president a traitor who aspired to absolute power by bribing a majority in the House of Representatives. A letter corroborating Buckskin's charge was said to be in the possession of one William Pollard, who resided in the district. But Pollard denied that such a letter existed. That was not good enough for Secretary of State Pickering, who, upon hearing the charge, proposed to Edward Carrington, Polly Marshall's brother-in-law, that Clopton be prosecuted under the Sedition Act. Luckily for Marshall, Carrington dissuaded Pickering from pursuing the prosecution; the spectacle of a prosecution of Marshall's opponent, no less, under the hated act would almost certainly have doomed his chance for election.

By late October, Marshall was greatly discouraged about the political climate in Virginia, where, despite the thorough airing of the XYZ Affair, there appeared to be a pervasive anti-Federalist and anti-British sentiment. "The real French party of this country [the Virginia Republicans] again begins to show itself," he wrote Pickering. "Publications calculated to soften the public resentments against France, to excite an apprehension of Britain as our natural enemy and to diminish the repugnance to pay money to the French republic are appearing every day. There are very many indeed in this part of Virginia who speak of our own government as an enemy infinitely more formidable and infinitely more to be guarded against than the French Directory."

Equally ominous, Marshall had heard reports that the Virginia legislature was prepared to take up what would be known as the Virginia Resolutions. "Immense efforts are made to induce the legislature of the state which will meet in December to take some violent measure which may be attended with serious consequences," Marshall wrote Pickering. "I am not sure that these efforts will entirely fail. It requires [one] to be in this part of Virginia to know the degree of irritation which has been excited and the probable extent of the views of those who excite it."

At Monticello, Jefferson harbored his own apocalyptic vision of the nation's political future. Whereas Marshall feared disunion at the hands of the radical Republicans, Jefferson was certain that the Federalists were attempting to establish an American monarchy, supported by strong-armed Alien and Sedition Act prosecutions. "For my own part," Jefferson wrote Senator Stevens Thomson Mason of Virginia, "I consider those [the alien and sedition] laws as merely an experiment on the American mind, to see how far it will bear an avowed violation of the Constitution. If this goes down, we shall immediately see attempted another act of Congress declaring that the President shall continue in office during life, reserving to another occasion the transfer of the succession to his heirs, and the establishment of the Senate for life."

At the same time that he was expressing his worst fears, Jefferson continued to promote his antidote to the alien and sedition laws: the proposed Kentucky and Virginia Resolutions. He was convinced that the state governments were "the very best in the world," he wrote John Taylor, and that the federal government "has swallowed more of the public liberty than even that of England."

Madison's Virginia Resolutions, introduced into the state legislature on December 10, 1798, began, significantly, with a declaration of loyalty to the union. Nonetheless, Madison's draft insisted that the Constitution derived its authority from a compact among the states and that, "in case of a deliberate, palpable, and dangerous exercise of powers (by the federal government) not granted by the compact," the states had the right to intervene to arrest "the progress of the evil." Echoing Jefferson's fears, Madison charged in the resolutions that the unauthorized extension of power of the federal government threatened to "transform the present republican system of the United States into an absolute, or at best, a mixed monarchy." Specifically, Madison's resolutions attacked the Alien Act as an unconstitutional consolidation of executive and judicial power, and the Sedition Act for undermining the freedom of the press guaranteed by the First Amendment.

When John Taylor introduced the resolutions into the House of Delegates, they contained Jefferson's suggested phrase that Virginia ask her sister states "to concur with this commonwealth in declaring, as it does hereby declare, that the said [Alien and Sedition] Acts are, and were *ab initio,* null, void, and of no force or effect." But on Taylor's own motion, before the final vote was taken on December 21, he restored Madison's original wording, inviting the states to "concur with this commonwealth in declaring, as it does hereby declare, that the aforesaid acts are unconstitutional." Several years later, Madison pointed to the change as proof that the legislature was only expressing its opinion, not attempting to invalidate a federal law.

The resolutions were fiercely debated, provoking Marshall to declare that he "never saw such intemperance as existed in the Virginia Assembly." The Federalists issued a spirited defense of the Alien and Sedition Acts and a rejoinder to the resolutions, entitled "Address of the Minority of the Virginia Legislature," declaring that the Constitution's authority derived from the people, not the states. Neither Virginia nor any other state could, therefore, nullify legislation that had been duly passed by the people's representatives in Congress.

That constitutional theory had been publicly propounded by Marshall himself at the beginning of his congressional campaign, and Marshall's biographer, Albert Beveridge, wrote that Marshall was the author of the "Address." Beveridge based his claim on letters from the New England High Federalist Theodore Sedgwick to Alexander Hamilton and to Rufus King, in which Sedgwick referred to Marshall's authorship. But later Marshall scholars have suggested that both the elaborate style and uncompromising content (a strong defense of the Alien and Sedition Acts, which Marshall had publicly criticized) point to Henry Lee, another Federalist candidate for Congress who was then a member of the state legislature, as the author.

Soon after the resolutions passed, Marshall received a letter from George Washington, who said the Alien and Sedition Acts debate in the Virginia Assembly had been put "to a very pernicious purpose" by the Republicans. Washington also sent Marshall a pamphlet written by Alexander Addison, a state judge in Pennsylvania, offering a spirited defense of the alien and sedition laws. The former president held out little hope that Addison's pamphlet would have much effect on the Republican opposition. "My opinion is," Washington wrote Marshall, "that if this or other writings flashed conviction as clear as the sun in its meridian brightness, it would produce no effect in the conduct of the leaders of opposition, who have points to carry from which nothing will divert them in the prosecution."

Marshall replied promptly, thanking Washington for the judge's pamphlet and expressing general admiration for Addison's effort. Commenting on the pamphlet, Marshall wrote, " 'Tis certainly well written," and said he wished other publications on the subject were more widely read. Although Marshall did not believe that any argument could persuade Republican leaders, he thought it was possible "to make some impression on the mass of the people." For that purpose alone, Marshall wrote Washington, "the charge of Judge Addison seems well calculated."

In the same letter, Marshall reinforced Washington's impression that the Republicans were determined, through demagoguery, to exploit every instance of voter discontent. If there were no alien and sedition laws, Marshall was certain that the Republican opposition would find some other target for their political attacks on the Adams administration.

Marshall's criticism of the Alien and Sedition Acts is a matter of public record, but as his letter to Washington indicates, that criticism was significantly muted in his private correspondence. He was just as offended by the excesses of the Republican press as was Washington or Pickering, and distrusted the motives of Republican leaders as much as either of them did. In private, he appeared to be considerably more sympathetic to defenders of the laws than his public statements during his congressional campaign suggested.

Marshall never mentioned Jefferson by name in his letters to Washington and Pickering denouncing the Republicans, or in his public declarations during his congressional campaign. And it is highly unlikely he knew that Jefferson was the author of the Kentucky Resolutions or adviser to Madison on the Virginia Resolutions. Even so, Marshall's general antipathy for the Republicans' political doctrines and tactics could have, by inevitable association, been attributed to Jefferson. He was, after all, the acknowledged Republican leader, and his party's prohibitive favorite to be its presidential nominee in 1800.

The distrust between Jefferson and Marshall was palpable, if stated in general terms, in 1798, when each man viewed the other as a leader of political forces the other believed could devastate the nation.

Three days before the state assembly passed the Virginia Resolutions, Jefferson began the return journey to Philadelphia for the new session of the Fifth Congress. Shortly after his arrival in the capital on Christmas Day, he received a letter from Elbridge Gerry "with great satisfaction." Gerry, the Paris envoy who Jefferson had long believed held out the best hope for a successful diplomatic settlement with the French, beseeched the Republican leader to provide him with counsel on matters of state and party politics.

Jefferson's response to Gerry covered ten handwritten pages and demonstrated his talent for melding high principle with his partisan political interests. First, he laid out his general political philosophy in bold, succinct terms, pledging loyalty to the federal Constitution, but with a distinctly Republican reading of the document. He wrote that he was opposed to the "monarchising" of the Constitution, fearing that the Federalists would first provide the president and the Senate with terms for life, and gradually grant them hereditary tenure that would "worm out the elective principle." He was in favor of "preserving to the States the powers not yielded by them to the Union, and to the legislature of the Union its constitutional share in the division of powers," and he was opposed to "transferring all the powers of the States to the general government, and all those of that government to the Executive branch."

After offering his views on specific national policies (he opposed a standing army and supported a frugal federal budget to discharge the national debt), Jefferson addressed the "X.Y.Z. inflammation." He voiced sympathy for Gerry's much-maligned role in the Paris negotiations, noting that the American people had originally held out high hopes for a peaceful resolution of differences with France primarily because Gerry, a moderate Federalist from Massachusetts, was a member of the negotiating team with Marshall and Pinckney. Too bad, then, Jefferson suggested, that Marshall had prepared his despatches from Paris "with a view to their being made public." It was "truly a God-send to them [the Federalists] and they made the most of it," Jefferson wrote. Jefferson charged that the Federalists had purposely misled the American public into thinking that the French government had tried to swindle Gerry and the other envoys.

Fortunately for the American people, Jefferson wrote, the whole issue had been put in proper perspective by Gerry's subsequent correspondence with Talleyrand, reporting that France, as Gerry had written, "was sincere and anxious to obtain a reconciliation, not wishing us to break the British treaty, but only to give her equivalent stipulations, and, in general, was disposed to a liberal treaty."

Jefferson ended his masterly polemic with a plea to Gerry to join his natural allies, the Republicans. He reminded Gerry that the Federalists "openly wished you might be guillotined, or sent to Cayenne, or anything else." The Republicans, on the other hand, wished only his good counsel and support in the worthy Republican cause.

At the time that Gerry wrote his letter to Jefferson, he was under relentless attack from Secretary of State Pickering, who accused him of treason in his negotiations with Talleyrand. Pickering enlisted Marshall in his cause, seeking corroboration for his view that Gerry had been shamelessly manipulated by Talleyrand, to the nation's profound detriment. Specifically, Pickering sought confirmation from Marshall that, despite Gerry's protestations to the contrary, Talleyrand had been fully aware of the attempted bribe of the American envoys in Paris, and indeed had conspired to see that it was successful.

Marshall himself had been disturbed by Gerry's representations of Talleyrand's benign intentions during their Paris negotiations. After Marshall and Pinckney had left Paris in April 1798, Talleyrand had expressed indignation and pleaded innocent to the charge that he was a party to the French demand for a bribe from the American envoys. To make his point, Talleyrand had asked Gerry to provide him with the names of the extortionists. To Marshall and Pickering's chagrin, Gerry had readily complied, identifying X, Y, and Z for Talleyrand, implying that Gerry believed the French foreign minister when he had insisted that he did not know about the bribery attempt.

During Marshall's congressional campaign in the fall of 1798, Pickering had kept the candidate closely apprised of Gerry's public declarations and private representations to the Adams administration of Talleyrand's honorable intentions. In response, Marshall adamantly disagreed with Gerry's reported version of events. He wrote Pickering that Gerry and Talleyrand had attended a small private dinner party in Paris in which X, Y, and Z not only were in attendance but renewed their demand for a bribe. Further, Marshall said, Gerry had told Marshall and Pinckney, who were not present, about the dinner and the renewed bribery attempt. Marshall wrote Gerry a long, detailed letter on November 12, the very day Gerry had written Jefferson, recounting his vivid recollections and ending with a veiled threat: "I must hope, sir, that you will think justly on this subject and will thereby save us both the pain of an altercation I so much wish to avoid."

On the same day he wrote to Gerry, Marshall stated under oath at a deposition in Richmond that he "was so struck with the shameless effrontery of [Talleyrand] affecting to Mr. Gerry ignorance of the persons so designated and of demanding their names from him that I stated to Colo. Pickering the fact which I now certify." Marshall sent a copy of his deposition to Pickering, who used it in his sustained attack on Gerry's conduct in his negotiations with Talleyrand.

Elbridge Gerry, then, became another issue in the antagonism between Marshall and Jefferson. While Jefferson was attempting to lure Gerry away from the Federalists, Marshall was questioning his fellow envoy's memory, and integrity. Gerry, for his part, soon announced his candidacy for governor of Massachusetts, as a Republican challenging the incumbent, a Federalist.

In early January 1799, with less than four months remaining before the congressional election, Marshall's mood was gloomy, his pessimism spread far beyond his own election chances. His deep concern, he wrote George Washington, focused on recent actions by the Virginia legislature, particularly the passage of the Virginia Resolutions. He was appalled by the Republicans' accusation that the Alien and Sedition Acts were transforming the government of the United States into "an absolute, or at best, mixed monarchy." Such vicious attacks, Marshall believed, demonstrated the Republicans' malicious distortion of the Adams administration's intentions and actions. Equally disturbing, Marshall noted, was that another measure had been introduced* "which seems calculated to evince to France and to the world that Virginia is very far from harmonizing with the American government or her sister states."

Marshall was convinced that the political health of the nation, at least as reflected by the actions of the Republican-dominated Virginia legislature, was cause for serious alarm. "To me," Marshall wrote, "it seems that there are men who will hold power by any means rather than not hold it, and who would prefer a dissolution of the union to the continuance of an administration not of their own party. They will risk all the ills which may result from the most dangerous experiments, rather than permit that happiness to be enjoyed which is dispensed by other hands than their own." Yet again, Marshall did not mention Jefferson by name, but his leadership of the Republicans and outspoken states'-rights philosophy, most recently reflected in the Kentucky and Virginia Resolutions, were familiar to Marshall and undoubtedly seen as inviting "a dissolution of the union," which he so feared.

*The resolution introduced was critical of Congress's suspension of commercial intercourse with France.

The spring elections held a greater importance to Marshall than simply the partisan advantage that would result from Federalist victories at the polls. If moderate Federalist candidates like Marshall himself failed, he suggested, the steady progress of the young republic could be seriously, perhaps irreparably, jeopardized.

As to his own chances, Marshall was not sanguine. But the fight, he assured Washington, was crucially important. His reluctant candidacy was now seen as one of his "obligations of duty to make sacrifices and exertions for the preservation of American union and independence, as I am more convinced of the reality of the danger which threatens them." Secure in his decision to run for Congress, Marshall nonetheless continued to bristle at what he considered the unprincipled attacks on him.

By early winter, the Republican attacks on Marshall had begun to achieve their desired effect, and Clopton appeared to gain the advantage in the congressional race. To clinch the victory for Clopton, Republicans circulated the rumor that one of the American Revolution's great heroes, Virginia's Patrick Henry, favored the Republican candidate. Though ill and retired from public office, Henry still could deliver a knockout blow for any candidate for political office in the state. If Henry were to support Clopton publicly, Marshall's defeat was certain.

Archibald Blair, the longtime clerk of the state's executive council and a friend of both Henry's and Marshall's, wrote the great orator a letter informing him of the rumor of his support for the Republican candidate. Henry's reply not only stanched Clopton's momentary advantage, but gave the Marshall campaign a critical boost.

If Marshall had written the response, he could not have drafted a more astute statement on behalf of his own candidacy. Henry first denounced the Virginia Resolutions as a severe threat to the survival of the union. He also labeled the government of France an opponent of "virtue, morality, and religion." As to the Marshall candidacy, Henry asked rhetorically: "Can it be thought that with these sentiments I should utter anything tending to prejudice General Marshall's election? Very far from it indeed. Independently of the high gratification I felt from his public ministry [to France], he ever stood high in my esteem as a private citizen. These things are sufficient to place that gentleman far above any competitor in the district for Congress. But, when you add the particular information and insight which he has gained and is able to communicate to our public councils, it is really astonishing that even blindness should hesitate in the choice." With a final flourish, Henry exclaimed, "Tell Marshall I love him, because he felt and acted as a republican, as an American."

Jefferson would not have been happy with any endorsement that helped Marshall's candidacy, but Henry's support for Marshall carried a special sting. As a young man, Jefferson had been awed by Henry's oratorical powers. But later, upon close dealings with Henry when both served in the state government, Jefferson concluded that just below the surface of Henry's luminous oratory was a closed, ignorant mind. Jefferson considered Henry to be an unprincipled demagogue driven only by raw ambition.*

Even with Henry's endorsement, Marshall's congressional victory was not assured. Jefferson, who followed the contest closely, hoped and believed that voters would ultimately reject what he termed "Marshall's romance," allowing Clopton to win in a very close race. And Marshall himself was hardly brimming with confidence, as he wrote his younger brother, James, in early April. "The fate of my election is extremely uncertain. The means used to defeat it are despicable in the extreme and yet they succeed. Nothing I believe more debases or pollutes the human mind than faction."

On April 24, 1799, voters walked, rode, and sometimes were carried to the Richmond green to vote. Eligible voters—white male property owners over twenty-one years old—approached a long rectangular table set up across from the county courthouse. There the county magistrates, seated next to the two candidates, prepared to record the votes. No

---

*After his endorsement of Marshall, Henry himself successfully stood for election to the Virginia legislature in the spring of 1799, with the enthusiastic support of the Federalists. But Jefferson discounted Henry's influence in the state assembly, confident that he would be overmatched when confronted with the superior talents of Republicans like Madison. "Still," Jefferson wrote bitterly, "I fear something for his [Henry's] intriguing and cajoling talents to which he is still more remarkable than for his eloquence. As to the effect of his name among the people, I have found it crushed like a dried leaf the moment they become satisfied of his apostasy."

written ballots were used; the voters simply announced their choices.

The voting exercise was one part civic ceremony, one part county festival. Each party leavened the atmosphere, and enticed prospective supporters, by offering whiskey from two large barrels strategically located under trees near the voting table. An indecisive voter could have the merriest time of all, imbibing from each party's barrel before making his decision.

The public nature of the voting could also create ugly scenes. As the day wore on, the crowd grew larger and tempers, lubricated by drink, frequently flared. Fistfights broke out among voters and partisan, sometimes disgruntled, onlookers who did not like the vote that they heard. "You, sir, ought to have your mouth smashed," one Republican shouted angrily at a voter who had announced his preference for Marshall.

The vote was so close that the lead swung from one candidate to the other. Though the tightness of the contest did nothing to calm the nerves, or tempers, of partisans in the crowd, the candidates themselves maintained their composure and good humor throughout the day. Each rose to shake hands with, and thank, each man who voted for him:

"I vote for Clopton," one voter announced.

"May you live a thousand years, my friend," Clopton responded, to the accompaniment of shouts of approval from Republican partisans in the crowd.

"I vote for John Marshall," another voter exclaimed.

"Thank you, sir," Marshall responded, while his supporters yelled, "Hurrah for Marshall."

Late in the afternoon, Marshall supporters escorted two of Richmond's most prominent ministers to the county green, certain that they would both cast their votes for Marshall. As they approached, one observer shouted, "Here comes two preachers, dead shot for Marshall."

The first clergyman, Parson Blair, voted for Marshall, as predicted. "Your vote is appreciated," Marshall responded gratefully.

But the second, Parson Buchanan, surprised everyone by announcing that he favored Clopton.

"Mr. Buchanan, I shall treasure that vote in my memory," Clopton responded. "It will be regarded as a feather in my cap forever."

Later, Parson Buchanan confessed to Blair that he had voted for Clopton with an ulterior motive in mind. "Brother Blair, we might as well have stayed at home," Buchanan said. "When I was forced against my will to go, I simply determined to balance your vote, and now we shall hear no complaints of the clergy interfering with elections."

Marshall won the election by only 114 votes (out of more than fifteen hundred cast), and his narrow victory was attributed to Patrick Henry's endorsement. "With infinite pleasure I received the news of your election," George Washington wrote Marshall soon after hearing of his victory. "For the honor of the district, I wish the majority had been greater; but let us be content and hope, as the tide is turning, the current will soon run strong in our favor."

In fact, the Federalists had done surprisingly well in the congressional elections in strongly Republican Virginia, winning eight of the nineteen seats in the state's delegation, an increase of four representatives over the previous Congress. Jefferson, naturally, was disappointed in the results, particularly in the election of Marshall and other Federalist candidates from the eastern region of the state. The election "marks a taint in that part of the state which I had not expected," he wrote his friend Archibald Stuart.

But Jefferson did not despair. He noted that only five of the eight members of the opposing party elected were "certain federalists." The other three, he wrote, were "moderate men, and I am assured will not go with them on questions of importance." He did not name Marshall as one of the three moderate men.

The Federalist gains in the congressional delegation were the result, Jefferson concluded, of "accidental combinations of circumstances, and not from an unfavorable change of sentiment." The Republican cause, he believed, was in the ascendancy, confirmed by the party's strong showing in the state elections (including the election as governor of Virginia of his protégé, James Monroe). But he was not prepared to predict how long the Republican advantage would last, since he suspected the Federalists of a continuing effort to corrupt the political process (just as Marshall was convinced of the corrupting influence of the Republicans). "How long we can hold our ground I do not know,"

Jefferson wrote. "We are not incorruptible; on the contrary, corruption is making sensible though silent progress."

Marshall also viewed the state elections as a solid victory for the Republicans. He was prepared for the worst. Noting Republican dominance in those elections, Marshall observed pessimistically: "The consequence must be an antifederal senator [Wilson Cary Nicholas] and governor [Monroe]. In addition to this, the baneful influence of a legislature hostile perhaps to the Union—or if not so—to all its measures, will yet be kept up."

In December 1799, Marshall would take his seat in the Sixth Congress, his political perspective expanded far beyond Virginia's borders. New England's High Federalist congressional contingent nervously anticipated the appearance of their new colleague. Would Marshall now close ranks with his more conservative Federalist colleagues? No one knew. But House Speaker Theodore Sedgwick of Massachusetts was certain of one thing: "There never has been an instance where the commencement of a political career was so important as is that of General Marshall."

[4]

Defending the President

WHILE JOHN MARSHALL slogged through Richmond in the winter of 1799 searching for votes, Vice President Jefferson presided over the Federalist-controlled Senate in Philadelphia and kept a watchful eye on the activities in the House of Representatives. "The army and navy are steadily pursued," Jefferson wrote his son-in-law, Thomas Mann Randolph. Underscoring Jefferson's observation, the Federalist congressional majority voted substantially increased military appropriations and authorized a loan of $5 million from the federal government to pay for it.

Putting the nation on a war footing was central to the political ambitions of the High Federalists, who were determined to discourage new diplomatic initiatives that might bring a settlement between the United States and France. They successfully sponsored the Logan bill, which prohibited communication between any private American citizen and a foreign government. The bill's immediate target was Dr. George Logan, a close friend of Jefferson's who had embarked on a personal diplomatic mission to France in an attempt to repair the relations between the two countries. Logan had returned to the United States in November 1798 convinced that a peace settlement was possible. In a four-hour harangue on the floor of the House in support of the Logan bill, the High Federalist leader Robert Goodloe Harper denounced Logan's mission and hinted that Logan and his sponsor, Jefferson, were guilty of treason.

As the High Federalists prevailed in Congress, the president was moving in a different direction. On February 18, 1799, Adams announced that he would appoint William Vans Murray, the American envoy at the Hague, to represent the United States in new peace negotiations with the French government. This was a stunning reversal of policy by the president, who, having shocked friend and foe, quickly left Philadelphia to join his ailing wife, Abigail, at their home in Quincy, Massachusetts.

Only ten months earlier, Adams had encouraged the spreading anti-French martial spirit with bellicose rhetoric. But the pledges of patriotism were followed by demands from the High Federalists for a large standing army, to be commanded by their leader, Alexander Hamilton. Adams had favored a modest navy, solely for defensive purposes, and only reluctantly acquiesced in the High Federalists' call for a peacetime standing army led by Hamilton, a man Adams deeply distrusted.

Congress had been forced not only to borrow large sums of money but to raise new taxes. And for what purpose? Presumably, to prepare for a war that neither the United States nor France seemed to want. Since the failed negotiations with Paris the previous spring, France's military fortunes had taken a dramatic turn for the worse. Britain's Admiral Horatio Nelson had defeated the French fleet at the Nile, and French troops had suffered surprising defeats in land battles. Those setbacks, coupled with the militancy of the Adams administration toward France, helped persuade the French government that it should make peace with the United States.

Adams began cautiously to give credence to reports from Murray at the Hague as well as from Gerry that the French now sought an honorable peace. When the president announced his decision to appoint Murray as the new American envoy to France, he insisted on terms that would assure the United States representative a status equal to that of diplomats of other sovereign nations. But conspicuously absent from his announcement was the angry tone of his earlier declarations. The president offered a guarded message of hope for honest reconciliation.

Historians of the Adams administration (and Adams himself in retirement) have pointed to the president's peace initiative as the major achievement of his presidency. At the time, however, Adams received meager encouragement. The High Federalists were incensed. Hamilton was reported to have dismissed Adams as "a mere old woman and unfit for a President." Massachusetts's George Cabot wrote bitterly,

"Surprise, indignation, grief and disgust followed each other in quick succession in the breasts of the true friends of our country."

Jefferson was no kinder to the president, even though he had long called for just such an initiative. He took grim satisfaction in the fact that Adams's party was "graveled and divided" but noted that the Federalists continued to prepare for war. As to Adams's initiative, Jefferson wrote that it had been taken both "grudgingly" and "tardily." At least, he concluded, it "silences all arguments against the sincerity of France."

John Marshall was one of the few prominent Federalists to endorse Adams's initiative. He did so in a letter to Adams's Attorney General Charles Lee a month after the president's announcement.

Marshall's gesture was the first of many instances of political support for the president over the remainder of his term, which endeared him to Adams. Once he was in the House, Marshall rallied other Southern Federalist congressmen to support Adams's policy. Working toward an honorable peace settlement with France was clearly in the best foreign-policy interests of the United States. At the level of pragmatic politics, the peace initiative also made good sense. Adams, and presumably Marshall, had appraised the president's chances for re-election and realized that the High Federalists' policies—intractable opposition to peace negotiations with France, an increasingly expensive standing army, new taxes—were political dead weights that would probably doom his candidacy.

After Adams nominated Murray for the new peace mission, irate High Federalists blocked his appointment in Senate committee. The president responded by expanding the delegation, adding Chief Justice Oliver Ellsworth and Virginia's Patrick Henry (who declined and was replaced by North Carolina Governor William R. Davie). It was a tactical move by Adams to salvage his peace initiative in the face of stiff opposition from conservatives within his own party. Jefferson brooded nonetheless, fearing that the addition of Ellsworth and Davie was a dilatory tactic (the new envoys could not leave for Paris until the fall) calculated to diminish the mission's chance of success.

Although both Jefferson and Marshall supported Adams's goal of peace negotiations with France, they continued to maintain their long-held and diametrically opposed views of the intentions of the French and the British. Marshall remained skeptical of France, whereas Jefferson was confident of France's desire for an honorable peace. Each claimed neutrality. But Jefferson accepted the French government's good faith and questioned Great Britain's; Marshall's judgment was the mirror opposite.

Marshall remained suspicious of negotiations with France even as American envoys were preparing for another round of diplomatic discussions. In a letter to Secretary of State Pickering dated August 25, 1799, Marshall wrote that any concession to France concerning commercial claims on the high seas, without reciprocal provisions, would encourage the view that France's conduct had not been hostile to the United States, a view that he found naïve. As to future discussions with France, Marshall had no confidence that French representatives would negotiate in good faith. "It appears to me that in a contest with another nation," he wrote, "a Frenchman can never see wrong in his own government."

As to France's war on the high seas, which Marshall deplored, Jefferson considered France's treatment of U.S. commercial ships to be significantly less deplorable than Great Britain's. And occasionally he credited the French with high-minded, even generous, conduct toward American vessels and crews.

Jefferson charged that any French aggression against American commercial ships paled in comparison with that by the British—a conclusion, he contended, that was backed by maritime insurance companies, which were in the best position to know. And now, even in the face of the manifest good intentions of the French government, he believed that the peace process was being jeopardized by the willful obstruction of Federalist war hawks.

On December 6, 1799, four days after Marshall entered the House as the new congressman from Richmond, he undertook the difficult assignment of drafting the official congressional response to President Adams's State of the Union speech. In his address, Adams had recounted the accomplishments of his administration, including his dramatic peace initiative with France. If Marshall were to praise the initiative too much, he invited the wrath of the High Federalists in Congress. If he ignored the president's initiative, or devalued it, he risked undercutting Adams and his moderate Federalist supporters. A tepid response to the peace negotiation could also encourage open rebellion by the Republicans who, if they withheld credit from Adams for the initiative, nonetheless supported it.

Marshall began the official response with praise for the president, who, by sending a second delegation to Paris, was prepared "to meet the first indications on the part of the French Republic of a disposition to accommodate the existing differences between the two countries." His words were not welcomed by the High Federalists, but they were reassuring. He said that it was the *first* indication of France's genuine desire to negotiate in good faith, reinforcing the Federalists' (both moderates and conservatives) position that blame for the failure of the earlier Paris mission lay squarely with the French.

Marshall made it clear, moreover, that Adams was correct to have insisted that U.S. envoys be accorded the status of equals in any negotiations with France. Again, he had found common ground between the rival factions of his party. To be sure, the Republicans could not have been happy with Marshall's congratulatory words for Adams, but their interest in seeing that negotiations went forward discouraged open protest.

Finally, Marshall struck a theme that he had repeated often since returning from Paris: a strong national defense was essential if U.S. negotiations with France were to be fruitful. "The most pacific temper will not always insure peace," he declared. "Experience, the parent of wisdom and the great instructor of nations, has established the truth of your [Adams's] position that, remotely as we are placed from the belligerent nations . . . yet nothing short of the power of repelling aggression will secure to our country a rational prospect of escaping the calamities of war or national degradation." Marshall's emphasis on military preparedness for defensive purposes supported Adams's position, not the more aggressive ambitions of the High Federalists. There was, however, sufficient steel in Marshall's words to discourage revolt by the conservative members of his party. The draft was accepted without amendment.

Less than two weeks later, Marshall walked into the House chamber visibly distraught. He had just received word, still a rumor, that George

Washington had died. A day later, there was no longer doubt. "Our Washington is no more!" Marshall announced. "The hero, the sage and the patriot of America–the man on whom in times of danger every eye was turned and all hopes were placed, lives now only in his own great actions and in the hearts of an affectionate and afflicted people." He ended his tribute with the famous words (borrowed from a draft by his Virginia colleague Henry Lee), "First in war, first in peace, and first in the hearts of his country."

Marshall not only offered the official congressional eulogy for his hero but led (with House Speaker Sedgwick) the solemn six-block funeral procession from Congress Hall to the city's German Lutheran Church. Vice President Jefferson, still in transit to Philadelphia from his Virginia home, missed the funeral.

Jefferson offered no reason for his absence, but it could have been explained on grounds other than the difficulty of travel from Monticello to Philadelphia in the depths of winter. Jefferson possessed a well-known aversion to elaborate ceremony, particularly ceremony that served a political purpose, and the elaborate and lengthy public mourning for Washington, Republicans suspected, was staged by the Federalists, at least in part, for political advantage. Jefferson may also have been sensitive to the continued Federalist attacks on him for his Mazzei letter (with its veiled reference to Washington), and wished to avoid calling attention to himself during the solemn occasion of Washington's funeral.

The presidential election of 1800 was very much on the minds of Marshall and every other member of the Sixth Congress as they conducted the nation's business. From Marshall's perspective, the High Federalists posed a threat almost as great as Jefferson's Republicans. He was alarmed by reports of a strategy by the conservative wing of his party to dislodge Adams from office. "I can tell you in confidence," Marshall wrote his brother, James, "that the situation of our affairs with respect to domestic quiet is much more critical than I had conjectured. The eastern people [i.e., the High Federalists] are very much dissatisfied with the President on account of the late mission to France. They are strongly disposed to desert him, and to push some other candidate."

According to rumors Marshall had heard, the High Federalists intended to promote their own candidate for the presidency. The list of possible candidates included Rufus King, the American minister to Great Britain; Chief Justice Oliver Ellsworth; and Marshall's fellow envoy to France Charles Cotesworth Pinckney. Marshall wrote: "If they are deterred from doing this [i.e., replacing Adams] by the fear that the attempt might elect Jefferson, I think not improbable that they will vote generally for Adams and Pinckney so as to give the latter gentleman the best chance, if he gets the southern vote, to be the President."

Marshall expressed no opinion on the High Federalists' strategy beyond the concern that any divisiveness within his party could lead to the disastrous result of Jefferson's election to the presidency. He also worried that the pressure from the High Federalists to expand the standing army, and with it the national debt, in a time of peace could provide Jefferson with a decisive popular issue.

It was imperative, Marshall believed, that he and other moderate Federalists keep congressional debate and actions on an even keel. "I hope a mutual spirit of toleration and forbearance will succeed to the violence which seemed in too great a degree to govern last year," he wrote his brother-in-law, John Ambler, at the beginning of the congressional term. "As far as I can judge from present appearances, this will be a temperate session, and I wish devoutly that the prevalence of moderation here may diffuse the same spirit among our fellow citizens at large."

Toward that end, Marshall played a crucial leadership role in the House. To the shock and surprise of the High Federalists and even fellow Federalist moderates, Marshall redeemed his campaign pledge to his Virginia constituents to abide by their wishes on the Sedition Act, casting a vote with the Republicans in their unsuccessful attempt to repeal the law. He continued to reveal an independent streak by opposing a bill that would have authorized a joint committee of the Senate and House to make the final determination in a contested presidential election. With the Federalists holding a firm congressional majority, such a bill would have opened the 1800 election to potential partisan abuse that could have dealt a fatal blow to Jefferson's presidential ambitions. (Even Marshall's work on behalf of a more moderate electoral bill failed to impress Jefferson, who refused to give Marshall credit for bipartisanship, dismissing his effort as a "dexterous maneuver" of questionable effectiveness.) Marshall, in another act of defiance of his more conservative colleagues, urged the House to pass military appropriations for defensive purposes only, as President Adams had long urged.

If Marshall was concerned about the High Federalists' disappointment in him during the congressional term, he did not record it. He was, in any event, more than compensated for any disillusionment on the part of conservatives in his party by the enthusiastic support of his most important sponsor, President Adams. With an unwavering eye on Adams's reelection chances, Marshall, more than any other Federalist member of the House, assiduously protected the president's interests. No issue better demonstrated Marshall's commitment to Adams—as well as his forensic talents—than his celebrated argument in the enigmatic case of Jonathan Robbins.

The Robbins controversy was rooted in a mutiny on the British thirty-two-gun frigate HMS *Hermione,* sailing in the Caribbean. On September 22, 1797, the crew of the *Hermione* overthrew the harsh rule of the ship's captain, Hugh Pigot. The crew attacked the captain on the deck with a tomahawk, then followed him to his cabin, where he was bayoneted and thrown through a porthole into the sea. The crew then killed three lieutenants, the purser, the ship's doctor, and several other members of the ship's staff "in a most cruel and savage manner," according to one commentator, "dragging [the victims] from their beds, cutting and hacking them with tomahawks and other weapons, and thrusting many overboard whilst yet alive."

The mutineers then sailed the *Hermione* into the Spanish port of La Guaira, in what is now Venezuela, and turned the ship over to Spanish authorities in exchange for a pledge that they would not be returned to Great Britain. The British naval command vowed to bring the mutineers to justice. And for the next two years, the British relentlessly tracked down the crew of the *Hermione*—on captured Spanish vessels, on other English ships, and, in the Robbins case, in the port town of Charleston, South Carolina, where the American schooner *Tanner's Delight* was docked.

On the basis of information provided by an eighteen-year-old member of the crew of the *Tanner's Delight* in February 1799, British authorities identified a sailor on the *Tanner's Delight* known by the name of Robbins as the British citizen Thomas Nash, who had been listed as a member of the mutinous *Hermione* crew. According to the informer, who claimed to have overheard an earlier conversation in a Santo Domingo bar, a drunken Robbins had admitted that he had been a member of the *Hermione* crew and that he wished "bad luck to her." Based on that reported conversation, the man called Robbins was arrested and jailed in Charleston.

The British consul general moved to have the prisoner extradited under terms of the Jay Treaty. Before the extradition proceeding took place in the summer of 1799, a British naval officer who had served on the *Hermione* before the mutiny swore that he was certain, based on depositions given in other *Hermione* courts-martial, that Robbins was in fact Nash and "was one of the principals in the commission of the . . . acts of murder and piracy."

As British authorities were building their case against the sailor they claimed was Thomas Nash, the arrested man in the Charleston jail had in his possession a document attesting that he was a twenty-three-year-old resident of Danbury, Connecticut, named Jonathan Robbins and, most important for the purposes of the extradition proceeding, that he was an American citizen.

U.S. District Judge Thomas Bee for the District of South Carolina refused to act unless President Adams approved of the extradition. The British consul in Philadelphia, therefore, requested the prisoner's extradition but omitted any mention of the prisoner's claim of American citizenship. Secretary of State Pickering advised Adams that the South Carolina federal judge "should be directed to deliver up the offender in question, on the demand of the British government by its minister."

President Adams, in a brief response, wrote: "I have no doubt that an offence committed on board a public ship of war on the high sea is committed within the jurisdiction of the nation to whom the ship belongs. How far the President of the U.S. could be justifiable in directing the judge to deliver up the offender is not clear. I have no objection to advise and request him to do it."

On the basis of that ambiguous approval, Secretary Pickering advised

Judge Bee that the president had consented to the extradition. At the extradition hearing, the prisoner made a formal declaration in court that he was Jonathan Robbins, an American citizen and a resident of Danbury, Connecticut, who had been forced by the British into involuntary service on the *Hermione*. In support of his claim, Robbins submitted a notarized certificate, dated May 1795, attesting to his American citizenship. But such certification (often granted without independent corroboration) was not difficult to come by in those days. Counsel for the British government dismissed the certificate as a forgery and insisted that the extradition provision of the Jay Treaty, which called for extradition of a fugitive charged with the crime of murder, be honored.

The prisoner's two attorneys, both faithful Republicans, offered no corroboration of their client's claim of American citizenship. They nonetheless insisted that he was an American citizen who had been involuntarily stripped of his rights. He was, they argued, entitled under the U.S. Constitution to a trial by jury and should not, in any event, be handed over to a foreign power, and a monarchy at that, merely at the consent of the president.

Why, asked Judge Bee, would an American sailor serve at length on a British frigate under an assumed name and citizenship and later sit in a Charleston jail for several months without divulging his true identity? The answer, the judge surmised, must be that he was lying. Rejecting the prisoner's claim of American citizenship, the judge concluded, "There was sufficient evidence of criminality to justify the apprehension and commitment of the prisoner for trial." The prisoner was delivered in leg irons to His Britannic Majesty's sloop *Sprightly,* then anchored in Charleston Harbor, which immediately set sail for Jamaica, where the prisoner faced a court-martial and, if found guilty, death.

The British court-martial began in Jamaica on August 15, 1799. Four witnesses from the *Hermione* testified that they knew Robbins as Thomas Nash, and that he was the mutineer who had killed one of the *Hermione*'s officers. No defense was offered. Four days after the trial had begun, the prisoner was found guilty and executed.

Moments before the prisoner was executed, British authorities reported, the man who claimed to have been the American citizen Robbins had confessed to being an Irishman. The *Hermione*'s records showed that one of her crew, Thomas Nash, was a native of Waterford,

Ireland. Shortly thereafter, the Adams administration made its own inquiry of officials in Danbury, Connecticut, who reported that they found no record of a man named Jonathan Robbins residing in the town at the time that the prisoner claimed to have lived there.

The Republican newspaper *Aurora* denounced the president's action of handing over the prisoner to the British authorities as beyond his constitutional power, a charge reiterated by leading Republicans. The Jay Treaty, they argued, was not self-executing but required implementing legislation by the House of Representatives before any extradition could occur. Absent such legislation, the president had acted unlawfully in the Robbins case, with the result, the *Aurora* declared, that "BRITISH INFLUENCE threatens destruction to these United States!"

After the execution, Jefferson's South Carolina ally Senator Charles Pinckney (cousin of Federalist Charles Cotesworth Pinckney, the Paris envoy) wrote a series of letters, widely circulated as *Letters of a South Carolina Planter* (and published in the *Aurora*), condemning the Adams administration's handling of the Robbins case. Pinckney criticized Judge Bee's decision to hand the prisoner over to the British, arguing that his judicial duty was to commit the matter to a jury trial in an American courtroom. He called for Congress to pass legislation prohibiting the extradition of fugitives unless an American grand jury authorized it. He also accused the Adams administration of "extreme impropriety" in effectively ignoring the prerogatives of the judiciary.

Jefferson congratulated Pinckney on the soundness of his arguments. The alleged martyrdom of Jonathan Robbins was embraced by the Republicans. Here was a lone American citizen (the Republicans, despite British and Adams-administration reports to the contrary, did not doubt the claim that the man executed was the American Jonathan Robbins), stripped of his freedom and all other natural rights, who had been executed on foreign soil by representatives of the British monarchy. At worst, Robbins had been guilty of participating in a justifiable mutiny against a tyrannical British captain. The Republicans charged that Robbins's death had been the direct result of the precipitous action of President Adams, whose sympathies for Great Britain as well as his own monarchial tendencies had led to his unbridled, and unconstitutional, use of executive power.

The Jeffersonian Republicans extended their assault on the Adams administration's handling of the Robbins case to the floor of the House of Representatives. On February 2, 1800, Republican Congressman Robert Livingston of New York declared that the Jay Treaty was "unjust, impolitic, and cruel." Livingston offered the example of the Robbins case, in which "a citizen of the United States might be dragged from his country, his connections and his friends, and subjected to the judgment of an unrelenting military tribunal." Following Pinckney's line of reasoning, Livingston attacked President Adams's intervention as constituting "a dangerous interference of the executive with judicial decisions," thereby sacrificing the constitutional independence of the judiciary.

Argument of the finer legal points was left to the Republicans' floor leader, Albert Gallatin, who insisted that under the Jay Treaty the president had no authority to carry into effect the extradition provision (article 27) without implementing legislation by Congress. He believed that his argument was made stronger by the nature of the questions raised by the extradition: issues of jurisdiction (if the charge was piracy as well as murder, American courts would have jurisdiction regardless of the terms of the Jay Treaty) and the definition of murder (if the prisoner had been involuntarily impressed on the *Hermione,* the charge could not be murder). Gallatin argued that the American Robbins had been deprived of his liberty and, ultimately, his life without due process in an American courtroom—that the issues raised by the Robbins case should have been addressed by the American judiciary under Article III of the U.S. Constitution, which provides that "the judicial power shall extend to all cases in law & equity arising under treaties & to all case of admiralty & maritime jurisdiction."

The Republicans' attacks on the Adams administration's handling of the Robbins case included a demand for censure of the president and were calculated to dominate the congressional agenda only months before the presidential election. No legitimate congressional business could be accomplished, Marshall complained, because of the Republicans' filibuster.

The stage was set for Marshall's rebuttal to the Republican charges. Recognized by Speaker Sedgwick on the morning of March 7, 1800, Marshall, his clothes in their usual rumpled condition, moved slowly to the well of the House. Gallatin sat a few feet away, notebook in hand, planning his reply to Marshall's arguments.

Marshall assumed at the outset of his three-hour speech that the man executed was the British sailor Thomas Nash, not the American citizen Jonathan Robbins as the Republicans claimed. Throughout, Marshall referred to the prisoner as Nash. "The case really was that he was an Irishman who had committed a horrid murder on board a British frigate for which he was given up," Marshall later wrote Reuben George. "After he had been several months in prison, he was induced to declare himself an American seaman in the hope that this untruth would save him."

On the assumption that the man executed was a British subject who had, upon supporting proof, been charged with murder on the British frigate *Hermione* Marshall declared to the House that the extradition was clearly required by article 27 of the Jay Treaty. That article provided for extradition of a fugitive who was a British subject charged with murder on British territory (as the British frigate *Hermione* must be considered under international law, Marshall convincingly argued). Even if there was an additional charge of piracy (for confiscating the ship), which it could be argued was a crime against all nations and, therefore, within American as well as British jurisdiction, the British could still try the prisoner on murder charges. "For the murder, not the piracy, Nash was delivered up," Marshall asserted. "Murder, and not piracy, is comprehended in the 27th article of the treaty between the two nations."

Marshall challenged Gallatin's argument that it was the constitutional duty of the judiciary, not the president, to take primary responsibility for the prisoner's fate. Marshall first agreed with Gallatin's contention that the American judiciary possessed the constitutional authority to decide all *cases* arising under treaties. But in the matter at hand, said Marshall, there was no *case* at issue, only a *question* arising under the Jay Treaty. Marshall observed that the Constitution had never been intended to confer on the judiciary the authority to decide political questions, as distinct from legal cases. The distinction between a *case* in law and a *question* arising under the Constitution or a treaty was crucial for Marshall. "A case in law or equity was a term well understood, and of limited signification," he stated. "It was a controversy between parties which had taken shape for judicial decision. . . . To come within this description, a question must assume a legal form for forensic litigation and judicial decision." But it was a political question—the extradition of a fugitive under the terms of the Jay Treaty—that was at issue here. "The judicial power cannot extend to political compacts—as the establishment of the boundary line between the American and British dominions," he declared, "or the case of the delivery of a murderer under the 27th article of our present treaty with Britain."

Marshall then rebutted the Republicans' argument that the prisoner was entitled to an American trial by jury. The U.S. Constitution, he noted, does not even guarantee a trial by jury to an American seaman accused of murder on an American ship. How, then, could it be argued that a British citizen could not be tried for the crime of murder on a British ship by the proper British tribunal?

Defending Adams's action, Marshall went on to describe the president's foreign-affairs authority. "The case was in its nature a national demand made upon the nation," Marshall said. "The President is the sole organ of the nation in its external relations, and its sole representative with foreign nations. Of consequence, the demand of a foreign nation can only be made on him."

The president, Marshall continued, is charged by the Constitution with executing the laws, including the terms of a treaty. And although Congress may prescribe the means of executing the treaty, absent such procedures in the Jay Treaty, the president's constitutional duty was "to execute the contract [between the United States and Great Britain] by any means it possesses."

"It has then been demonstrated," Marshall concluded:

> 1st. That the case of Thomas Nash, as stated to the President, was completely within the 27th article of the treaty between the United States of America and Great Britain.
> 2ndly. That this question was proper for executive and not for judicial decision, and
> 3rdly. That, in deciding it, the President is not chargeable with an interference with judicial decisions.

Marshall's future colleague on the Court, Justice Joseph Story, would write that Marshall's speech on the Robbins case was "one of the most consummate juridical arguments which was ever pronounced in the halls of legislation . . . a *Réponse sans réplique,* an answer so powerful that it admitted no reply." President Adams's great-grandson Henry wrote that the Marshall argument reduced the Republican opposition to silence. Marshall's biographers have accepted that version of history. One describes a distressed Albert Gallatin, who had retreated to the rear of the House chamber, rejecting his Republican colleagues' urgent request for a reply to Marshall's argument. "Gentlemen," Gallatin was reported to have said, "answer it yourself. For my part, I think it is unanswerable."

But recent research strongly suggests that, as impressive as Marshall's arguments were, they did not render the opposition speechless. Gallatin's papers, for example, show that he made extensive notes on Marshall's speech and several points of rebuttal in the right-hand margin. There is also evidence that Jefferson, who extended to Marshall a rare compliment on the quality of his argument, found much in it to disagree with. Specifically, Jefferson wrote on a copy of the speech printed in pamphlet form: (1) that the primary charge against Robbins should have been piracy, which could be prosecuted in an American court; (2) if Robbins was, in addition, charged with murder, the court was required to determine whether he was an American sailor involuntarily impressed by the British; and (3) even if the president was unwilling to hear Robbins's defense, the American judiciary, under the U.S. Constitution, was required to do so.

And, in truth, Marshall's conclusions depended crucially on his basic premises, which were by no means self-evident. Consider, for example, Marshall's rendering of the facts. He was certain that the man executed was the British subject Thomas Nash, who was guilty of the crime of murder on the *Hermione*. But even Marshall admitted that if the Republicans' factual assumptions were correct his conclusions would be different. "Had Thomas Nash been an impressed American, the homicide on board the *Hermione*, would, most certainly, not have been murder," Marshall conceded. "Of consequence, the decision of the President was so expressed, as to exclude the case of an impressed American liberating himself by homicide." Although Marshall and his biographers considered the evidence of the identity of the prisoner as Thomas Nash to be overwhelming, at least one modern historical study has presented strong circumstantial evidence that he was, in fact, an American citizen named Jonathan Robbins.

In addition to his presumption that the man executed was Nash,

Marshall insisted on another crucial premise that was also debatable. In the Robbins case, as discussed above, Marshall argued that the controversy involved only a *question* under the Jay Treaty, and that such a question, as opposed to a *case* in law, did not require judicial resolution. But it could be argued that the Robbins controversy contained key elements of a *case* in law.

There were differences between the extradition proceeding in Judge Bee's courtroom and that of an ordinary trial. Unlike a trial, the arguments in the Robbins case encompassed the meaning of a binding treaty between two nations and the proper authority to see that the terms of the treaty were carried out. But the proceeding also had trappings of an ordinary case, with a federal judge presiding and hearing arguments from opposing counsel. And, significantly, Judge Bee was required to determine whether there was sufficient evidence of criminality to bind the prisoner over for a British court-martial. The purpose of the proceeding was, in effect, to determine probable cause of a crime, a determination that must be made in an ordinary criminal case. Judge Bee's decision, in turn, dictated whether the prisoner would ultimately be deprived of his liberty and his life without the due-process rights that, under the U.S. Constitution, are protected by the judicial branch of the government.

Regardless of the serious questions raised about Marshall's arguments, he carried the day on the floor of the House of Representatives in the spring of 1800. To the immense relief of President Adams, Marshall's bravura performance effectively ended congressional debate in the Robbins case. After Marshall's speech, the Republicans' motion for censure of the president was soundly defeated, and the Federalists, pressing their advantage, quickly passed a resolution approving of Adams's action.

With Marshall's considerable assistance, Adams had managed to deflect serious challenges to his policies from the Republicans during the crucial congressional session prior to the 1800 presidential election. But the president was less successful in quelling opposition from the High Federalists. They had never forgiven him for his peace initiative with France. From the moment of his announcement in February 1799 that he would send a second diplomatic mission to Paris, through the presidential election more than a year and a half later, Hamilton and his High Federalist allies were determined to undermine Adams's presidency and his chance for reelection.

An increasingly bitter Hamilton began to lump Adams and the rival Jeffersonians together, viewing both as poisonous spirits infecting the American body politic. The High Federalists struggled valiantly at home, Hamilton wrote to American Minister Rufus King in England, but were always faced with the "perverseness and capriciousness of one [Adams] and the spirit of faction of many [the Jeffersonians]." Adams was subject to "momentary impulse," Hamilton wrote; "vanity and jealousy exclude all counsel," and "passion wrests the helm from reason." But Hamilton was unsure of the course the High Federalists should take. "In our councils there is no fixed plan," he wrote.

Soon enough, however, the High Federalists agreed upon a strategy that they hoped would deny Adams a second term. At Hamilton's insistence, the High Federalists agreed to give equal public support to the two Federalist candidates, Adams and South Carolina's Charles Cotesworth Pinckney. With their strong endorsement of Pinckney, the High Federalists expected South Carolina's electors to withhold their support for Adams, thereby guaranteeing the election of Pinckney to the presidency.

Adams was not oblivious to the intrigue surrounding him. As early as December 1799, three of his Cabinet members well known for their loyalty to Hamilton—Secretary of War James McHenry, Secretary of State Pickering, and Secretary of the Treasury Oliver Wolcott—sensed that they no longer enjoyed the president's trust. Adams now considered the three Cabinet members "his enemies," Wolcott wrote Massachusetts's Fisher Ames, adding that the president's "resentments against General Hamilton are excessive."

Adams, it often seemed, was bereft of a true political friend in all of Philadelphia—except for John Marshall. Through the entire rancorous session of the Sixth Congress, Marshall not only remained loyal to the president in his votes, but valiantly and effectively defended the Adams administration's policies. And when necessary, as the Robbins case demonstrated, Marshall brilliantly defended the conduct of the president himself.

In typically abrupt fashion, Adams attempted to reward Marshall and, at the same time, rid himself of one of his Cabinet members whom he suspected of disloyalty. On the evening of May 5, 1800, the president demanded that Secretary of War McHenry leave a dinner party to discuss departmental business with him. After settling the departmental business, Adams launched into a blistering attack on Hamilton and accused McHenry of being his stealthy accomplice. In McHenry's account of the incident, the shaken Cabinet secretary tried to defend himself, which only infuriated the president. Adams castigated McHenry for what he charged were the War Department's woeful inefficiencies. Left little choice, McHenry submitted his resignation, which the president accepted on the spot.

Less than forty-eight hours later, without consulting Marshall, Adams sent his name to the Senate as the replacement for McHenry. With the extraordinary self-assurance that he had earlier displayed in turning down President Adams for a seat on the U.S. Supreme Court, Marshall carefully considered the reasons why he should not accept the president's latest offer. First of all, he did not consider himself well qualified to be secretary of war. Second, he was not yet willing to abandon his hopes of returning to the Richmond bar. His once-thriving law practice had suffered severely as a result of his long absences, first as envoy in Paris and now as a member of Congress. If he had any hope of resuscitating his practice, he knew he must return soon to Richmond. Marshall was also aware that his wife, Polly, had been extremely unhappy living in Philadelphia and wanted desperately to reside permanently in Richmond. Marshall therefore wrote Adams privately (so as not to embarrass the president) that he must reluctantly decline his offer. Yet, even after he had also received Marshall's formal public letter respectfully declining the appointment, Adams did not withdraw the nomination, and on May 9, 1800, the Senate duly confirmed Marshall as secretary of war.

Although John Adams knew that he could not persuade Marshall to serve as secretary of war despite the Senate confirmation, the president was still determined to make Marshall a member of his Cabinet. The opportunity arose on May 10, after Adams, in a confrontation with Secretary of State Pickering—another Cabinet member he had long suspected of disloyalty—demanded that his secretary of state resign. The proud, arrogant Pickering refused, and so Adams dismissed him.

Two days later, the president sent the name of John Marshall to the Senate, this time to be his new secretary of state. The incorrigible Adams had neglected, once again, to inform Marshall of his intention to appoint him to his Cabinet. In fact, Marshall was en route to Richmond to attend to legal matters in the state courts at the moment that the Senate received his name for a second Cabinet post.

With his second Cabinet appointment within a week pending, Marshall's reasons for returning to Richmond permanently still weighed heavily on him. But there were attractions to being secretary of state. Most important, Marshall considered himself well qualified to supervise the administration's foreign policy. He possessed extensive high-level experience as a diplomat in Paris, and he continued to hold strong views on the direction that U.S. foreign policy should take. Accepting the position, moreover, would allow him to serve his country and his party at a salary ($5,000) that would support a comfortable lifestyle. The cabinet post might also shield him from the ugly partisan attacks of the Republicans. He later wrote:

> The office was precisely that which I wished, and for which I had vanity enough to think myself fitted. I should remain in it while the party remained in power; should a revolution [i.e., Jefferson's election as president] take place, it would at all events relieve me from the competition for Congress without yielding to my adversaries, and enable me to return once more to the bar in the character of a lawyer having no possible view to politics. I determined to accept the offer.

[5]

Prelude to a Revolution

REPUBLICAN LEADERS in the House of Representatives were dealt a maddening defeat by the Federalist majority when they had attempted to debate the merits of the Alien and Sedition Acts in January 1799. Whenever a Republican spoke, Jefferson reported to Madison, the Federalists "began to enter into loud conversations, laugh, cough, etc., so that for the last hour of these gentlemen's speaking, they must have had the lungs of a vendue master to have been heard."

But Jefferson, understandably irritated, realized that his opponents were making a tactical error. He was convinced that the furor over the XYZ Affair—which he labeled "the X.Y.Z. delusion"—had begun to dissipate, thanks largely to the public's general revulsion at the Alien and Sedition Acts. He noted with satisfaction that Congress was almost daily bombarded with petitions—sent primarily from the states of New York, New Jersey, and Pennsylvania—protesting the laws. The petitions were tangible evidence that Republican arguments against the oppressive laws, most dramatically articulated in the Kentucky and Virginia Resolutions, were having the desired effect on public opinion.

What Jefferson feared most was that the protests against the laws would turn violent, as, reportedly, appeared likely in several sections of Pennsylvania. "Firmness on our part, but passive firmness, is the true course," he wrote Madison. "Anything rash or threatening might check the favorable dispositions of these middle states and rally them again around the measures which are ruining us."

Outside of Philadelphia, the Republicans were more than holding their own in the state elections in the Southern and Middle Atlantic states, as Republican victories in the Virginia gubernatorial and assembly races demonstrated. Jefferson knew that Republican successes in state legislative elections were crucial if the Republicans were to win the 1800 presidential election, since more than half of the states provided that the state legislatures appoint their presidential electors. Jefferson was intent on making certain that the Republicans' message was effectively spread through word of mouth, the Republican press, and the publication and wide distribution of political pamphlets.

By the late summer of 1799, almost a year after he had drafted the Kentucky Resolutions, Jefferson wrote to Wilson Cary Nicholas, the neighbor who had delivered the Resolutions to John Breckinridge, proposing that the Republicans renew their protest by responding to Congress and to states that had ignored or rejected their arguments in the Kentucky and Virginia Resolutions. Jefferson recommended that they reiterate his basic objection that Congress, by ignoring the essential compact among the states, had exceeded its constitutional authority in passing the laws. Repeated violations of the compact, Jefferson believed, would justify overt defiance by the states.

Realizing that his arguments could be construed as advocating secession, Jefferson suggested to Nicholas that the Republicans "express in affectionate and conciliatory language our warm attachment to union with our sister-states, and to the instrument and principles with which we are united." Indeed, Jefferson conceded, union was worth the sacrifice of everything—except the rights of self-government. Confident that the good sense of the American people would prevail, and that the Alien and Sedition Acts would be overturned, Jefferson nonetheless reserved the right of the states to secede if all else failed. Union, he wrote to Nicholas, was not worth the price of self-government, "which we have never yielded and in which alone we see liberty, safety, and happiness."

In this remarkable letter, Jefferson proved himself a political purist, willing to sacrifice everything, even the union for which he had been such an eloquent spokesman. But even as he wrote this radical declaration of principle, he acknowledged that he needed the counsel of the more pragmatic Madison. His arguments, he emphasized, were only a basis for discussion. In fact, Jefferson had met with Madison, before he wrote Nicholas. And Madison, predictably, toned down Jefferson's declaration and ultimately eliminated his call for secession as a last resort.

Jefferson was not particularly disappointed by the moderation imposed upon him by Madison. As he wrote Nicholas, his recommendations had only been for the purpose of expressing "some general ideas for consideration and consultation." He reported that "Mr. Madison does not concur [with Jefferson's position on secession] . . . and from this I recede readily, not only in deference to his judgment, but because . . . we should never think of separation but for repeated and enormous violations."

Before closing his letter to Nicholas, Jefferson warned that "the visit of the apostle Marshall to Kentucky excites anxiety; however, we doubt not that his poisons will be effectually counterworked." Jefferson's attack on Marshall was puzzling, because, of all the Federalist leaders, Marshall had been the most critical of the Alien and Sedition Acts. Marshall, in fact, had not gone to Kentucky to spread "poisons" but to visit his father, who was dying.

By early fall, Jefferson's attention had turned to Republican prospects in the presidential election. He happily reported to his South Carolina ally Senator Charles Pinckney that there were indications that the Republicans would win majorities in both houses of the Pennsylvania legislature. With Republican victories in Pennsylvania and other Middle Atlantic states as well as in the South, Jefferson believed the Republicans would win control of the executive and legislative branches of the federal government.

Jefferson continued to denounce the work of the third branch of the federal government, the judiciary, not just for the Federalist judges' complicity in prosecutions under the Alien and Sedition Acts, but also for their recognition of a unifying federal common law based on evolving judicial principles, not statutes passed by the popularly elected legislatures.

The emergence of a federal common law was just one more example to Jefferson of the "monarchising" policies of the judicial and executive branches of the federal government. It was urgent, therefore, that Republican leaders like Pinckney continue to work toward what Jefferson would later refer to as a peaceful revolution. Jefferson was confident that, once the monarchial designs of the Federalists had been exposed, the American people would reject them and allow his party to rededicate the nation to its essential republican principles.

Early in 1800, Jefferson received the shocking news from Paris that Napoleon Bonaparte had seized power from the French Directory. "You have seen the afflicting details from Paris," Jefferson wrote Dr. William Bache. "On what grounds a revolution has been made, we are not informed, and are still more at a loss to divine what will be its issue: whether we are to have again the history of Robespierre, of Caesar or the new phenomenon of a usurpation of the government for the purpose of making it free."

A passionate supporter of revolutionary France, Jefferson was alert to the despotic dangers posed by the new regime. He drew important lessons for the United States from the coup. Napoleon's seizure of power should remind Americans of the "necessity to rally firmly and in close bands round their Constitution." The first constitutional duty of U.S. citizens was to abide by the will of the majority, but always with a respect for the rights of the minority. They must "beware a military force, even of citizens, and to beware of too much confidence in any man."

Jefferson believed that republican principles continued to be in danger at home as well. He feared the concentration of power in a single executive, then President Adams, but even more he feared Hamilton, whom he termed "our Bonaparte." And that executive power could too easily be expanded by the vigorous prosecutions of critics of the Adams administration under the Sedition Act as well as by the threat posed by a large, potentially menacing standing army.

Still, Jefferson distinguished between the American and French experiences. He noted that Americans, unlike the French, had been committed since their revolution almost a quarter-century earlier to the natural law of self-government. "Of the sacredness of this law our countrymen are impressed from their cradle," he wrote John Breckinridge, "so that with them it is almost innate."

In their most blatant effort to stay in power, the Federalists stepped up their campaign to silence critics of the Adams administration by targeting three Republican "scribblers"—William Duane, Thomas Cooper, and James T. Callender. According to the Federalist press, the three foreign-born "scribblers" took their orders directly from Jefferson—labeled "the Chief Juggler"—and together they had conspired to spread subversive Republican invective across the country.

The first of the writers singled out, William Duane, inspired both scorn and trepidation among Federalist leaders (including Washington, Adams, and Pickering). Although born in colonial New York to Irish parents (a fact disputed by his Federalist detractors, who insisted that the "wild Irishman" had been born in Ireland), Duane had spent his early adulthood in the British Empire, demonstrating an exceptional talent for vituperative attack on the governing establishments in both India and Great Britain. As editor of Calcutta's *Indian World,* he so infuriated the provincial governor with his attacks on the powerful East India Company that he was seized, divested of his property, and deported without a trial.

Duane returned to the United States in 1796, at the age of thirty-six, to become assistant to Benjamin Bache, the editor of Philadelphia's *Aurora.* When Bache died of yellow fever in 1798, Duane succeeded him and quickly introduced his confrontational style of journalism into the columns of the *Aurora.*

Three months after he took over the *Aurora,* Federalist prosecutors made their first attempt to transfer Duane from his editorial office to a federal jail. Their effort followed a scuffle outside of St. Mary's Catholic Church in Philadelphia in the spring of 1799, where a small group of Irish immigrants had attempted to obtain signatures on a petition protesting the Alien Act. Duane and three other men were arrested and charged with maliciously stirring up a seditious riot with intent to subvert the government of the United States. It became known as "Duane's case," even though the prosecution never established that Duane was present at the church. A jury acquitted all four defendants after only thirty minutes of deliberation.

The following summer, Secretary of State Pickering called President Adams's attention to Duane's accusation, repeatedly published in the *Aurora,* that the administration was improperly influenced by British interests. With Pickering himself supplying the offending articles from the *Aurora* to the federal prosecutor, Duane was arrested for seditious libel.

While Duane's sedition trial was pending, the Federalists made their most audacious effort to gag the *Aurora*'s editor. It occurred in March 1800, after Republican senators furnished to Duane a copy of the Federalists' proposed Ross bill, named for Senator James Ross of Pennsylvania, which would have given a Federalist–dominated congressional committee of twelve, presided over by Federalist Chief Justice Oliver Ellsworth, the authority to scrutinize and, presumably, throw out electoral votes for Jefferson in the impending presidential election. Duane promptly published the bill, along with fiery editorials assaulting the legislation, before it passed the Senate.

The enraged Federalists invoked a novel notion of Senate privilege to punish the *Aurora*'s editor. This theory held that there could be no publication of the Senate's business that brought the body into disrepute. A special Senate committee on privileges was convened and quickly found Duane guilty of seditious utterances. He was ordered to appear before the Senate in a special proceeding that required the presiding officer of the Senate, Thomas Jefferson, to read the charges against Duane.

It seemed that the Federalists had finally trapped Duane, and ensnared the Republican presidential aspirant in the process. But the feisty Duane was more than equal to the challenge. He refused to recognize the legitimacy of the Senate's charge. Denouncing its action as a "monstrous attempt" to muzzle him, Duane vowed to continue to comment on the Senate's proceedings "with all freedom that the Constitution secures to the press."

Duane also met with two prominent Republicans—Alexander Dallas, secretary of the commonwealth of Pennsylvania, and Thomas Cooper, a Pennsylvania lawyer and writer—to devise a legal strategy for his defense. They decided that Duane should try to delay the Senate proceeding for as long as possible but, ultimately, to challenge the legality of the proceeding, including the jurisdiction of the Senate to punish Duane. Cooper informed Jefferson of the strategy in a letter that began with a formal request by Duane to the vice president, as presiding officer of the Senate, for the assistance of counsel at the Senate proceeding and the right to call witnesses in his behalf.

Before the Senate could act on his request, however, Duane was ordered to appear before the Senate, where he repeated his request for legal representation. He was informed that legal counsel could appear on his behalf only to deny any of the charges or to offer "in excuse and extenuation of his offense." His attorneys could not challenge the jurisdiction of the Senate or present evidence of his innocence, such as the defense that what Duane had printed was true.

Without legal representation, Duane declared that he would not voluntarily appear before the Senate, which, therefore, found him guilty of contempt on March 25 and issued a warrant for the sergeant-at-arms to take him into custody. The warrant, signed by the Senate's presiding officer, Vice President Jefferson, enlisted every officer of the federal government to assist the sergeant-at-arms in bringing the fugitive to justice. But somehow, over the next few months, Duane managed to stay just out of reach of the authorities, all the while taunting his pursuers by continuing to publish his attacks in the *Aurora*.

Publicly, Jefferson was scrupulously nonpartisan during the Duane proceedings in the Senate. He was, nonetheless, fully informed by Duane's attorney Thomas Cooper of every strategic legal move that the *Aurora* editor would make during the confrontation with the Senate, and may well have participated in the strategy sessions. In any event, he was surely relieved that the editor of the leading Republican newspaper in the country remained free throughout the election campaign.

John Marshall, who was not directly involved in the Duane case, made written observations on both the legal and the political aspects of the controversy, whereas Jefferson, who presided over the proceedings, wrote nothing. Marshall defended the legality of the Senate's action against Duane, although he considered it a political mistake for the Federalists.

Marshall's denunciation of Duane's published attacks ("a [daily] falsehood & an insult") was uncharacteristically dogmatic. And his defense of the Federalist Senate majority's action appeared somewhat strained. The usually deliberate Marshall relied exclusively on precedent—that it had been done before and accepted by both political parties. Conspicuously missing from his arguments was any suggestion of the danger that the partisan Senate attack on Duane could pose for a free press during a presidential campaign year.

Thomas Cooper found himself the object of a Sedition Act prosecution shortly after Duane had failed to appear in the Senate to hear the charges against him. Like Duane, Cooper had earlier gained a measure of notoriety in England with his outspoken verbal attacks on the established British order; he was denounced in Parliament for his radicalism by Edmund Burke. But, unlike Duane's, Cooper's reputation was not acquired solely from his work as a journalist. Born in England, Cooper was an Oxford-educated barrister who was also a serious chemist as well as a successful Manchester businessman. The freedom to express his political beliefs was more important to Cooper, and as a result, he immigrated to the United States in 1794, where he expected that he could more freely express them. Cooper settled in rural Northumberland County, Pennsylvania, became a U.S. citizen, practiced law, and eventually wrote articles and pamphlets criticizing the Adams administration.

In 1799, Cooper wrote an article in the *Northumberland Gazette* in which he imagined himself a power-hungry president of the United States. Cooper described the policies that his despotic president would need to pursue to consolidate his power—measures that were remarkably similar to the policies of the Adams administration, including the expansion of a standing army and prosecutions of the opposition press. In conclusion, Cooper dispensed with the imaginary president and specifically attacked Federalist prosecutions under the Alien and Sedition Acts.

After Secretary of State Pickering had a copy of Cooper's article (which had been reprinted in the *Aurora*) sent to the president, Adams wrote Pickering that such "libels and satires" were "lawless things, indeed!" The president said he had not read "a meaner, a more artful, or a more malicious libel. I despise it; but I have no doubt it is libel against the whole government and, as such, ought to be prosecuted."

Cooper was soon accused in print by an anonymous writer of attacking Adams because the president two years earlier had refused to appoint him to a federal commission arbitrating American and British debts. Cooper vehemently denied the charge and was further incensed because the anonymous writer could have known about his request for a federal appointment only through a leak from the president of their confidential correspondence. He published a denial of the charge in a handbill, commenting acidly that the president was "hardly in the infancy of his political mistake" when Cooper's request for federal appointment had been turned down.

Though Adams and Pickering had targeted Cooper for reprisal, Federalist prosecutors only brought charges against him under the Sedition Act after Cooper served as legal adviser to William Duane. With Duane on the run in April 1800, Cooper was arrested for seditious libel and prosecuted before U.S. Supreme Court Justice Samuel Chase, who was serving as circuit judge, sharing the bench with U.S. District Judge Richard Peters.

From the outset, it was clear that Justice Chase, the most zealous Federalist on the bench, was in charge and actively engaged in helping the prosecutor prove Cooper guilty. In his remarks during trial and in his instruction to the jury, Chase systematically undermined Cooper's two defenses—that what he wrote was true and, alternatively, that even if it was not shown to be true, the writer lacked the requisite bad motive. Although the Sedition Act's language made it clear that the burden was on the government to prove Cooper's writings false, Justice Chase shifted the burden to the defendant to prove that what he wrote was true. The defendant "must prove every charge he has made," Chase told the jury, "he must prove it to the marrow." Chase also declared in open court that the evidence showed that the defendant "intended to dare and defy the government and to provoke them," concluding that that was proof enough of Cooper's bad intent.

After brief deliberation, the jury brought in a verdict of guilty for what was essentially Cooper's criticism of the public policies of the president of the United States. Chase sentenced Cooper to six months in prison and assessed a $400 fine.

Throughout the Cooper trial, Jefferson said nothing publicly and offered little comment in his correspondence. Jefferson's reticence about the Federalist assault on Cooper (as well as on Duane and Callender) was probably due to his fear that any written communication from him might be intercepted by Federalist postal officials and used against him or his party.

James T. Callender, the third target for the Federalists in the spring of 1800, first gained public notice for his writings in Great Britain challenging the established political order. The Scottish-born Callender was indicted for seditious criticism of the government in Edinburgh in

1793 for his publication *The Political Progress of Great Britain, or An Impartial History of Abuses in the Government of the British Empire,* which attacked King George III, Parliament ("a phalanx of mercenaries"), and the British constitution ("a conspiracy of the rich against the poor"). He fled to the United States, and was forbidden by British authorities from returning to his homeland.

Callender was a cruder version of the political radical than either Duane or Cooper. For much of his life in the United States, Callender was debt-ridden and suffered periodic bouts of alcoholism. His political writings were filled with venomous personal attacks on his political targets. It was Callender who first publicly exposed Alexander Hamilton's affair with a married woman, Maria Reynolds. In 1798, after Callender had joined the staff of the *Aurora,* the rival Federalist newspaper, the *Gazette of the United States,* demanded the ultimate sanction. Callender had published "sufficient general slander on our country," the *Gazette* charged, "to entitle him to the benefit of the gallows."

Callender fled Philadelphia and turned up in Virginia, where he joined the staff of the South's leading Republican newspaper, the *Richmond Examiner.* While at the *Examiner,* Callender wrote his best-known pamphlet, *The Prospect Before Us,* a bristling attack on the Federalist party and an unadorned plea for Jefferson's election to the presidency.

Callender's broadside assault did not spare even John Marshall and may explain, in part, Marshall's great interest in Callender's sedition trial. Marshall's successful 1798 congressional campaign, Callender wrote, could be attributed to his hypocritical guile and base pandering to the masses. According to Callender, Marshall had duped Richmond's Republican voters by persuading them that his views did not differ from those of his Republican opponent. All the while, Callender wrote, Marshall was courting them shamelessly by plying them with liquor and dancing foolishly around expensive barbecues that Marshall himself had paid for. He was "the paymaster of strong liquors," Callender wrote, "the barbeque representative of Richmond."

Callender saved his most acrimonious attacks for President Adams. "The reign of Mr. Adams has been one continued tempest of malignant passions," Callender wrote. "As President, he has never opened his lips, or lifted his pen without threatening and scolding; the grand object of his administration has been to exasperate the rage of contending parties to calumniate and destroy every man who differs from his opinions."

For Callender, the choice for the voters was between "paradise and perdition," between an exemplary Jefferson and an unprincipled, warmongering Adams, "between that man whose life is unspotted by crime, and that man whose hands are reeking with the blood of the poor, friendless Connecticut sailor [Jonathan Robbins]." He concluded: "Take your choice, then, between Adams, war and beggary, and Jefferson, peace and competency."

Jefferson had praised *The Prospect Before Us* after Callender sent him a proof of the manuscript. "Such papers cannot fail to produce the best effect," Jefferson wrote. Soon after *Prospect* was published, Callender wrote a series of articles further attacking Adams and reported to Jefferson that he was "now firing through five port holes at once, which is enough for one hand."

With the Federalists already on the attack against Duane and Cooper, it was only a matter of time until they targeted Callender. Writing to Jefferson in early May 1800, Virginia's Governor James Monroe predicted, "An attempt will be made to carry the sedition law here, as an electioneering trick, in the course of the summer." Justice Samuel Chase, fresh from the trial of Thomas Cooper, was given a copy of Callender's *The Prospect Before Us* en route to Virginia for his first tour of the Southern federal judicial circuit. Chase later recalled that his "indignation" was strongly aroused by Callender's "atrocious and profligate libel." Even before he had arrived in Virginia, the justice had decided that Callender had violated the Sedition Act.

After a warrant for Callender's arrest was sworn out, Chase expressed his fear "that we shall not be able to get the damned rascal in this court." But Callender was soon arrested and brought before Chase, who released him on $400 bail pending trial.

The question for Jefferson and other Republican leaders was how vigorously Callender should be defended. He was not the most reputable spokesman for Republican principles. But he had, in his inimitable way, done the party a distinct political service. Jefferson wrote Monroe that Callender should be "substantially defended" in the Richmond courtroom in which Justice Chase presided.

At the trial, Justice Chase rendered Callender's attorneys virtually powerless to defend their client. He harassed all three of Callender's lawyers, each a leader of the Virginia bar. The Justice interrupted George Hay, son-in-law of Governor James Monroe, when Hay attempted to make the argument that Callender's attacks were opinions protected under the Sedition Act, not "fact falsely and maliciously asserted." Chase abruptly challenged Hay, declaring that Callender's pamphlet was false, and that the defendant's bad intentions appeared "sufficiently obvious."

The first defense witness was John Taylor, a leader in the Virginia Assembly and a confidant of Jefferson. Before Taylor could say a word, Chase challenged the witness by insisting that he know in advance what the defense hoped to prove by Taylor's testimony. When he was told that Taylor was expected to testify that he could corroborate Callender's opinion with his own previous conversations with President Adams showing that the president was indeed "a professed aristocrat," Chase demanded that all questions to Taylor be put in writing in advance for his review. When the questions were listed, Chase ruled them inadmissible.

A second defense attorney, William Wirt, attempted to argue that the Sedition Act was unconstitutional. Chase interrupted Wirt and finally ordered him to sit down because, he insisted, his argument was inadmissible. When Hay tried once more to defend Callender, he was again interrupted by the judge. Frustrated that he could not plead his case for his client, Hay folded his papers and withdrew from the case.

After the jury returned a guilty verdict against Callender, Justice Chase praised the panel "because it [the verdict] showed that the laws of the United States could be enforced in Virginia, the principal object of this prosecution." Until he had read Callender's book, Chase said, he had not thought such a bad man existed in the United States. He was relieved, therefore, to know that Callender "was not a native American." Callender was sentenced to nine months in jail, and would not be free until the day the Sedition Act expired, during Jefferson's first year in office as president.

Although the Callender prosecution was a direct attack on the Republican opposition to the Adams administration and a blunt attempt to silence one of the party's most effective propagandists, Jefferson himself was not directly involved in the trial and did not comment extensively on it in writing. On the other hand, John Marshall, recently appointed secretary of state by President Adams, attended the trial, and after Chase had sentenced Callender, accompanied the justice on a stagecoach returning to Philadelphia.* Marshall's presence at the trial was somewhat puzzling, since his attendance could hardly have been inconspicuous. He was, by then, Adams's most trusted Cabinet officer and perceived as one of the president's most enthusiastic supporters for reelection. Did he, by his presence, willingly give his imprimatur to the prosecution?

There is no written record of Marshall's opinion of the Callender trial when it occurred, but he later defended the conduct of Justice Chase. It is fair to say, based on Marshall's later comments, that he disagreed on technical legal grounds with some of Chase's rulings, but that he stopped short of outrage at the justice's conduct at the Callender trial.

Jefferson was not "the Chief Juggler" of Duane, Cooper, and Callender that the Federalist press supposed. There is no record of strategy meetings between Jefferson and the journalists, and no correspondence revealing that Jefferson ordered, or made editorial suggestions on, the work of the three "scribblers." That does not mean that he was unaware of their work or discouraged them from spreading word of what he considered to be the blasphemies of the Adams administration or the need for a new Republican order.

Jefferson read William Duane's scorching editorials in the *Aurora* and, no doubt, approved of them. As presiding officer of the Senate, he was, moreover, an involuntary participant in the Federalist plan to jail Duane in March 1800 for his verbal transgressions against senators of the ruling party. Jefferson's only tangible act in support of Thomas Cooper was a request earlier in the year to the Republicans' state chairman in Virginia that eight dozen copies of Cooper's pamphlet *Political Arithmetic,* a dense analysis of the nation's economy that favored agricultural and inland trade interests championed by the Republicans, be

---

*The Marshall family was represented at the Callender trial by, in addition to John, John's brother William, who was the clerk of the court.

distributed to party committees in every county in the state. Only with regard to Callender is there ample evidence that Jefferson had long encouraged his diatribes. Earlier in the decade, he had read and admired Callender's published attack on the British monarchy and governing establishment. After Callender immigrated to the United States and enthusiastically enrolled as a scribe in the Republican cause, Jefferson wrote him letters of support, including the one praising *The Prospect Before Us*. And from time to time, he answered pleas for money from the desperate Callender, who always seemed to be in debt. According to Jefferson, his modest donations (no single contribution of more than $50) were charitable gestures; his detractors considered them payoffs for Callender's attacks on the Federalists.

Marshall's utter disdain for Callender—and, to a slightly lesser degree, Duane—may suggest why the more radical members of his party were fierce in their pursuit of Callender and the other Republican "scribblers" who offended them. But whereas the pragmatic Marshall admitted that the attacks on Callender and Duane were political mistakes, his more zealous Federalist colleagues, such as Pickering, Justice Chase, and even the president himself, could not rein in their disgust or drive for revenge.

The Federalists' pursuit of William Duane made them look oppressive and, ultimately, incompetent, when they failed to capture the elusive Republican editor. Though the Federalists did corner Thomas Cooper, their success only made a martyr of him. When he was released from jail, shortly before the presidential election, Cooper was made the toast of Philadelphia by the Republicans, the triumphant symbol of freedom over Federalist tyranny. And thanks, in particular, to the tactics (biases) of Justice Chase, the Federalists even cast a scoundrel like James T. Callender in a sympathetic light, as the victim of an overzealous and patently unfair prosecution.[*]

If Jefferson had, in fact, been "the Chief Juggler," he could hardly have planned it better.

---

[*] As a postscript to his prosecution, it should be noted that Callender published the second volume of *The Prospect Before Us,* another unbridled attack on the Federalists, from his jail cell.

[6]

"The Fangs of Jefferson"

AFTER HE WAS SELECTED to lead the Republicans' presidential ticket in 1800, Jefferson projected the image of a political ascetic, wishing only that his pure republican principles be put before the voters. He told his opponent, John Adams, that the presidential contest had nothing to do with their personalities, and everything to do with their conflicting political principles. "Were we both to die today," Jefferson told Adams, "tomorrow two other names would be put in the place of ours, without any change in the motion of the machinery."

As the candidate of lofty principle, Jefferson often appeared to view the day-to-day business of winning the presidency as beneath him, or at least irrelevant to his role as the Republican standard-bearer. His determination to avoid any opportunity to bring public attention to himself was apparent when he made plans to return to Virginia after the adjournment of the spring congressional term. He wrote Virginia Governor Monroe that he hoped to meet with him in Richmond before returning to Monticello. But he cautioned Monroe that their meeting should take place without the public's knowledge.

"Besides my hatred of ceremony," Jefferson wrote Monroe, "I believe it better to avoid every occasion for the impression of sentiments which might drag me into the newspapers." He acknowledged that the Federalists had put public displays to powerful political use, rallying support by furnishing occasions for "the flame of public opinion to break out from time to time." But Jefferson thought such public events unnecessary, even detrimental, to the achievement of his ambitious goals.

Despite his public image of detachment, Jefferson was anything but aloof in his behind-the-scenes political activities. He and Madison, in particular, discussed both broad issues of political principle and specific strategies for partisan advantage. Jefferson had firm ideas on how to exploit the growing fissure between the moderate and conservative Federalist factions over the second Paris peace mission and the related issue of a standing army. He knew that Adams and Marshall supported the peace mission and wanted to maintain the army only for defensive purposes, whereas the High Federalists, led by Hamilton, opposed any settlement with France and favored an expansive, permanent military presence.

Jefferson believed it was important that the Republicans give the warring Federalist factions no reason to unite on the issues. Republicans should continue to advocate a peace settlement with France without saying or doing anything that could provide the Federalists a pretext for keeping a large standing army in peacetime.

At the same time that he was setting the broad parameters of the Republicans' national strategy, Jefferson maintained a very active interest in his party's organization, down to the local county level–as his directive to Virginia's Republican chairman to distribute Thomas Cooper's *Political Arithmetic* demonstrated. He was, moreover, vigilant in urging that the party's message be widely disseminated by the fervent Republican press and the party's most effective pamphleteers. He could justifiably deny that he was "the Chief Juggler" of partisan Republican writers like Duane, Cooper, and Callender–but he knew and encouraged their work.

Jefferson also demonstrated a sure grasp of the electoral process. He prided himself on his ability to know how each state's electors were likely to vote, and indeed boasted that in the 1796 presidential election his prediction was within one or two votes of the outcome. He was somewhat less confident of his prognostications in 1800, but nonetheless ventured to make an educated estimate of the Republicans' chances. He conceded the New England states to Adams and counted most of the Southern and Western states in the Republican column, though he was concerned about Federalist inroads in the Carolinas. The election, Jefferson thought, would be decided in the Middle Atlantic states.

Jefferson had received reliable reports that the two houses of the Pennsylvania legislature—one controlled by Federalists, the other by Republicans—were deadlocked and would not agree on an electoral law, thereby neutralizing the state in the presidential election. Despite assurances from Republican supporters in New Jersey that his party would prevail, Jefferson was not prepared to make such a prediction. His attention, therefore, turned to New York, and more particularly to New York City, where the April election of the city's representatives to the state assembly would determine which party would control the state's electors—and probably the national election.

The fate of the presidential election was, in effect, placed in the hands of the rival political leaders in New York, the Federalists' Alexander Hamilton and the Republicans' Aaron Burr. During the campaign, Burr not only demonstrated superior organizational skills but also proved to be a better strategist than Hamilton. Hamilton's task appeared somewhat easier than Burr's, since the Federalist incumbents already held a majority in the state assembly. But the Federalists made a fatal miscalculation by naming a lackluster list of candidates from New York City for the new assembly. Burr had shrewdly withheld his own slate of Republican candidates until the Federalists had named theirs. Once the Federalist candidates had been announced, Burr stunned Hamilton and other members of his party by announcing a dazzling Republican ticket that included some of the most illustrious names from the American Revolution—former Governor George Clinton, Judge Brockholst Livingston, and General Horatio Gates.

Hamilton was furious that he had been outmaneuvered by Burr, whose Republican slate in New York City won, and took the desperate step of pleading with Governor John Jay to call a special session of the state legislature to nullify what appeared to be a certain Republican electoral victory in the state. Since the old Federalist-dominated assembly was still in office, Hamilton reasoned, the governor could ask the lame-duck legislature to adopt an electoral plan that would take the presidential vote away from the new Republican majority in the assembly and give it to the state's districts, where the Federalists were likely to be victorious.

To Hamilton, such an extraordinary measure was necessary to prevent a Jefferson victory, a catastrophe he compared to "the overthrow of the government . . . a revolution after the manner of Bonaparte." And if that specter of national disaster did not move Jay, Hamilton provided another: the governor must act "to prevent an *Atheist* in religion, and a *Fanatic* in politics, from getting possession of the helm of state." Despite Hamilton's dire warnings, Governor Jay refused the invitation to participate in the electoral scheme.

The New York City election, which appeared to clinch the presidency for Jefferson, dramatically lifted Burr's political fortunes within the Republican party. Although Burr had been on the Republican presidential ticket with Jefferson in 1796, he had never been fully accepted by Virginia's Republican establishment. Jefferson himself had met with Burr only once before the election. The 1796 election had only deepened Burr's distrust of the dominant Southern wing of the party when all but one of Virginia's electors withheld their votes from him.

With his brilliant success in New York City's election, Burr's name was again prominently mentioned for vice president on the Republican national ticket. The Republican House leader, Albert Gallatin, made inquiries about the availability of either George Clinton or Burr to run with Jefferson. Clinton declined for reasons of age and poor health.

Burr could well have afforded to turn down an offer to run with Jefferson, for he was almost assured election as New York's next governor if he chose to make the race. He let it be known, nonetheless, that he was interested in the vice-presidency, if he could be assured that there would be no recurrence of the 1796 electoral slight by Southern Republicans. He would agree to be on the ticket with Jefferson only if he received the total allegiance of his party, including the Virginia electors. After those assurances were made, Burr was officially nominated to the ticket with Jefferson at the Republican congressional caucus in Philadelphia.

Meanwhile, the Federalists were in disarray. Their hopes of retaining the presidency had plummeted with news of the Republican victory in New York City's election. Inside the party, the feud between Adams and Hamilton intensified. For more than a year, Hamilton and his followers had condemned Adams for sending a second peace delegation to Paris. With Adams's determination to support the peace initiative and his resolve to resist the High Federalists' demand for a large standing army, Hamilton had thoroughly soured on the prospect of a second Adams presidential term.

As John Marshall had reported to his brother James during the congressional session, Hamilton intended to undermine Adams's candidacy by urging Federalists to divide their support between the president and South Carolina's Charles Cotesworth Pinckney *equally*. Hamilton expected Federalist electors in all states but South Carolina to give Pinckney the same number of votes as Adams. In Pinckney's home state, Hamilton calculated, Pinckney would split the vote with Jefferson, not Adams. The result, Hamilton hoped, would be the presidential election of Pinckney, over both Adams and Jefferson.

It was a devious plan but one, Hamilton insisted, that was necessary to save the country from both Adams and "the fangs of Jefferson."

On May 15, Jefferson left Philadelphia for the last time.* The three years he served there as vice president had been pocked with relentless political rancor, so he had few regrets about his departure. Jefferson returned to Virginia by way of the Eastern Shore, stopping briefly for a private visit with Governor Monroe in Richmond before reuniting with his daughter Maria at her home in Mont Blanco. At Monticello, Jefferson harvested his wheat crop (the best ever) and continued to work on a manual for Senate parliamentary procedures, which he had begun during the last congressional term, and which, when finished, would serve the Senate for the next two centuries.

That summer and fall, Jefferson the presidential candidate appeared to await the judgment of the voters with equanimity. He did not campaign, or in any other public way call attention to his candidacy. Within those self-imposed restraints, Jefferson nonetheless continued to make certain that his followers fully understood the political principles that would guide him in elective office. In a letter to Gideon Granger, a forlorn Connecticut Republican in overwhelmingly Federalist New England, Jefferson assured his supporter that a Republican majority in Congress would return government to the people, as the Constitution had intended. He wrote Granger that Republicans would

*When the Sixth Congress reconvened for its first session in December, it would do so in the nation's new capital of Washington, D.C., then little more than a festering swamp on the banks of the Potomac.

restore freedom of the press and religion, trial by jury, and an "economical government" and, at the same time, oppose "standing armies, paper [currency] systems, war and all connection, other than commerce, with any foreign nation."

When Jefferson described the prospects for his Republican administration, as he did to Granger, his discussion was of policy and theory. Although Jefferson's opponents faulted him on those terms, their most vicious attacks on the Republican candidate were personal. Jefferson was accused anew of cowardice for fleeing from British troops two decades earlier, when he was Virginia's governor. He was suspected of being a Jacobin at heart, bent on Robespierrean treachery. He was attacked as an incorrigible debtor who owed British creditors more than the worth of his entire estate (a charge that was originally attributed to John Marshall, who later denied being the source of it). He was rumored to have cheated a poor widow out of her estate and to have had sexual relations with the wife of one of his best friends.

Worst of all, Federalists charged that a Jefferson presidency threatened to destroy America's soul. Voters had only to ask one question of themselves, suggested the leading Federalist newspaper, the *Gazette of the United States:* "Shall I continue in allegiance to God—and a religious President, or impiously declare for Jefferson—and no God!" During the campaign, the Federalists reprinted and widely distributed a sermon of President Timothy Dwight of Yale, a Congregationalist divine, who asked: "Can serious and reflecting men look about them and doubt that, if Jefferson is elected and the Jacobins get into authority, those morals which protect our lives from the knife of the assassin, which guard the chastity of our wives and daughters from seduction and violence, defend our property from plunder and devastation and shield our religion from contempt and profanation, will not be trampled upon?"

Jefferson had written Monroe the previous spring that he had no intention of responding to his critics' attacks, particularly about his suspected atheism. "It has been so impossible to contradict all their lies that I have determined to contradict none," he wrote, "for while I should be engaged with one, they would publish twenty new ones." In a letter a few months later to his friend Dr. Benjamin Rush, Jefferson did, however, offer an explanation for the attacks on him and a defense of his religious beliefs, which he did not think would offend either "the rational Christian nor Deists." He strongly suspected that the motivation of his harshest critics, New England clergymen and especially Episcopalians and Congregationalists (like Timothy Dwight), was that their power and ambition were threatened by his insistence on religious liberty for all Americans. "The returning good sense of our country threatens abortion to their hopes, and they believe that any portion of power confided to me will be exerted in opposition to their schemes," Jefferson wrote Rush. "And they believe rightly, for I have sworn upon the altar of god eternal hostility against every form of tyranny of the mind of man."

John Adams had his own formidable problems. He started well enough, attending a celebration in his honor in Alexandria, Virginia, where the president noted how prosperous the upper South had become since his last visit, during the American Revolution. And in Washington and Philadelphia, he spoke again of his experience in the fight for independence, and defended his current Paris peace initiative.

But at the same time that Adams was promoting his candidacy and policies, the Federalist leader most adamantly opposed to both, Alexander Hamilton, was engaged in his own campaign trip. In June, Hamilton made a tour of New England, ostensibly to review military troops and the progress of recruitment, but actually to evaluate the relative strength of Adams and his preferred candidate, Charles Cotesworth Pinckney. Adams himself was well aware of what he termed Hamilton's "imprudent and brazened" attempt "to persuade the people to choose electors who will give a unanimous vote for General Pinckney."

Relations between Adams and Hamilton deteriorated even more in the months before the election. That deterioration was due, in part, to the continuing efforts of the Adams administration to negotiate a peace settlement with France. Since the previous spring, the American envoys in Paris had sent encouraging reports to the administration of progress between their delegation and that of the French government, led by Napoleon's brother Joseph.

Reports of that progress had reached Jefferson in the spring, and he, like Secretary of State Marshall, waited anxiously for further word throughout the summer and early fall. By this time, both men, who only a year earlier had held such diametrically opposed views of

French intentions, were cautiously optimistic about prospects for a peace settlement.

Marshall, as a member of the first American delegation in Paris, had earlier concluded that a just peace settlement with the ruling Directory was impossible. Now he attributed his more sanguine attitude toward a settlement to his greater confidence in the good faith of the new French government.

At the same time that Marshall was looking favorably on a peace treaty with France, he assumed a tougher stance toward Great Britain over that nation's continued violations of American neutrality on the high seas. In a letter to Rufus King, the American minister to Great Britain, Marshall laid out the demands of the U.S. government for a change in British policy. The British navy must abandon its practice of seizing goods on American commercial ships, and the British admiralty courts must stop condoning the practice, which, Marshall wrote, "converted themselves from judges into mere instruments of plunder." He also denounced the impressment of American sailors into service in the Royal Navy, which he described as an act "of violence for which there is no palliative."

If the foreign-policy positions of Marshall and Jefferson toward Great Britain and France, as reflected in their private correspondence in 1800, were placed side by side, it would be difficult to discern major differences between them. Both insisted that Great Britain and France respect American neutrality. They favored free commercial intercourse with each nation but rejected encumbering alliances. And they encouraged peaceful relations with both Great Britain and France on honorable terms that recognized the sovereignty of the United States.

Neither Jefferson nor Marshall credited the other with those reasonable foreign-policy principles. Jefferson never acknowledged Marshall's highly competent work as secretary of state in forging a strong and independent U.S. foreign policy. And Marshall continued to associate Jefferson with a naïvely benign attitude toward France that threatened American interests.

By October 1800, American and French negotiators had reached agreement on the basic issues of a peace treaty that neither side had dared hope for six months earlier. On October 3, the American and French delegations traveled eighteen miles north of Paris to the country estate of Joseph Bonaparte, where they signed the Convention of

Mortefontaine, which provided for "a firm, inviolable, and universal peace" between the two nations.

Although news of the Mortefontaine agreement did not reach the United States for more than a month, earlier reports from Paris of progress in the negotiation provided Hamilton and the High Federalists with one more reason to dread the presidential victory of either Adams or Jefferson. It was during the same month that the Convention of Mortefontaine was signed that a portion of a private letter that Hamilton had written to Federalist leaders, castigating Adams, fell into Aaron Burr's hands. After excerpts were published in the Republican press, Hamilton decided to have the letter published as a pamphlet. In the letter, Hamilton had condemned Adams's peace initiative but saved his most savage words for what he called the president's personal shortcomings, including "disgusting egotism, the distempered jealousy and the ungovernable indiscretion of Mr. Adams's temper."

The publication of Hamilton's attack probably came too late in the presidential campaign to affect its outcome, but it distressed Adams loyalists, including John Marshall. "I wish for his [Hamilton's] sake that it had never been seen by any person," Marshall wrote. "I have no doubt that it wounds & irritates the person at whom it is directed infinitely more than [Callender's] *The Prospect Before Us,* because its author is worthy of attention & his shaft may stick."

In October and early November, the election returns dribbled in from the various states, and it was soon apparent that the Republicans would take control of both houses of Congress. Jefferson's earlier analysis of the presidential election appeared to be borne out by the early returns. New England remained solidly Federalist; Republicans carried New York, thanks to Burr's ingenuity and organizational skills, but lost New Jersey and had to settle for a one-vote margin in Pennsylvania as a result of a compromise between the divided houses of the state legislature. Jefferson won his native Virginia decisively, and most of the other Southern states. But the contest in South Carolina, which Jefferson had expected to go to the Republicans, turned out to be excruciatingly close. By the middle of November, with all but South Carolina's electors chosen, the opposing presidential candidates stood in a virtual tie. Both Adams and Jefferson and their supporters awaited word from South Carolina.

Although Marshall was deeply involved with his official duties as secretary of state, he nonetheless found time to write two anxious letters to the Federalist candidate, South Carolina's Charles Cotesworth Pinckney, reporting the critical position that Pinckney's state held in the election. While emphasizing South Carolina's decisive role in the presidential election, Marshall may also have been subtly exhorting Pinckney to see that all efforts were made to help the Federalist ticket. "I believe the Senate of Pennsylvania will maintain their ground," Marshall wrote Pinckney on November 20. "This, however, will not do for us if Mr Jefferson gets any votes in South Carolina." Even if the Federalist-controlled Senate in Pennsylvania held out for a compromise that deprived Jefferson of a decisive electoral advantage in that state (as it did), Marshall concluded, "it is now reduced to an absolute certainty that any success in your state elects him." Two days later, Marshall again wrote Pinckney to underscore the urgency of his state's election: "On your legislature, I believe, depends absolutely the election."

Jefferson was no less eager to receive the results from South Carolina than Marshall as he awaited word from Senator Charles Pinckney, who had been assigned primary responsibility for a Republican victory in the state. In October, Pinckney had sent Jefferson an optimistic report of Republican prospects. A month later, Pinckney remained confident that Republicans would win a majority in the state legislature, where the electors were selected. But when he realized that Jefferson's fate depended crucially on the results in his state, Pinckney took personal control of his party's efforts. Setting up a command post in Columbia, the state capital, he caucused, cajoled, and bargained for the Republican slate of electors. On December 2, he exultantly reported to Jefferson, "The election is just finished, and we have (thanks to Heaven's goodness) carried it."

By the time Pinckney's letter arrived at Monticello, Jefferson had left for Washington to preside over the final session of the Sixth Congress. The new capital was a sorry sight. Pennsylvania Avenue was a coach-rutted, muddy mess running from the President's House to the incomplete Capitol building. Whereas the old national capital, Philadelphia, boasted a thriving commercial district with hotels, clothing stores, and bookshops, Washington could claim only the barest amenities—one tailor shop, a dry-goods store, a grocery, a laundry, an oyster bar, and a few boarding houses with modest accommodations.

Jefferson took up residence at Conrad and McMunn's boarding house (known as Conrad's), just south of the new Capitol building, where his accommodations of a bedroom and a parlor for receiving guests provided him with greater comfort than the other boarders enjoyed. Among Jefferson's fellow boarders were, agreeably, many members of the Republican congressional delegation. But what should have been a felicitous Jefferson victory celebration at Conrad's turned into a protracted nightmare.

As the state returns were received in Washington for the official count in early December, it became increasingly clear to Jefferson and his fellow Republicans that their party's electors had kept their word to Burr too well. They had voted equally for Jefferson and Burr, even in South Carolina, the state on which the election hinged. By the middle of December, Jefferson believed that the final electoral count would likely be seventy-three votes each for him and Burr, sixty-five for Adams, and sixty-four for Pinckney (one Federalist elector in Rhode Island voted for John Jay instead of Pinckney). If that tie vote held, the Constitution mandated that the decision be made in the Federalist-controlled House of Representatives, where a majority vote of the sixteen state delegations would determine the election.

Before the final electoral-vote count was official, Jefferson held out hope that at least one Republican elector would withhold his vote from Burr. He had been told that several Republican electors from Georgia would do so, assuring Jefferson the presidency, but also guaranteeing that Burr would finish ahead of Adams, so that he would be elected vice president. When that hopeful expectation was not realized, Jefferson appeared to accept the news calmly. He was confident that his leadership of the Republicans was unchallenged, and therefore that his running mate would graciously withdraw from presidential consideration. He had already begun to name his Cabinet, informing Madison that he would be secretary of state and writing New York's Robert Livingston on December 14 that he was his choice as secretary of the navy.

Jefferson even wrote Burr to express regrets that Burr could not serve in Jefferson's Cabinet, since, he presumed, Burr's vice-presidential duties would forbid it. He also probed delicately for assurances of Burr's loyalty to him. "I understand several of the high-flying Federalists have expressed their hope that the two Republican tickets may be equal," he wrote Burr, "and their determination in that case to prevent a choice by the House of Representatives (which they are strong enough to do) and let the government devolve on a president of the Senate."

By Jefferson's own estimate, seven state delegations were committed to him (later revised to eight), and he thought he might reasonably expect to receive the votes of two more. But he was discouraged by the uncertainty of the arithmetic, which depended on "the operation of caucuses and other federal engines," he wrote Madison. He worried that the Federalists might cynically throw their support to Burr. And before long, the Federalists were, in fact, plotting just such a scheme. The month of February 1801 (the month when the House was scheduled to decide the issue), Jefferson predicted, "will present us storms of a new character."

Jefferson feared that the Federalists might snatch the election from the Republicans altogether. As he had speculated in his letter to Burr, a deadlocked House might pass legislation electing an interim president until a new election could be called. Jefferson had originally suggested that the Federalists might elect a president of the Senate (a president *pro tempore*) to serve in that interim capacity. Later, he reported to Madison that "the Feds appear determined to prevent a election, and to pass a bill giving the government to Mr. Jay, appointed Chief Justice,[*] or to Marshall as Secretary of State."

Shortly after Jefferson wrote to Madison, Marshall, the third man on Jefferson's list of potential Federalist usurpers, expressed his most expansive and hostile views of Jefferson in letters to Federalist leaders and family members. He had already written to Charles Cotesworth Pinckney of his profound disappointment in the electoral results that appeared to make Jefferson the next president. Now that a Jefferson-Burr tie seemed inevitable, Marshall wrote Edward Carrington, he really had no interest in the outcome. Marshall's letter to Carrington,

---

[*]Adams had asked John Jay to serve a second term as chief justice, succeeding Oliver Ellsworth, but the president had not yet received Jay's answer; Jay ultimately declined the offer.

however, belied a lack of interest in the result. "I consider it as a choice of evils, & I really am uncertain which would be the greatest." But his description of what was in store for the nation if Burr were elected suggested, by implication, that he would prefer Burr to Jefferson. "It is not believed that he [Burr] would weaken the vital parts of the Constitution, nor is it believed that he has any undue foreign attachments."

In a letter to Alexander Hamilton a few days later, Marshall indicated that he believed Jefferson, unlike Burr, would be susceptible to "undue foreign attachments" and would pursue policies that "weaken the vital parts of the Constitution." Marshall's negative views of Jefferson were offered in response to a letter from Hamilton, who had urged Marshall to use his considerable influence with his former colleagues in the House of Representatives to help elect Jefferson. Hamilton had sent similar letters to other influential Federalists, imploring them to support Jefferson. "Jefferson is to be preferred," Hamilton wrote Oliver Wolcott. "He is by far not so dangerous a man; and he has pretensions to character." Burr, on the other hand, whom Hamilton termed "the Catiline of America," had nothing to recommend him. "Disgrace abroad and ruin at home are the probable fruits of his [Burr's] elevation," Hamilton predicted.

Marshall's reply to Hamilton left no doubt of his deep aversion to Jefferson. "To Mr. Jefferson, whose political character is better known than that of Mr. Burr, I have felt almost insuperable objections," he wrote. "His foreign prejudices seem to me totally to unfit him for the chief magistracy of a nation which cannot indulge those prejudices without sustaining deep & permanent injury." Marshall's attack on Jefferson's "foreign prejudices" was exaggerated and unfair, at least in regard to his attitude toward France, as Jefferson's private correspondence that year demonstrated. Fair or not, Marshall's appraisal of Jefferson's "foreign prejudices" contrasted markedly with his opinion that Burr possessed none.

In addition to his "solid & immoveable objection" to Jefferson's suspected foreign prejudices, Marshall wrote Hamilton that "Mr. Jefferson appears to me to be a man who will embody himself with the House of Representatives." To Marshall, a president who did not exercise the constitutional prerogatives of his office would effectively distort the constitutional structure and undermine the fragile balance of powers provided by the framers. Both Federalist presidents, Washington and Adams, had understood and acted upon their conviction (and Marshall's) that the chief executive must fully exercise his constitutional authority. "By weakening the office of President he [Jefferson] will increase his personal power," Marshall wrote, suggesting that Jefferson would identify with the popular will of the legislative majority and abandon the essential constitutional duties of his office. "He will diminish his responsibility, sap the fundamental principles of the government, & become the leader of that party which is about to constitute the majority of the legislature." Marshall's gloomy forecast of a Jefferson presidency, so far as constitutional structure was concerned, contrasted with his view that Burr "would not weaken the vital parts of the Constitution." Marshall was not indifferent to the contest between Jefferson and Burr, as he professed.

Marshall's final condemnation of Jefferson in his letter to Hamilton had nothing to do with foreign policy or the Constitution, but was instead a deeply personal indictment. Marshall told Hamilton that he could never support Jefferson, because "the morals of the author of the letter to Mazzei cannot be pure." Marshall could not forgive Jefferson for his 1796 letter to his friend Philip Mazzei which appeared to defame George Washington. Jefferson would later deny that he had meant to make any reference to Washington in the letter, but neither Marshall nor any other Federalist ever believed him. For Marshall, Jefferson's insult of his mentor and hero was morally indefensible and, as if an additional reason was needed, disqualified him for the presidency.

Why did Marshall choose to ignore Hamilton's dismal assessment of Burr's character and destructive potential? He was surely as aware of Burr's suspect reputation as were Hamilton and other Federalist leaders, including John Adams, who found the belated Burr presidential candidacy scandalous. And yet Marshall, who could have used his immense influence within the Federalist party to thwart Burr, refused to do so. By refraining from taking an active role during the crisis, the moderate Marshall did as much as the most zealous Federalist partisan to deny the presidency to the undisputed democratic choice, Thomas Jefferson. The explanation must be that the judgment of the usually fair-minded Marshall was severely skewed by his fear and loathing of a prospective Jefferson presidency.

One man could have instantly spared the nation the agony of the election stalemate, and that man was Aaron Burr. No one, including Burr himself, doubted that he had been placed on the Republican presidential ticket for the second position only. He acknowledged that fact in mid-December, after all the votes had been cast but, significantly, before the final count was known. He had first made a post-election declaration of his allegiance to Jefferson in a letter, dated December 16, to one of Jefferson's fellow boarders at Conrad's, Senator Samuel Smith of Maryland. In that letter Burr stated that, in case of a tie (it had not yet been officially confirmed), he would "utterly disclaim all competition" and would never consider "counteracting the wishes and expectations" of the voters to elect Jefferson to the presidency.

A week later, Burr wrote to Jefferson, offering the reassurance that the Virginian had cautiously sought in his letter to Burr of December 15. "My personal friends are perfectly informed of my wishes on the subject [of the presidential election] and can never think of diverting a single vote from you." He was confident, he added, that Jefferson would receive the votes of the majority of state delegations in the House, if the issue was decided there. "As far forth as my knowledge extends, it is the unanimous determination of the Republicans of every grade to support your administration with unremitted zeal," Burr wrote, adding that his loyalty to Jefferson was compelled "by the highest sense of duty as by the most devoted personal attachment."

Jefferson seemed satisfied by Burr's assurances when he wrote his daughter Maria on January 4, 1801. "The Federalists were confident at first they could debauch Col. B. [Burr] from his good faith by offering him their vote to be President, and have seriously proposed it to him," Jefferson wrote. "His conduct has been honorable and decisive, and greatly embarrasses them. Time seems to familiarize them more and more to acquiesce, and to render it daily more probable they will yield to the known will of the people, and that some one state will join the eight already decided as to their vote."

Once Burr had learned that the official results gave him the same number of votes as Jefferson, he began to equivocate about his intentions. He did not repeat his private declarations of loyalty to his running mate and made no attempt to concede the election to Jefferson. The defeated candidate, President John Adams, was appalled by the possibility that Aaron Burr might be the next president of the United States. "All the old patriots, all the splendid talents, the long experience, both of federalists and antifederalists, must be subjected to the humiliation of seeing this dexterous gentleman [Burr] rise, like a balloon, filled with inflammable air, over their heads," Adams wrote Elbridge Gerry. "What a discouragement to all virtuous exertion, and what an encouragement to party intrigue, and corruption!"

While the lame-duck president remained detached from the electoral crisis, he was busy on other matters that would affect the nation long after he left office. Both he and Marshall were stunned when the High Federalists in the Senate initially mustered the votes to reject the treaty between France and the United States that had been signed at Morte-fontaine. But the High Federalists soon realized that the agreement was popular with the general electorate as well as with businessmen in the mercantile towns, who were staunch supporters of the Federalist party. Bolstered by that widespread public approval, the Adams administration resubmitted the treaty to the Senate for a second vote, and it was ratified.

The president also signed into law the Judiciary Act of 1801 after the outgoing Federalist majority in Congress had hurriedly passed a bill creating a new level of federal appellate judgeships, which would be filled promptly by Adams with loyal members of the Federalist party. The Federalists justified the legislation as a reform measure that relieved the six justices of the Supreme Court of their circuit-court duties, which had forced them to travel far from the nation's capital on bad roads and in inclement weather. The Judiciary Act was nonetheless perceived by Republicans as an attempt by the Federalists to control the judicial branch of the federal government for years. Because of the life tenure of the new federal judicial appointees, Jefferson condemned the passage of the Judiciary Act above all other last-minute Federalist measures.

Jefferson showed himself to be less than prescient in focusing his greatest criticism on the Federalist appointments under the Judiciary Act. For there was another judicial appointment that winter, one destined to be by far more historic and antithetical to Jefferson's own political ambitions: President Adams's nomination of John Marshall to be chief justice of the United States.

The president knew that he must act quickly, before the Republicans took office, if he was to replace Chief Justice Oliver Ellsworth, who had announced his resignation in December. Adams had initially offered the chief justiceship to New York's governor, John Jay, but in January, Jay officially declined the nomination. Attention then focused on two members of the Court, Associate Justices William Cushing, sixty-eight years old, and William Paterson of New Jersey, who was the favorite of the High Federalists. But Adams, typically keeping his own counsel, rejected elevating either man in favor of the forty-five-year-old Marshall, whose moderate Federalist views and loyalty to the president were unquestioned.

Marshall recalled the moment when the president made him aware of his choice. He was meeting with Adams to discuss Jay's letter declining the appointment as chief justice. "Who shall I nominate now?" the president asked. Marshall replied that he could not advise him (though privately Marshall had earlier speculated that the appointment would go to Cushing). Hesitating a moment, Adams then answered his own question. "I believe I must nominate you," he told Marshall.

"I had never before heard myself named for the office and had not even thought of it," Marshall later wrote. "I was pleased as well as surprised, and bowed in silence." The day after the president told Marshall of his decision, Marshall's name was sent to the Senate for confirmation. At first, the nomination drew unexpected opposition from the High Federalists, who held up the appointment for a week in hopes that Adams would withdraw Marshall's name in favor of their candidate, Justice Paterson. But Adams stood firm, and Marshall was unanimously confirmed as chief justice of the United States on January 27, 1801.

Meanwhile, the choice of the next president remained unresolved. As Jefferson had feared, the contest was to be decided in the House of Representatives, where the Federalists, with Aaron Burr's acquiescence, were determined to deprive him of the presidency. Jefferson continued to hold out hope that any one of six representatives in key states, all "of moderate disposition," could change their vote and bring him the decisive ninth state delegation. But that hope was mixed with despair, because, as he told his daughter Martha, "there is such a mixture of bad passions in the heart that one feels themselves in an enemy's territory." The worst of it, he wrote, was that most of the Federalist representatives who were to decide his fate were "of the violent kind."

Even Jefferson conceded that defeat in the House might not be the worst outcome. He had heard the rumors, rampant in Washington as well as in the states, that a continued stalemate could lead to the total dissolution of the federal government. Virginia's Republican governor and Jefferson confidant, James Monroe, promised that his state militia stood ready to prevent the Federalists from voiding the election. At the same time, the editor of the Federalist newspaper *Gazette of the United States* reported that if it came to a test of military strength Massachusetts, a Federalist stronghold, could field a state militia greater than the combined strength of those of Pennsylvania and Virginia, which were loyal to Jefferson. Jefferson ignored the insurrectionist threats from both sides and continued to hope for a peaceful, constitutional solution. "At present there is a prospect that some, though Federalists, will prefer yielding to the wishes of the people rather than have no government," he wrote Martha.

The House vote was scheduled for the second week in February. By prior agreement between the two parties, the representatives would meet and vote in continuous session until a winner was declared. At the outset, Jefferson counted eight state delegations solidly supporting him. Six states, all controlled by Federalist majorities, were committed to Burr. Two states, Maryland and Vermont, remained uncommitted.

Members of the House soon realized that a resolution would not come quickly. Some sent home for nightcaps and pillows. And it was well that they did, for the balloting continued for six days. After five days and thirty-five ballots, the delegations were still deadlocked, eight to six, in favor of Jefferson, with Maryland and Vermont uncommitted.

The break came on the thirty-sixth ballot, after moderate Federalists secretly caucused and concluded that Burr could not win. To continue their futile pursuit of a Burr presidency, said James Bayard, the lone congressman from Delaware (who had voted for Burr on all previous ballots), was "to exclude Jefferson at the expense of the Constitution."

On the next ballot, moderate Federalists from the two uncommitted delegations, Maryland and Vermont, submitted blank ballots, giving Jefferson supporters majorities in both states and ten overall, one more than he needed for election. At the same time, Delaware's Bayard and South Carolina's Federalist majority (both of whom had previously cast their delegations' votes for Burr) also cast blank ballots and were recorded as not voting, reducing Burr's total to four states.

Later, Bayard claimed that he had swung the election to Jefferson only after he had been assured that Jefferson would maintain the fiscal integrity of the federal government and retain several important Federalist appointees. There is no evidence that Jefferson made any such promise, though such commitments would not have contradicted his basic principles. The man who was supposed to have extracted the promises from Jefferson, Senator Samuel Smith, declared that, although he had engaged in general discussions with Jefferson, he had never asked the candidate directly for any commitment. Jefferson denied making any commitment to Bayard or any other Federalist, maintaining that he did not trade promises for votes. "Many attempts have been made to obtain terms and promises from me," he wrote Monroe. "I have declared to them unequivocally that I would not receive the government on capitulation, that I would not go into it with my hands tied."

The prolonged election crisis did not appear to dampen Jefferson's conviction that his republican principles would ultimately prevail. Even at the height of the crisis, when the House had voted more than thirty times without resolution, he wrote his old colleague John Taylor offering reassurance. Despite "the gales of monarchy" that the nation had endured, he was hopeful that, "when put on her republican tack, she will show herself built for that." When his victory was secure, he told Taylor, he would be prepared to lead the people in a return to what he considered to be the nation's first political principles. And "even if the old rigging may for a while perhaps disorder her motion," Jefferson concluded, he was confident that he could return the ship of state to her proper constitutional moorings, where power resided with the states and the people. It would be the peaceful revolution that Jefferson had long anticipated.

On March 2, less than two weeks after he had been declared the president-elect of the United States, Jefferson wrote to John Marshall, the new chief justice, with a request. "I propose to take the oath or oaths of office as President of the U.S. on Wednesday the 4th [of March] at 12. o'clock in the Senate chamber. May I hope the favor of your attendance to administer the oath?"

"I shall with much pleasure attend to administer the oath of office on the 4th," Marshall replied the same day, "& shall make a point of being punctual."

[7]

"The Least Dangerous" Branch

ON THE RAW, rainy day of February 4, 1801, John Marshall took his oath as chief justice of the United States in a small committee room on the first floor of the nation's new Capitol. The Supreme Court's meager physical space, later described by the building's architect, Benjamin Latrobe, as "meanly furnished" and "very inconvenient," suggested the Court's lowly status. The quarters for the presumed third coequal branch of the federal government were embarrassingly inferior to the accommodations for the president and Congress. In contrast to the Court's committee room, the President's House, with its four ionic columns at the north entrance, and Congress's official home, located on the upper floors and in the grander spaces of Latrobe's classic Capitol, suggested, even in their unfinished condition, a simple but impressive dignity. The Court's modest accommodations appeared to be an afterthought—as, indeed, they were. The commissioners of the city of Washington did not recommend a space for the Court until late December 1800, and Congress only began to take action a month later, the very day that President Adams's nomination of Marshall as chief justice was sent to the Senate for confirmation.

The Supreme Court of the United States in 1801 could not, in fact, claim parity with the executive or legislative branch of the federal government in either prestige or power. During the first ten years of the Court's existence, no one, including members of the Court itself, appeared impressed with the authority of the federal judiciary. Only four of the six members of the Court attended its first meeting, in New

York in 1791. One of those members, John Rutledge, soon resigned to take what he considered a more important position, that of chief justice of the South Carolina Supreme Court. Like Rutledge, the first chief justice of the United States, John Jay, had also resigned, after he was elected governor of New York.

While in office, Chief Justice Jay and his successor, Oliver Ellsworth, did little to encourage the image of an independent judiciary. Both suspended their Court duties when the president asked them to take on diplomatic assignments. At Washington's request, Jay negotiated the 1794 treaty with Great Britain that bore his name; Ellsworth became a member of Adams's second diplomatic mission to France, which resulted in the Convention of Mortefontaine. But at least Jay's and Ellsworth's extrajudicial duties were widely perceived to be in pursuit of important government business, which could not always be said of the activities of other members of the Court. No one did more to undermine the early image of the Court as an independent and nonpartisan institution than Associate Justice Samuel Chase, first by his aggressively biased conduct of the Sedition Act trials of Republican critics of the Adams administration, and later by his active campaigning for Adams in the 1800 presidential campaign.

At the first official meeting of the Court in 1801, just a few days before Marshall took his oath, only one member, Associate Justice William Cushing, showed up. A second meeting that week still did not produce a quorum. Finally, on February 4, a quorum was achieved when Marshall was joined by three of his colleagues; the two remaining members of the Court, Justices Alfred Moore, and William Paterson, skipped the entire winter session.

The Court's calendar in those early days was uncluttered, and its cases rarely attracted national attention. There were few constitutional cases or crucial interpretations of federal statutes. Most of the work involved technical analyses of narrow legal questions, such as the resolution of a dispute between citizens of different states over the meaning of a private contract or land title. The Court's opinions[*] were so legalistic that the nation's newspapers, both Federalist and Republican, routinely ignored them.

---

[*]Before Chief Justice Marshall encouraged the unanimous Court opinion (usually written by Marshall himself), the justices wrote *seriatim,* each filing a separate opinion.

Marshall anticipated, even in the early months of 1801, that the Federalist-dominated Court would serve as a crucial counterweight to the authority of the first Republican president and Republican-controlled Congress. "Of the importance of the judiciary at all times, but more especially the present, I am very fully impressed," Marshall wrote Charles Cotesworth Pinckney shortly before Jefferson's inauguration, "& I shall endeavor in the new office to which I am called not to disappoint my friends."

Jefferson's Republican dream was Marshall's nightmare. "So far as relates to our domestic situation," Marshall wrote to Rufus King, the American minister to Great Britain, "it is believed & feared that the tendency of the [Jefferson] administration will be to strengthen the state governments at the expense of that of the Union & transfer as much as possible the powers remaining with the general government to the floor of the House of Representatives." As to Jefferson's foreign policy, Marshall saw only mischief and malevolence. "My private conjecture," he wrote King, "is that the government will use all its means to excite the resentment & hate of the people against England without designing to proceed to actual hostilities."

On the morning of March 4, only hours before he was to administer the presidential oath to Jefferson, Marshall wrote Pinckney, describing what he considered to be the dismal prospects for the nation. In the process, Marshall offered the president-elect the most damning words of faint praise. "The democrats are divided into speculative theorists & absolute terrorists," Marshall wrote. "With the latter I am not disposed to class Mr. Jefferson."

Marshall had joined many of Jefferson's vocal detractors in the Federalist party who predicted that the "speculative theorist" at the head of the national government would be totally absorbed with elaborate and, at best, useless political theories that would do the nation no practical good. Things could be worse. If Jefferson joined the "absolute terrorists" in his party, Marshall surmised, "it is not difficult to foresee that much calamity is in store for our country." And if Jefferson did not join his more violent brethren, Marshall speculated, "they will soon become his enemies & calumniators."

Marshall's dark assessment of the nation's prospects under the Republicans was echoed by the leading Federalist newspapers. On Jefferson's inauguration day, Boston's *Columbian Centinel* wrote a eulogy for the nation, appropriately encased in a black border, that mourned the passing of twelve exemplary years of Federalist government, "animated by a Washington, an Adams," as well as other prominent Federalists, including Hamilton, Pickering, and Marshall.

John Adams himself could not bear to witness the transfer of power to his successor, and left Washington by stagecoach at 4 A.M., eight hours before Jefferson was scheduled to take the oath of office. Under any circumstances, Adams's long ride to his Quincy home would not have been pleasant. But the president's companion surely did not help: he was another fleeing Federalist, Speaker of the House Theodore Sedgwick, who, with his High Federalist colleagues, had visited much political misery on the moderate Adams.

Meanwhile, Thomas Jefferson had been happily contemplating the Republican administration that Adams, Marshall, and Sedgwick so dreaded. By design, Jefferson drew an immediate, and vivid, symbolic distinction between his administration and that of his predecessor. Four years earlier, President-elect Adams had ridden to his inaugural ceremony in an elegant coach especially purchased for the occasion; Jefferson walked the few hundred yards from his rooms at Conrad's to the Capitol. And whereas Adams had worn a splendid new suit of pearl-gray broadcloth, a cockaded hat, and a full sword sheathed at his side, Jefferson dressed in plain clothes, swordless, his attire not very different from that of many who watched the Alexandria militia lead the president-elect to the spacious, circular Senate chamber.

Since his election was assured barely two weeks earlier, Jefferson had worked and reworked his speech through three drafts. And at noon on March 4, his speech in hand, Jefferson was welcomed into the Senate chamber by enthusiastic Republican colleagues and well-wishers. After the extraordinary electoral crisis that Jefferson had only just survived, the setting for his inaugural address was awkward. The president-elect took his seat between Vice President Aaron Burr—his Republican running mate, who had only reluctantly acquiesced in his election—and Chief Justice John Marshall.

If Jefferson was discomforted by the presence of the two men who shared the stage with him, he did not show it. He appeared supremely content, as did his many Republican friends and admirers in the gallery. All rejoiced for the same reason: the Republicans had effected a dramatic, but entirely peaceful, transition of political power. "The changes of administration, which in every government and in every age have most generally been epochs of confusion, villainy and bloodshed, in this our happy country take place without any species of distraction or disorder," wrote one exultant onlooker. "This day, has one of the most amiable and worthy men taken that seat to which he was called by the voice of his country."

Jefferson's inaugural address was a masterpiece, demonstrating his talent for articulating his political philosophy in exquisitely crafted, often poetic phrases of great power and beauty. It was also a work of uncommon shrewdness that blurred many of the differences between Jefferson and his opponents, who had predicted that his election would bring irreparable division and destruction to the union. Unfortunately, Jefferson's words, uttered in his soft, high-pitched voice, were inaudible to almost everyone in the Senate chamber except the handful of listeners in the front rows. Fortunately, Jefferson had the good sense to make written copies of the speech so it could be published.

The most stunning theme of Jefferson's address was reconciliation between Republicans and Federalists. Now that the voters had made their choice known, Jefferson said, it was time for Americans of all political persuasions to "arrange themselves under the will of the law, and unite in common efforts for the common good." All could agree on at least one sacred principle: "That though the will of the majority is in all cases to prevail, that will, to be rightful, must be reasonable; that the minority possess their equal rights, which equal laws must protect, and to violate which would be oppression."

Jefferson then hazarded a reference to the wars in Europe, including the French Revolution ("the agonizing spasms of infuriated man, seeking through blood and slaughter his long-lost liberty"), which had caused Americans to divide their sympathies. Admitting that Americans of different political persuasions had reacted differently to the "throes and convulsions of the ancient world," Jefferson nonetheless insisted that "every difference of opinion is not a difference of principle."

To make his point that Americans were united in principle, if divided in transitory opinion, Jefferson penned one of his most quoted passages: "We are all republicans; we are all federalists." Those who heard the statement and the newspapers that reprinted it assumed that the President had capitalized "Republicans" and "Federalists." But that was not his intention; in his original draft he used lowercase letters. His meaning, which he explained more fully in later correspondence, was that all but the most radical Americans believed in a republican form of government, as opposed to a monarchy, and all supported a strong federal government, though moderate Federalists favored a strong executive branch whereas moderate Republicans preferred that the greatest federal power reside in the popularly elected legislature.

Besides delivering felicitous phrases of reconciliation, Jefferson attempted to assuage the worst fears of his Federalist opponents, such as John Marshall. He turned the charge that he was a hopeless visionary and willing participant in the disintegration of the union against his accusers. "I know, indeed, that some honest men fear that a republican government cannot be strong; that this government is not strong enough." His response to that concern contained a subtle dig at his detractors. "But would the honest patriot, in the full tide of successful experiment, abandon a government which has so far kept us free and firm, on the theoretic and visionary fear that this government, the world's best hope, may by possibility want energy to preserve itself? I trust not. I believe this, on the contrary, the strongest government on earth."

Jefferson's libertarian creed was much in evidence as he accepted harsh political dissent as both the price and strength of a vibrant democracy. "If there be any among us who would wish to dissolve this Union or to change its republican form, let them stand undisturbed as monuments of the safety with which error of opinion may be tolerated where reason is left free to combat it." And he applauded Americans, prematurely, for having the conviction to eliminate all religious intolerance from their shores.

There was, to be sure, a distinct Republican flavor to the address, an implicit promise that the new administration would make good on its pledge to restore the nation to its republican principles. Jefferson advocated "a wise and frugal government" and proclaimed his "support of the state governments in all their rights, as the most competent administrations for our domestic concerns and the surest bulwarks against anti-republican tendencies." But there were also assurances that there must be "the preservation of the general government in its whole con-stitutional vigor, as the sheet anchor of our peace at home and safety abroad."

He specifically addressed one of Marshall's abiding concerns about a Jefferson administration—that it would favor French interests and push the nation to the very brink of war with Great Britain. Jefferson expressed no such intentions. On the contrary, he declared that he sought "peace, commerce, and honest friendship with all nations—entangling alliances with none." Such a policy was entirely consistent with Marshall's.

And as if to salve every Marshall wound, Jefferson offered an elo-quent tribute to George Washington. No president who followed Washington, Jefferson conceded, could possibly emulate his great achievements. His preeminent service to the nation "entitled him to the first place in his country's love and destined for him the fairest page in the volume of faithful history." Jefferson promised to do his duty as best he could, humbly asking the indulgence of citizens for the errors of judgment he expected to make. Undoubtedly, he hoped his tribute to Washington would put to rest, once and for all, the furor raised by his letter to Mazzei.

On returning to his lodgings in the late afternoon after administer-ing the presidential oath, Marshall expressed guarded, somewhat grudging admiration for Jefferson's inaugural entreaty. "It [the inau-gural address] is in the general well judged & conciliatory," Marshall wrote Charles Cotesworth Pinckney, completing the letter he had begun that morning. But Marshall could not resist contrasting Jeffer-son's words with the Republicans' attacks on the Adams administra-tion during the presidential campaign. Jefferson's soothing speech of reconciliation "is in direct terms giving the lie to the violent party decla-mation which has elected him." Despite the "well judged" address, Marshall remained skeptical. In his careful appraisal of Jefferson's speech, Marshall concluded that it "is strongly characteristic of the gen-eral cast of his political theory." No inaugural address, however elo-quent, could remove the chief justice's distrust of President Jefferson and the political philosophy that had brought him to power.

Given the content of several letters that Jefferson wrote after his inauguration, Marshall's skepticism was well placed. In his private correspondence, Jefferson described the transition of power in sharply partisan terms that had been absent from his ecumenical public address. In his letters, Jefferson returned to his favorite nautical metaphors to express exhilaration over the Republican victory, and undisguised resentment of the Federalist past. "The storm through which we have passed has been tremendous indeed," he wrote John Dickinson. "The tough sides of our Argosy have been thoroughly tried. Her strength has stood the waves into which she was steered with a view to sink her. We shall put her on her republican tack, and she will now show by the beauty of her motion the skill of her builders." To General James Warren, Jefferson wrote: "It is pleasant for those who have just escaped threatened shipwreck to hail one another when landed in unexpected safety." And to Samuel Adams (the former president's cousin), he wrote, "The storm is over, and we are in port. The ship was not rigged for the service she was put on."

Jefferson was confident that the Republicans were better and more benign sailors than the crew that had been thrown overboard. In scorning past Federalist tactics and policies, he abandoned his nautical imagery. Americans had been "led hoodwinked from their principles," he told Dickinson. He grieved with General Warren over the "subversion" of principles under the Federalists, but, fortunately, they could rejoice "that the ground from which fraud, not force, had for a moment driven us" had been retaken.

If Marshall had read only those passages from Jefferson's private letters, he would no doubt have felt justified in holding to his long-standing suspicion of Jefferson's good faith and judgment. But there was, of course, more to Jefferson's thoughts and intentions than exalting republican theory and condemning the political opposition. In his letters and in many of his decisions as president, Jefferson revealed a practical and conciliatory side. As an early example of Jefferson's pragmatism, the new president ignored pressure from his Republican brethren to remove the Federalist minister to Great Britain, Rufus King, in favor of a party loyalist. Jefferson was aware that King had served well and built valuable relationships with British diplomats that would be extremely important in concluding the negotiations initiated by President Adams and Secretary of State Marshall to settle private American debts to British creditors. Marshall never recognized that pragmatic side of Jefferson (nor, for that matter, did Jefferson ever accept that Marshall's positions as a moderate Federalist were both reasonable and principled).

Beneath the soaring phrases of his inaugural, Jefferson proved that he could protect himself politically much more effectively than his predecessor. Adams had won the presidency by only three electoral votes and, understandably, had felt considerable pressure to stress continuity with the popular Washington administration, which had preceded his. But the key members of Washington's Cabinet he chose to retain—Secretary of State Pickering, Secretary of the Treasury Wolcott, and Secretary of War McHenry—were loyal to Alexander Hamilton, not Adams.* Soon enough, they began to undermine Adams's moderate policies and, ultimately, worked to defeat him in the 1800 presidential campaign.

Since Jefferson expected to lead a Republican revolution, he could make a clean sweep of the Adams Cabinet. In replacing it, he exhibited care and calculation in choosing men who would be not only competent but loyal. His first Cabinet choice was James Madison as secretary of state. Madison and Jefferson had formed one of the closest and most productive political partnerships in all of American history. Eight years younger than Jefferson, the down-to-earth Madison was the perfect alter ego for the ideologically prone Jefferson. And together they built the Republicans' ideological base, with Jefferson becoming the party's democratic symbol and standard-bearer while Madison served as the day-to-day strategist.

Jefferson's second Cabinet choice, Albert Gallatin as secretary of the treasury, was as sure and shrewd as his first. The Swiss-born Gallatin had proved to be a loyal and effective minority leader for the Republicans in the House of Representatives. Despite his foreign background and accent (cruelly ridiculed by High Federalist nativists), the forty-year-old Gallatin was not just a superb political tactician in Congress but also a man with a sophisticated understanding of the financial challenges facing the young republic. Gallatin was said to be the only man in American public affairs who could effectively debate Alexander Hamilton on the intricacies of public finance. Besides their service in

---

*Adams also retained Attorney General Charles Lee from Washington's Cabinet, but Lee remained loyal to the president.

Jefferson's Cabinet, Gallatin and Madison served the president in the informal, and equally valuable, capacity of confidential advisers on issues that ranged far outside their official portfolios.

The other members of Jefferson's Cabinet did not enjoy the same intimate relations with the president. But all of them—Henry Dearborn as secretary of war, Robert Smith as secretary of the navy, Levi Lincoln as attorney general—were, like Gallatin and Madison, in complete agreement with Jefferson on issues of broad policy. So certain was Jefferson of the judgment, and loyalty, of all his Cabinet members that he rarely felt the need to call a meeting of the collective body. Instead, following Washington's earlier example, he supervised the activities of each department by means of frequent meetings and correspondence with individual Cabinet members.

After his presidential reelection defeat was assured, Adams had used his remaining months in office to fill executive and judicial offices with loyal Federalists. At 9 P.M. on the night of March 3, 1801, only three hours before officially leaving office, Adams was busy signing commissions. Jefferson bitterly disagreed with many of Adams's policies, but no action distressed him more than his predecessor's last-minute political appointments, which "Mr. A crowded in with whip & spur." Nonetheless, Jefferson determined to underscore his inaugural theme of reconciliation with the Federalists; he pledged to remove from office only those Federalist appointees who were either incompetent or corrupt. Principle, not partisanship, would be his guiding rule. That credo not only was admirable in theory but had the added virtue of offering moderate Federalists assurances that the Jefferson administration would be both fair and inclusive.

Jefferson harbored no illusions that his policy would be greeted with the broad approbation that his inaugural address received. And, predictably, outspoken Republican leaders, such as Virginia's William Branch Giles, were quick to protest. The Federalists had so debauched the system, Giles asserted, that turnabout was not only fair play but highly desirable. "It can never be unpopular to turn out a vicious one and put a virtuous one in his room," Giles advised Jefferson, "and I am persuaded from the prevalence of the vicious principles of the late administration and the universal loyalty of its adherents in office, it would be hardly possible to err in exclusions."

Drawing partisan fire from the Federalist press as well as members of his own party, Jefferson struggled to adhere to his policy. He declared that all executive appointments (except life-tenured judgeships) after December 12, 1800, the day Adams knew that he had been defeated in the presidential election, would be considered nullities. He also removed the Federalist marshals and district attorneys who had committed "legal oppression" under the Sedition Act.

Jefferson considered Adams's appointments to the federal judiciary the most objectionable. He conceded that his rules of removal did not apply to the judges who were appointed to life terms. And yet the Federalist-dominated judiciary promised to perpetuate well into the nineteenth century a philosophy Jefferson detested. The Federalists "have retreated into the judiciary as a stronghold," Jefferson complained, "the tenure of which renders it difficult to dislodge them."

For years, the federal judiciary had been identified with the political interests of the Federalist party. Federalist judges, trained in the English common law, regularly applied that common law in the federal courts, much to the chagrin of Jefferson and other Republicans, who insisted that the only legitimate law to be applied was that created by statute by the popularly elected legislature. The federal courts, moreover, were widely viewed as sympathetic to large land companies and wealthy creditors, both businessmen and bankers, who were often influential Federalists. Debtors, in general, and small farmers in the South and West, in particular, voted Republican and eagerly sought to settle their disputes in state courts, whose judges were usually elected and more likely to be responsive to their claims. Add to this general impression the phenomenon of biased Federalist judges like Samuel Chase and it is not difficult to understand the disdain and trepidation with which Jefferson and other Republicans viewed Adams's last efforts to pack the federal judiciary.

Whereas Jefferson viewed the federal courts as centralizing, partisan obstacles to his republican vision, Marshall considered them bulwarks of union and protectors of law and, not incidentally, private property from irresponsible debtors. As a congressman, Marshall had worked diligently on the Judiciary Committee of the House of Representatives to prepare the legislation that would become the Judiciary Act of 1801. Adding a new tier of federal circuit courts with expanded jurisdiction was viewed by Marshall as a true reform measure that would strengthen the entire federal judicial system and relieve the justices of the U.S. Supreme Court of needless, and enervating, circuit riding.

After Marshall left Congress to serve as Adams's secretary of state, he was as determined as Adams to secure control of the federal judiciary for the Federalist party. During his nine months as secretary of state, Marshall supervised much of the work of the federal judiciary. His duties included issuing instructions to federal marshals and attorneys whose actions under the Sedition Act Jefferson so resented. He was also responsible for the preparation of all presidential commissions, including appointments to the federal judiciary. Given his close personal relationship with Adams, Marshall was almost certainly consulted on all important policy matters concerning the judiciary. Though Jefferson resented Adams's frenzy to sign the last Federalist judicial commissions on the eve of his inaugural, he could just as well have blamed Marshall, for the very last commissions were signed and sealed in Marshall's office.

Adams and Marshall had taken care in their judicial commissions to reward family affiliation as well as party loyalty, a nepotistic practice that Jefferson refused to follow.[*] Adams's nephew William Cranch and Marshall's brother James were named to the federal circuit court for the District of Columbia, created under a second Judiciary Act that was passed less than a week before Jefferson's inauguration.

The third and final position on the District of Columbia's new federal court, that of chief judge, was offered to another loyal Federalist, Thomas Johnson. But, much to the dismay of Marshall, Johnson officially declined the position after Jefferson took office, leaving the

---

[*]President Jefferson's opposition to appointments of family members was expressed in a letter to his nephew George Jefferson less than a month after he had taken office. "The public will never be made to believe that an appointment of a relative is made on the ground of merit alone, uninfluenced by family views; nor can they ever see with approbation offices, the disposal of which they entrust to their Presidents for public purposes, divided out as family property. Mr. Adams degraded himself infinitely by his conduct on this subject, as General Washington had done himself the greatest honor. . . . It is true that this places the relations of the President in a worse situation than if he were a stranger, but the public good, which cannot be effected if its confidence is lost, requires this sacrifice."

appointment to the new Republican president. Shortly after Jefferson had taken office, Marshall wrote his brother, James, expressing his mortification that Johnson's decision had come too late for Adams and Marshall to name a worthy Federalist replacement.

It did not take long for Judge James Marshall and his colleague William Cranch to serve notice to Jefferson that Federalist judges, even those like themselves who were appointed the day before his inauguration, could do calculable harm to his aspirations for a sustained period of political peace. In the first session of the District of Columbia circuit court, Judges Marshall and Cranch instructed the district attorney to bring a suit for seditious libel against the editor of the Republicans' Washington newspaper, the *National Intelligencer,* which had published a letter signed by "a friend of impartial justice" who, in attacking the political bias of the federal judiciary, found "the asylum of justice impure." From the bench, Judge Marshall, stating that he "was a friend to the freedom, but an enemy to the licentiousness of the press," demanded prosecution.

When Jefferson's appointee to the court, Chief Judge William Kilty, refused to take part in the action, the Federalist judges' instruction was perceived to be politically inspired. The law and control of the federal judicial machinery had changed, however, since the days of Sedition Act prosecutions under the Federalists. The Sedition Act had expired with Jefferson's assumption of the presidency, so the common law of seditious libel, invoked by Judges Cranch and Marshall, was the only instrument available to the federal judiciary to chastise a wayward Republican press. In June 1801, implementation of the circuit court's instruction was the responsibility of a grand jury no longer dominated by Federalists and a district attorney who was a Republican. The district attorney balked at the judicial order, and the grand jury refused to indict. The matter was quietly dropped.

In the early days of the Republican administration, when the president's popularity was ascendant, Jefferson's optimism was limitless. "We can no longer say there is nothing new under the sun," he wrote Dr. Joseph Priestley. "For this whole chapter in the history of man is new. The great extent of our republic is new." He could, at least momentarily, assume a tolerant, almost serene attitude toward the slings of the opposition party. As far as can be determined from Jefferson's correspondence, he did not condemn Judge James Marshall for his attack on the Republican *National Intelligencer*. And though he wanted to declare the Sedition Act unconstitutional, even after it had expired, and had drafted a statement for his first State of the Union address to that effect, he later deleted it to avoid controversy.

But even as he preached political harmony, Jefferson addressed what he perceived to be some of the grossest injustices perpetrated by the Adams administration and, particularly, the Federalist judges under the Sedition Act. Among his early executive actions as president, Jefferson pardoned two men who remained ensnared by the legislation. The first was David Brown, the penniless itinerant preacher who could not pay the $480 fine imposed by Justice Chase after he had served his eighteen-month prison term. Four days later, Jefferson pardoned James T. Callender under circumstances he would later regret.[*] He also halted the judicial proceeding against William Duane, the editor of the *Aurora,* who had been targeted by the Federalist Senate and still awaited trial. And he suggested to a Republican colleague that when Congress convened in December repeal of the Judiciary Act of 1801 would be in order.

John Marshall became head of the nation's highest court at a time when the judiciary was the weakest and least respected branch of the federal government. He and his colleagues would have to operate in a hostile political environment in which both Jefferson and the Republican-controlled Congress were intensely suspicious of the Court and prepared, no one could doubt, to curb what authority the justices possessed.

Marshall began with a modest but significant symbolic gesture. At the first session of the Marshall Court, the chief justice, unlike his new colleagues, wore a plain black robe, and he would continue to do so at every session for the next thirty-four years. It was the same judicial

---

[*]Callender resented the delay in refunding his fine (he had already served his jail sentence and paid his $200 fine) as well as Jefferson's failure to have him appointed federal postmaster in Richmond. That resentment turned to bitterness toward Jefferson, which exploded in print a year later, when Callender accused the president of having carried on a long-standing affair with his young slave, Sally Hemings.

attire worn by two friends of Jefferson's–Judge Edmund Pendleton of the Virginia Court of Appeals and George Wythe, who was chancellor of the High Court of Chancery. The other members of the Supreme Court favored either the scarlet-and-ermine robes of the British judiciary or equally colorful and magisterial academic robes. At the Marshall Court's second session, in August 1801, the other five members of the Court joined the chief justice in wearing unadorned black robes. For that August session, Marshall arranged for all the members of the Court to room and board at Conrad's, where Jefferson had only recently resided. It was the first time that the justices spent extended time together not just discussing cases, but eating, drinking, and sleeping under the same roof. In the past, the justices had found precious little time to congregate in the same city, much less in the same boarding house; instead, they were often riding circuit on horseback in six different directions from the nation's capital. Marshall's arrangements not only created an atmosphere of collegiality and stability but also allowed the chief justice's strong intellect and winning personality to work on his brethren.

An indication that Marshall established his leadership over the Court early on can be seen by the number of unanimous opinions the chief justice wrote in his first years on the Court. From 1801 to 1804, Marshall participated in forty-two cases and, remarkably, wrote unanimous opinions for the Court in all of them. Marshall's ability to forge consensus among the justices was impressive, not only because he came to the job with no prior judicial experience, but also because he had to develop unanimity among six diverse, highly independent men.[*]

The senior justice, sixty-nine-year-old William Cushing, was the first justice appointed to the Court by George Washington, in 1789, and a close friend of John and Abigail Adams. A graduate of Harvard College and the former chief justice of the Massachusetts Supreme Judicial Court, Cushing wore a three-cornered hat, buckled shoes, and a powdered English wig, reputedly the last American judge to do so. A resolute Federalist, he had faced down an unruly crowd protesting the state's collection of taxes, insisting that his court would operate on

---

[*]The unanimity of the Marshall Court did not mean that the justices always agreed. Those judges who disagreed with the majority sometimes honored the norm of "silent acquiescence" by withholding their objections and not recording their disagreement.

schedule. In 1793, Cushing wrote his most important opinion in *Chisholm v. Georgia,* joining the majority in ruling that a state could be sued by a private citizen of another state in federal court (the decision was repudiated by the passage of the Eleventh Amendment, which prohibited such a suit). By 1801, Cushing was considered well past his judicial prime; attentive but none too incisive, he found his greatest pleasure riding in a fine carriage pulled by two horses, while his wife read to him from his favorite literary works.

Associate Justice William Paterson joined the Court in 1793 after an illustrious career in New Jersey as a lawyer (primarily representing wealthy creditors in mercantile disputes), a U.S. senator, and the governor of the state. A graduate of the College of New Jersey (later Princeton), the fifty-five-year-old Paterson had signed the Constitution and, with Oliver Ellsworth, was the chief draftsman of the Judiciary Act of 1789, which created the federal court system. A judge of outstanding intellect and avid Federalist sympathies, Paterson was an outspoken champion of the Sedition Act prosecutions; he conspicuously assisted the jury that found Republican Congressman Matthew Lyon guilty of seditious libel. Not surprisingly, Paterson had been the choice of the Senate's High Federalists to succeed Chief Justice Oliver Ellsworth.

Only one member of the Court exceeded Paterson in his enthusiasm for Sedition Act prosecutions, and that was Justice Samuel Chase. Four years older than Paterson, Chase had earned his reputation for forceful advocacy, provoking controversy as a lawyer and legislator in his native Maryland. Ferocious in appearance, he stood well over six feet tall and had a massive head and a thick mane of hair, a broad, intimidating countenance, and auburn skin (he was called "baconface"). Chase had first shown his propensity for riotous action in colonial America as a member of the Maryland Assembly, protesting the Stamp Act. For his efforts, he was labeled by infuriated Annapolis officials a "busy, restless incendiary, a ringleader of mobs, a foul mouthed and inflaming son of discord and faction." Neither advancing age nor the successful revolution moderated Chase's political passions, though he tended to zigzag from cause to fiery cause. As a delegate to Maryland's Constitutional Convention, he opposed ratification of the Constitution, but he later gave unstinting support to President Washington. Appointed to the Court by Washington in 1796, Chase hewed to Federalist dogma in an opinion declaring the superiority of treaties over state laws. But in a second opinion, Chase took a position advocated by the rival Republicans, including Jefferson, and rejected the argument that federal courts had jurisdiction over crimes at common law. Despite Chase's intellectual independence, the Republicans never forgave him for his excesses during the Sedition Act trials.

Bushrod Washington, the fourth member of the early Marshall Court, was closest to the new chief justice in background and political outlook. Both men had studied law at the College of William and Mary, had served in the Virginia House of Delegates, and had voted to ratify the Constitution at Virginia's convention in 1788. A nephew of the first president, Bushrod had accompanied Marshall to Mount Vernon in 1798, when his famous uncle successfully implored them to run for Congress as moderate Federalists. After Marshall later that month turned down his first appointment to the Supreme Court, President Adams offered the position to Bushrod Washington, who, at the age of thirty-six, accepted and became the youngest justice. Small in stature, mild in manner, and cautious in his professional approach, Washington was not tepid once he had made up his mind in politics (he actively campaigned for Adams in 1800) or law. Though respected as a justice for his careful, studious opinions, he would be best remembered for his enduring friendship with Marshall. The two men rarely disagreed on anything of importance. Bushrod would assist Marshall in preparing his five-volume biography of George Washington, and in their twenty-nine years on the Court together, they differed in their judicial result in only three decisions.

The sixth member of the Court, Alfred Moore, had gained prominence in North Carolina as an attorney, state senator, attorney general, and judge on the state's highest court before his appointment to the Supreme Court in 1799. Only four feet five inches tall and weighing less than a hundred pounds, Moore compensated for his dwarfish size with a ready, biting wit and an intensely logical mind. Though his professional peers spoke of his brilliance at the bar, he did not make a significant mark at the Supreme Court, serving only five years and writing only one opinion.

The Marshall Court's first formidable challenge came in early August 1801 in a major prize case involving a dispute over the American frigate *Constitution*'s seizure on the high seas of an armed merchant ship flying the French flag. Just below the surface of the prize dispute lay the more important, and politically explosive, question of whether the United States' quasi-war with France, championed by the Federalists, gave constitutional sanction to the seizure. Four of the Federalist party's most prominent politicians and lawyers, including Alexander Hamilton (in the circuit court) and Congressman James Bayard (before the Supreme Court), represented the *Constitution*'s captain, Silas Talbot. They argued that his seizure was legal because the United States' quasi-war with France had been officially recognized by an act of the Federalist-controlled Congress in 1799. On the other side, an equal number of prominent Republican lawyers, including Aaron Burr (in the circuit court) and former Pennsylvania Attorney General Alexander Dallas (before the Supreme Court), defended the owner of the seized merchant ship, the *Amelia,* insisting that his ship was neutral and therefore that principles of international law protected him against seizure on the high seas.

The controversy began after the *Amelia,* a Prussian-owned merchant ship bound with valuable cargo from Calcutta to her home port of Hamburg, was intercepted by an armed French vessel, refitted with a French crew and flag, and appeared to be heading toward the French West Indies for salvage. At this point, Captain Talbot's *Constitution* commandeered the *Amelia* and brought her to New York Harbor to collect his prize from the merchant ship's owner, who, he contended, would have lost the entire cargo without Talbot's intervention. Talbot's claim (half the value of the captured ship's $188,000 cargo) rested on the proposition that, once the *Amelia* had been seized by the French, the ship was certain to be condemned in a French admiralty court. He argued that the *Amelia* was fair game for the *Constitution*'s crew under the terms of belligerents—that American ships were free to seize the cargoes of French vessels. But the *Amelia*'s owner insisted that his ship's neutral status had not changed as a result of the *Amelia*'s capture by the French, because, under international law, the French were prohibited from condemning the property of a neutral. He argued that Talbot's claim for compensation should be rejected.

Captain Talbot won his claim in federal district court, but the decision was overturned on appeal in the circuit court, setting the stage for the four-day argument in the Supreme Court's committee room, on the lower level of the Capitol. Chief Justice Marshall was presented with a legal controversy that was fraught with political consequences. If the Federalist Supreme Court ruled in favor of Talbot, it would give implicit endorsement to the quasi-war with France, a result urged by Hamilton and Bayard. But that conclusion carried obvious risks in the early months of the presidency of Jefferson, who had never viewed the French as the United States' belligerent.

In writing the Court's unanimous opinion in *Talbot v. Seeman*, Marshall essentially split the difference between the two adversaries, but arrived at that compromise through deft legal reasoning. Marshall appeared to side with his fellow Federalists on the major constitutional issues. He stated that, because Congress alone possessed the war-powers authority under the Constitution, the 1799 legislative act declaring a formal state of belligerency between the United States and France was constitutional. Although Marshall could not point to language in a specific statute, he said that Talbot's seizure of the *Amelia* was consistent with the intent of Congress.* That extrapolation of congressional intent, a bold exercise in statutory interpretation, would, in time, significantly expand the Court's discretionary authority.

Marshall concluded that, on the merits of the case, Captain Talbot was entitled to compensation for his ship's capture of the *Amelia*. He stated that the armed *Amelia,* once flying the French flag, could no longer be considered a neutral protected by international law. He took note of French decrees warning that neutral vessels carrying goods from British colonies, if captured on the high seas, would be subject to French condemnation, as well as of the obvious state of combat-readiness of the refitted *Amelia*. Under the circumstances, Marshall reasoned, Talbot was justified in assuming that he faced a belligerent vessel when he confronted the *Amelia*.

If he had stopped there, the chief justice would have handed the Federalists a stunning victory. But he also found that Captain Talbot's claim for remuneration was excessive. The chief justice, acting on the Court's discretionary authority alone, cut Talbot's reward from one-half to one-sixth the value of the spoils, and then cut it once more, rul-

---

*During oral argument, the justices had refused to hear evidence of President Adams's interpretation of the legislation, a significant step toward establishing the Court's independence from the executive branch of the federal government.

ing that the legal costs of the *Amelia*'s owner were to be taken out of the captain's award.

Certainly the Federalists could claim an important political victory, because the Court had given constitutional recognition to the quasi-war with France. But the Republicans could not have been very unhappy with the result either; the Court, after all, had acknowledged the now Republican-controlled Congress's broad war powers. And even though the Federalists' client, Captain Talbot, "won" the case, he came away almost empty-handed.

The only undisputed victor in the case was the Marshall Court. For the first time in the brief history of the Supreme Court, it had issued a unanimous opinion, lending dignity and authority to its judicial pronouncement. Marshall also revealed his uncanny skill for navigating safe passage between formidable political shoals, using powerful legal arguments to guide him to his destination. The chief justice's success in avoiding political controversy was evident when the Republican *National Intelligencer* called the decision in *Talbot v. Seeman* important and published the entire text without critical comment.

With his decision in *Talbot*, Marshall began to establish the Court, in the eyes of his countrymen, as "the least dangerous" branch of the federal government. Alexander Hamilton had used that phrase in *The Federalist* to describe the role he envisioned for the federal judiciary. Without constitutional power of the purse or the sword, he had observed, the Court must ultimately depend on its judgment alone for its authority and prestige. Marshall well understood Hamilton's maxim and was now building the reputation of the Court not as a partisan political institution but, rather, as a deliberative judicial body worthy of enhanced national stature because of the force of its judgment.

Because President Jefferson had not called a special legislative session after his inauguration, he had several months to prepare an agenda for the first formal session of the Seventh Congress in December. The president had carefully laid the foundation for the broad Republican policies of his administration. Working closely with his secretary of the treasury, Albert Gallatin, Jefferson was intent on achieving the "wise and frugal" government that he had promised in his inaugural. He and Gallatin developed a three-pronged strategy: reduce the federal debt, cut federal spending, and eliminate internal taxes. With remarkable financial dexterity, Gallatin devised a plan that accomplished all three. The key to the success of the plan was the slashing of federal expenditures. Jefferson and Gallatin were helped, crucially, in the pursuit of this policy by the serendipitous negotiation of a peace settlement between the long-warring superpowers of Europe, Great Britain and France. With the elimination of an external military threat, Jefferson and Gallatin could reasonably propose a drastic cut in military expenditures. In addition to paring the military budget, Jefferson was determined to deflate what he considered a bloated federal bureaucracy. He wanted to reduce the number of American embassies abroad to three (Great Britain, France, and Spain) and, looking homeward, to eliminate scores of federal offices, including the entire layer of circuit judgeships provided by the Judiciary Act of 1801.

Jefferson chose to send his first State of the Union message to Congress via his secretary, Meriwether Lewis, and have it read by a clerk of the House, rather than delivering it in person, as both Presidents Washington and Adams had done. He offered a good Republican reason for breaking with precedent: the reading by a congressional clerk would minimize the attention paid to the president and thereby begin reversing what he believed was a tendency toward "monarchising" of the executive branch. It also allowed Congress to get down to business without submitting a detailed reply. And it relieved Jefferson of the burden of making another major public address, a task he found onerous and for which he conspicuously lacked talent.

And so, on December 8, 1801, Jefferson sent his first annual message to Congress, reporting that the union was thriving under Republican leadership and could look forward to an even brighter future. The president could take no credit for the first piece of good news, that "the wars and troubles which have for so many years afflicted our sister nations have at length come to an end." He announced that France and Great Britain, after eight long, debilitating years of war, were prepared to make peace. For the United States, peace in Europe meant unfettered navigation on the high seas and, more important from the perspective of Jefferson's now public agenda, justification for a drastic reduction of both the army and the navy.

Jefferson also proposed a stringent federal budget that provided for the elimination of all internal taxes and paying down the national debt. To accomplish all of this, he cautioned, government spending would have to be reduced, not just by cutting military expenses, but also by stripping the federal bureaucracy of all excess. He singled out the federal judiciary for special attention, asserting that there were too many judges and too little judicial business. "The judiciary system of the United States, and especially that portion of it recently erected, will of course present itself to the contemplation of Congress," Jefferson said, in a subtle directive to Congress to repeal the Judiciary Act of 1801. That oblique presidential command would ignite one of the fiercest, and most partisan, fights of Jefferson's eight-year presidency.

John Marshall had adjourned the meeting of the Supreme Court during its December term so that the justices could listen to the president's State of the Union speech. Immediately after Jefferson's speech had been read in the Senate chamber, the justices returned to their cramped committee room to hear arguments in *United States v. Schooner Peggy,* another prize case arising out of the United States' quasi-war with France. In this case, the political trail led directly to President Jefferson.

The armed French merchant vessel *Peggy* had been captured in the Caribbean by the American ship *Trumbull* in April 1800 a few miles off the shore of Port-au-Prince. It was condemned as a lawful prize by the U.S. Circuit Court for Connecticut six months later and ordered sold. The condemnation was called into question a week later, when the United States signed the Convention of Mortefontaine, which provided that vessels captured during the quasi-war but "not yet definitively condemned" were to be restored to the original owners. The circuit court's decision had not been officially executed when the treaty at Mortefontaine was signed.

Intent on improving relations with France, President Jefferson concluded that the *Peggy* had not been "definitively condemned" and ordered the United States attorney for Connecticut to arrange for the proceeds of the *Peggy*'s sale to be paid to the schooner's French owners. But the court clerk refused the president's instruction and asked the new federal circuit court, created under the Judiciary Act of 1801, to rule on Jefferson's order. The court unanimously sustained the clerk's position, ruling that the president had no legal authority to demand that the money be paid to the French owners. The Federalist press reported the court's refusal to support "executive usurpation." Neither the ruling nor the Federalists' gloating over the decision went unnoticed by Jefferson, who again was reminded of the damage that could be done by what he considered a partisan Federalist judiciary.

A decision in which the Federalist judges of a circuit court found an order of the Republican president illegal was bad enough. An affirmation of that decision by the full Marshall Court would carry greater risks, as the chief justice surely realized. But such political considerations could not be openly considered by Marshall and his colleagues. Instead, their task, undertaken shortly after the release of Jefferson's State of the Union speech, was to listen to arguments on the central legal issue raised in the *Schooner Peggy* case—namely, the meaning of the Convention of Mortefontaine's phrase "definitively condemned."

Two prominent Federalist congressmen, Roger Griswold of Connecticut and James Bayard of Delaware, represented the American captors and argued before the Court that the federal court's judgment in the fall of 1800 condemning the *Peggy* as a lawful prize was a final legal decree and therefore fit the treaty's term of "definitively condemned." As a second argument on behalf of their client, the Federalist congressmen maintained that the Convention of Mortefontaine was not a binding legal document, because the procedural requirements of the Constitution to give effect to the treaty had not been completed. In support of their argument, Bayard and Griswold noted that, although the treaty had been ratified by President Adams with the advice and consent of the Senate in February 1801, one article of the treaty (dealing with the postponement of American shipping claims against France) had been excepted from ratification. The entire treaty, they concluded, had yet to be promulgated into law.

While the Court deliberated in the *Schooner Peggy* case, President Jefferson and the Republican-controlled Senate hastily worked together to ratify the treaty and eliminate all ambiguity about its legal status. In the process, they provided tacit assistance to the Supreme Court's effort to resolve the crucial legal issue in *Schooner Peggy*. Two days after final arguments in the case had been completed, Jefferson resubmitted the treaty for the Senate's advice and consent, which were promptly given, and the president quickly promulgated the treaty.

Although Jefferson and Marshall did not communicate with each other during this critical period of the Court's deliberations, the actions of both men suggested that they were eager to avoid a clash between the executive and judicial branches. As if their actions had been coordinated, Marshall issued his opinion for the Court immediately after Jefferson had promulgated the treaty. Marshall gave a resounding endorsement to the treaty's terms and, at the same time, supported Jefferson's interpretation of the document. The chief justice's succinct, four-paragraph opinion first dismissed Bayard and Griswold's argument that the lower federal court's judgment condemning the *Peggy* was final. That judgment could not be considered final, Marshall reasoned, if in fact it could be appealed and reversed, as it was. As a constitutional matter, Marshall asserted, the terms of the freshly promulgated treaty with France superseded any private contractual arrangements sanctioned by a court of law. Treaties had the same binding legal status as acts of Congress and were, under the Constitution, the supreme law of the land. The chief justice concluded that the nation's will, as reflected in the terms of the Convention of Mortefontaine, must prevail.

Marshall had once again rendered a carefully considered judgment that combined acute legal analysis with a peerless assessment of political risk and benefit to the Court. His overarching constitutional theme—that the terms of a treaty could not be undercut by a judicial decision in an ordinary civil suit—supported President Jefferson's position, and therefore eliminated any danger of a political backlash from the Republicans. But at the same time, Marshall struck another blow for one of his most passionately held political principles—the necessity of a strong federal government to speak for the nation in foreign affairs.

If Marshall's decision in *Schooner Peggy* appeared to signal an effort on the chief justice's part to work cooperatively with the Republican president, another development at the Court communicated just the opposite impression. During the same December term in which the Court had heard arguments in the *Schooner Peggy* case, former President Adams's attorney general, Charles Lee, appeared before the justices to request that the Court order Secretary of State James Madison to show cause why he should not be compelled to deliver the judicial commissions of four of Adams's "midnight judges," including one William Marbury, who had been appointed a justice of the peace for the District of Columbia one day before Jefferson had taken the presidential oath. The commissions had been signed in the office of Secretary of State John Marshall but, because of the rush of last-minute business of the president and his secretary, had not been delivered. Jefferson's secretary of state, acting on the orders of the president, had simply refused to deliver the commissions.*

After Lee made his request to the Court, Marshall turned to Jefferson's attorney general Levi Lincoln, and inquired whether the administration would like to reply. Lincoln told the chief justice that he had been given no instruction from the president or the secretary of state. Marshall consulted his colleagues about how they should proceed. Only Justice Samuel Chase wanted to rule on the request immediately. Marshall thought the issue required further deliberation and said that the Court would take the matter under advisement. But two days later, the chief justice issued the order requested by Lee to force Secretary of State Madison to show cause why he had failed to deliver the commissions and set argument for the next scheduled term of the Court in June 1802. It now seemed as if the case of *Marbury v. Madison* could put the chief justice and the president on a collision course that both men had indicated they wanted to avoid. If the justices decided that William Marbury and the other three plaintiffs were entitled to their commissions, would they order the secretary of state to deliver the commissions? And what if Madison, on the president's instructions, refused?

Before the Court presented him with the Marbury challenge, Jefferson had appeared to take a conciliatory view toward the Federalist-dominated judiciary. He had not publicly criticized Judges James Marshall and William Cranch of the District of Columbia Circuit Court after they ordered the initiation of a seditious libel suit against the editor of the Republican *National Intelligencer,* though other Republican leaders and the party's press had been outraged at the judges' action. Nor had he openly complained about the federal circuit court's decision rejecting his order in the *Schooner Peggy* case. And, in the inter-

---

*When the commissions were first discovered, Madison had not yet taken office as secretary of state. The president instructed his acting secretary of state, Levi Lincoln, not to deliver them. Jefferson reasoned that, because Adams's appointees as justices of the peace were not life-tenured, he could treat them as ordinary political appointments that could be nullified.

ests of national harmony, the president had deleted from the final draft of his State of the Union address his strongly held conviction that the Sedition Act was unconstitutional. Even his suggestion to the Seventh Congress that the legislators consider repealing the Judiciary Act of 1801 was muted and fell far short of what more radical Republican leaders, like William Branch Giles, had wanted.

But the Marshall Court's show-cause order in December 1801 to Madison in the Marbury dispute rankled the president. The Federalists "have retired into the judiciary as a stronghold," Jefferson angrily wrote John Dickinson, "and from that battery all the works of Republicanism are to be beaten down and erased." Two days later, he told Dr. Benjamin Rush that he expected the congressional Republicans to introduce a measure to repeal the Judiciary Act of 1801, and he predicted that "lopping off the parasitical plant engrafted at the last session on the judiciary" would produce the political controversy he had previously been at such pains to prevent. The Republican drive for repeal would soon become known as "the President's measure."

Having denounced the exercise of broad executive power by his predecessor, President Jefferson found his own ways to influence Congress. Jefferson claimed that he was only seeking cooperation between the branches of the federal government, not attempting to impose his will on the popularly elected legislature. Through his subtle but highly effective uses of the authority of his office, Jefferson was able to achieve virtually all his congressional goals. No piece of legislation was passed without his approval, and nothing he opposed became law. John Marshall had correctly predicted that Jefferson's election would move the federal government's center of gravity from the executive to the legislative branch, but that development in no way diminished the authority of the president. On the contrary, Jefferson's standing with the Republican Congress and the electorate was only enhanced.

In many ways, Jefferson appeared to be a passive president. He rarely made public appearances. But he held frequent meetings with individual members of his Cabinet and with his party's congressional leaders, and he spent many hours at his writing table, drafting suggestions and instructions. Three evenings a week, he entertained at the

President's House, offering Cabinet members and their wives, visiting diplomats, and congressmen, both Republicans and Federalists, fine food prepared by his French chef and wines personally selected from his superb wine cellar. And although the president insisted that politics and religion were subjects too controversial to be appropriate for his dinner-party conversations, the host's brilliance, graciousness, and desire to find common ground did not fail to impress most of his guests. Jefferson was perceived by friend and foe alike to be the undisputed leader of his party at both ends of Pennsylvania Avenue. "There is no doubt in my mind," wrote one Federalist, "that . . . at this moment, the Executive as completely rules both Houses of Congress as Bonaparte rules the people of France."

When Jefferson's old friend and Republican ally, Senator John Breckinridge of Kentucky, introduced a bill in the Senate on January 6, 1802, to repeal the Judiciary Act of 1801, it was widely assumed that Breckinridge was acting with the president's approval. After the motion was seconded by another close Jefferson ally, Senator Stevens Thomson Mason of Virginia, Breckinridge began his supporting speech by echoing some of the concerns Jefferson had expressed about the act in his State of the Union. The number of suits in the federal courts was decreasing, Breckinridge claimed, so the increase in the size of the judiciary provided by the Judiciary Act was an extravagance that the federal government could ill afford. He also pointedly criticized the expanded federal jurisdiction provided under the act in land disputes, which, he argued, were more properly resolved in the state courts. On the issue of the constitutionality of repealing the act, he claimed that Congress had authority independent of the other two branches of the federal government to judge whether its legislation comported with the Constitution.

Breckinridge lifted phrases from Jefferson's discarded draft of the State of the Union that claimed that both Congress and the president possessed authority equal to that of the Supreme Court to declare an act of Congress (the Sedition Act, for example) unconstitutional. In support of his argument that congressional repeal of the Judiciary Act of 1801 was constitutional, Breckinridge cited Article III of the Constitution, which provided that Congress alone had the authority to establish, and presumably abolish, inferior federal courts. If his interpretation was wrong, Breckinridge noted ironically, then the Judiciary Act of 1801, which abolished the former circuit courts, was also unconstitutional.

The Federalists countered that repeal would undermine the independence of the federal judiciary, making the judges mere pawns of the legislature. If Congress could abolish whole layers of the federal judiciary at will, then judges served at the pleasure of whichever party held a majority in the legislature. The Constitution, they argued, explicitly prevented such legislative tampering by providing, first, that all life-tenured members of the federal judiciary "shall hold their Offices during good Behavior," and, second, that the judges' salaries "shall not be diminished during their Continuance in Office." Once the circuit-court judges had been appointed under the Judiciary Act of 1801, the Federalists maintained, there was only one constitutionally sanctioned means of removing them: impeachment. "The fight over repeal is not now a contest between Federalists & Republicans, as they call themselves," declared John Rutledge, the Federalist senator from South Carolina, "but between the 'Virginia Party' & the friends of the Constitution."

The protracted and bitterly contentious Senate fight over repeal worried the president. He was concerned that the Federalists' unrelenting attacks on the constitutionality of the measure were beginning to persuade some of his party's moderates that a compromise might be in order. As the final vote approached, it was apparent that some wavering Republican moderates did not consider the constitutional issue to be as clear-cut as did the president.

The Republicans held an eighteen-to-fourteen advantage in the Senate, but the numbers were misleading. When debate on the repeal motion began, two Republican senators were absent, one detained because of his wife's illness, the other having resigned unexpectedly, with no successor yet named. The Republicans' diminished ranks were temporarily offset by the absence of two Federalist senators, although they were expected to arrive in Washington before the final vote. The anxiety of the Republican leadership increased after a Federalist attempt to amend Breckinridge's motion, and effectively moderate the language of the repeal, was narrowly defeated, fifteen to thirteen, with one moderate Republican voting with the Federalists.

Alarmed by the close vote and the expectation of the imminent arrival of the two missing Federalist senators, Breckinridge moved for the appointment of a committee to bring a bill for repeal to the floor of the Senate. The Republican-controlled committee produced a bill to rescind the Judiciary Act of 1801. But the Republicans' task was further complicated by the enigmatic vice president, Aaron Burr, who presided in the Senate and was authorized to break tie votes. Formal passage of the bill required three readings and approval by the full Senate. A narrow Republican majority prevailed after the first two readings, but by the third reading, the two missing Federalists had arrived. The Federalists quickly submitted a new motion to return the bill to committee to work out a compromise. The vote was fifteen to fifteen. Vice President Burr then irrevocably doomed himself to pariah status in Jefferson's party by breaking the deadlock in favor of the substitute motion favored by the Federalists.

If Jefferson and Republican loyalists in the Senate needed another reason to distrust Burr, they now had it. Jefferson continued to suspect that Burr's motives during the 1800 presidential election crisis were not honorable. Once he was elected president, Jefferson had excluded Burr from all policy-making councils of his administration. To Burr's additional displeasure, his efforts to secure patronage positions for his political friends had been rebuffed by Jefferson, whereas those of the vice president's New York Republican rivals had been rewarded.

Still ambitious, Burr may have realized that his only hope for political advancement was to carve out a niche independent of the president. The Federalists' substitute motion on the repeal gave him that opportunity. Exhibiting independence and desiring to appeal to both Republican and Federalist moderates, Burr may have hoped his vote would enhance his chances for a future presidential bid as an independent candidate. But by opposing a major legislative goal of the president and the Republican leadership in the Senate, Burr forfeited any opportunity he might have had for a leadership role with Jefferson's Republicans.

Burr's and the Federalists' hopes for a compromise measure quickly dissolved with the arrival of Republican Senator Stephen Bradley of Vermont, who had been detained because of his wife's illness. Now Breckinridge had a firm majority for his motion and successfully moved that his repeal bill be released from the special committee. On the Senate floor, it passed sixteen to fifteen. Without delay, the measure was sent to the House, where the Republicans enjoyed a comfortable majority. Although several moderate Republicans expressed misgivings about the repeal, and three actually voted with the Federalists, the measure passed handily and became law.

Jefferson's unwavering support for repeal of the Judiciary Act of 1801 undercut his carefully nurtured image as national conciliator, not just with moderate Federalists, but also with moderate Republicans. Although he regretted the acrimony in Congress, he was satisfied that repeal was a necessary corrective in the Federalist-dominated judiciary. In Jefferson's view, Congress had done nothing more than "restore our judiciary to what it was while justice & not federalism was its object."

The High Federalists were convinced that the repeal was only Jefferson's first step in an assault on the judiciary that would, ultimately, bring it under the complete control of the Republican Congress. The Republicans, according to Connecticut High Federalist Roger Griswold, were "determined at all events to destroy the independence of the judiciary & bring all the powers of government into the House of Representatives." The leader of the High Federalists, Alexander Hamilton, urged his colleagues to bring a constitutional challenge to the repeal before the Supreme Court.

The groundwork for such a challenge had been laid during the congressional debate on the repeal legislation. The Federalists had repeatedly contended that the Republican bill was unconstitutional, and they had expressed confidence that, even if the measure passed, it would be declared unconstitutional by the Marshall Court. They had also referred to the pending case of *Marbury v. Madison,* suggesting that it was another Damoclean sword held over the Jeffersonian Republicans by the Court. Since the repeal of the Judiciary Act of 1801 would not take effect until the first of July, the scheduled June meeting of the Court became a focus for both Federalists and Republicans. At that 1802 session, the Court, presumably, would deal with both politically charged issues—the constitutionality of the repeal legislation, and the justices' order demanding that Secretary of State Madison justify his failure to deliver the commissions to William Marbury and the three other justice-of-the-peace appointees of President Adams.

Senate Republicans promptly responded to the anticipated crisis by voting to appoint a special committee to reexamine the federal court system and recommend any necessary changes. Within a week, the Republican-dominated special committee had completed its deliberations and recommended that the circuit-court structure be revised, that new circuit duties be given to the Supreme Court justices, and the June and December terms of the Supreme Court be abolished, to be replaced by a single February term. If the legislation passed, it would prohibit official meetings of the Supreme Court for fourteen months, well beyond when the repeal measure would take effect. "Are the gentlemen afraid of the judges?" asked Federalist congressional leader James Bayard. "Are the gentlemen afraid that they will pronounce the repealing law void?"

Chief Justice Marshall had followed closely the progress in Congress of this second Republican bill to rein in the federal judiciary. He had received a copy of the bill from Adams's former secretary of the treasury, Oliver Wolcott, who had been appointed a federal circuit-court judge under the Judiciary Act of 1801, and now stood to lose his commission as a result of the repeal. Marshall appeared to accept the latest Republican assault calmly, assuring Wolcott that some provisions of the bill restructuring the circuit-court system could well correct "essential defects in the system." He admitted to "regret that the next June term will be put down," but, ever the political realist, he said he had "no doubt the immediate operation of the bill will be insisted on."

A day later, in a letter to his colleague Justice William Paterson, Marshall appeared unperturbed by the circuit-court duties the new legislation would impose on the justices. "Our future duties," Marshall remarked, "are less burdensome than heretofore, or than I expected." But then, as if to balance his reassurances with a note of alarm, Marshall raised concerns about the constitutionality of the legislation. He did not think, as a constitutional matter, that Congress could force the justices to serve at both the circuit and Supreme Court levels, suggesting that such an arrangement could put the justices in the untenable position of reviewing their own lower-court decisions. "If the question was new, I should be unwilling to act in this character without a consultation of the judges; but I consider it as decided & that, whatever my own scruples may be, I am bound by the decision." In other words, Marshall considered precedent—that the justices had already served as circuit-court judges for many years, under the requirements of the original Judiciary Act of 1789—as a bar to a legal challenge that such service was unconstitutional.

Marshall was also in communication with Congressman Bayard, a close friend who had been asked by Hamilton to initiate a suit testing the constitutionality of the repeal of the Judiciary Act of 1801. In a letter to Bayard written in April, during the Senate's deliberations on the second judiciary bill, Marshall made no mention of the pending legislation and gave no indication of his views on the constitutionality of the repeal legislation. But in face-to-face meetings with Bayard in Alexandria during the same month, Marshall was reported to have discouraged Bayard and other Federalist legislators from initiating a constitutional challenge. According to Bayard's accounts of his conversations with the chief justice, Marshall said it was his personal opinion that such a suit would fail, because Congress, as the Republicans had argued, possessed plenary authority under Article III to establish, or abolish, inferior federal courts. When told of Marshall's view, another Federalist leader, Senator Gouverneur Morris of New York, said, "I am neither surprised nor disappointed, for it accords with my idea of the judge."

Despite Marshall's advice, Morris and other Federalists vowed to press on with a constitutional suit. At the same time, the Federalists devised another strategy to accomplish their objective without a Supreme Court ruling, though nonetheless requiring the justices' overt cooperation. Conceived at a secret caucus of Federalist congressmen, the strategy required that the justices refuse to serve as circuit-court judges, as the repeal mandated. If the justices agreed to join in the Federalists' plan, the circuit-court judges appointed under the Judiciary Act of 1801 but relieved of their responsibilities under the repeal would again take up their judicial duties.

Marshall was directly contacted by the Federalists about their second strategy, as was Justice Chase. Chase was immediately receptive. "I believe a day of severe trial is fast approaching for the friends of the Constitution," he wrote to Justice Paterson, "and we, I fear, must be principal actors and may be sufferers therein." Two weeks later, Chase more emphatically expressed his view that the Repeal Act was unconstitutional. He believed that the only way the circuit-court judges provided by the Judiciary Act of 1801 could be deprived of their commissions was by the constitutionally sanctioned method of impeachment.

When the chief justice polled his other colleagues for their views, he was more circumspect than Chase in expressing his opinion of the Federalist strategy. He had already confided to Justice Paterson his view that the justices, having acquiesced in Congress's original directive in the Judiciary Act of 1789 to serve as circuit-court judges, could not now, as a matter of principle, deny the legality of that responsibility. When Marshall was informed of the Federalists' plan to enlist the justices in passive resistance, he questioned both the wisdom and the authority of the justices in defying the new law. "This is a subject not to be lightly resolved on," he wrote Justice Paterson. "The consequences of refusing to carry the law into effect may be very serious." In reiterating his view that precedent ought not be ignored, Marshall also expressed concern about public reaction to judicial defiance of duly enacted legislation. And although he said he would be bound by the views of the majority of his colleagues, Marshall made no secret of his hope that they would agree with him.

The chief justice's skillful lobbying effort among his colleagues produced the desired result. Justices Cushing, Paterson, and Washington agreed with Marshall, providing a Court majority for his position. Without further debate, the justices agreed to serve once again as circuit judges.

Abandoned by the justices in their challenge of the repeal, Federalists were left to fume at the destruction wreaked by the Republicans and, most particularly, the president. "The judiciary is certainly gone," lamented Adams's attorney general, Charles Lee. "And this is not all. Mr. Jefferson is well calculated to pull down any political edifice, and those will not be disappointed who have feared he would employ himself as industriously and indefatigably in taking to pieces stone by stone the national building as Washington employed himself in putting them together. Even the foundation will be razed in less than four years."

But even as Federalists such as Lee denounced the Republicans, they plotted their next move to overturn the repeal of the Judiciary Act of 1801. Their new strategy, like the last, attempted to draw the justices of the Supreme Court into the scheme. Lee and other prominent Federalist attorneys would initiate a series of lawsuits challenging the authority of the newly established circuit courts in which the justices presided. But again they were frustrated. In Hartford, Justice Bushrod Washington summarily dismissed such a suit, while Justice Cushing in Boston simply adjourned proceedings rather than hear arguments on the issue.

The last of the Federalists' major legal challenges was brought by Charles Lee in Richmond's circuit court in a case known as *Stuart v. Laird*. What made Lee's challenge particularly important was that the presiding judge was none other than Chief Justice Marshall. Lee represented John Laird, who in December 1801 had obtained a property judgment in the circuit court that had been established by the Judiciary Act of 1801. But that circuit court had been abolished by the Repeal Act. Lee, on Laird's behalf, insisted that his client's judgment was still valid and prevented appeal to Marshall's new circuit court. The repeal legislation was unconstitutional, Lee claimed, and, consequently, Chief Justice Marshall and the other justices could not be required to sit as circuit judges. Marshall dismissed both of Lee's arguments with alacrity but ordered that the judgment in favor of Laird be executed. When Lee's appeal of Marshall's decision to the Supreme Court failed,[*] it effectively put an end to the Federalists' grand strategy to resist the Republicans' assault on the federal judiciary.

Marshall had begun his tenure as chief justice quietly, but in only two years his and the Court's profile had risen dramatically. During that time, he struggled mightily, and successfully, to change the perception of the Court as the surrogate voice for the Federalists. The Court now spoke with one voice, and not always in support of Federalists' interests, as Marshall had shown both in his opinions and in his behind-the-scenes refusal to participate in Federalist intrigues. He had diffused several potential clashes with the Republicans and had done so without provoking the ire of a single Federalist colleague, even the volatile Justice Chase.

While Marshall was establishing himself as a strong and shrewd chief justice, Thomas Jefferson was no less successfully proving to be a strong and shrewd leader of the executive branch. Both appeared to

---

[*]Marshall did not take part in the Supreme Court's consideration of the appeal, because he had made the circuit-court ruling. But his colleague Justice Paterson gave Lee's argument equally short shrift. "Congress have constitutional authority to establish such inferior tribunals as they think proper; and to transfer a cause from one such tribunal to another," Paterson wrote for a unanimous Court. "In this last particular, there are no words in the Constitution to prohibit or restrain the exercise of legislative power."

avoid direct confrontation consciously. But they were still irreconcilable adversaries. Despite Marshall's ostensible efforts to cooperate with Jefferson, he privately brooded over the direction in which the president and Republican Congress were taking the nation. He wrote his old friend Charles Cotesworth Pinckney that he despaired over the political struggles in Washington: "There is so much in the political world to wound honest men who have honorable feelings that I am disgusted with it & begin to see things, & indeed human nature, through a much more gloomy medium than I once thought possible."

The Court had managed to stay above the swirling political battles that so concerned Marshall, thanks largely to his leadership. But whether the Marshall Court could continue to build its authority as "the least dangerous" branch was still an open question. And the case of *Marbury v. Madison*, still on the docket for argument before the justices, threatened to drag the Court into partisan politics at the highest level.

[8]

Mr. Marbury's Missing Commission

AS POLITICAL PLUMS GO, a commission to be a justice of the peace for the District of Columbia was a rather small serving.* President Adams had sent the name of William Marbury, a prosperous Georgetown businessman and loyal Federalist, along with forty-one others to the Senate on March 2, 1801, for confirmation. They were the last of Adams's "midnight judges."

What roiled the Republicans was certainly not the power or prestige of the positions, but the clear intent of Adams. All forty-two nominations for justice of the peace had been rushed to the President's House for Adams's signature on March 3, the day before he relinquished his office. These last judicial appointments would complete the Federalists' calculated plan to capture the entire federal judiciary for their party for years to come. They were seen by Jefferson as a final, brazen act of defiance.

The details of the last frenetic day of the Adams presidency are unclear, but some facts are known. A disgruntled Adams sat at his desk in the President's House until 9 P.M. signing commissions brought to him by a clerk from the State Department. Once the president had signed the documents, the clerk returned with the papers to the State

---

*A justice of the peace was not entitled to a salary but, rather, to the less predictable remuneration of fees, and his civil jurisdiction was limited to cases with no more than $20 at stake.

Department, where Secretary of State John Marshall (who continued briefly in that office after becoming chief justice) affixed the Great Seal of the United States on the documents.

Exactly what happened in Marshall's office is also not clear, despite the best efforts at recollection of Daniel Brent, a State Department clerk who shuttled between the State Department and the President's House. Brent recalled that he had turned the papers over to Adams's private secretary. James Marshall, the secretary of state's brother, who had been rewarded by Adams with a judicial appointment to the new circuit court for the District of Columbia, recalled that he had taken a batch of commissions to the newly appointed justices of the peace in nearby Alexandria, Virginia. But neither Brent nor James Marshall was certain that the commissions of William Marbury and his three fellow plaintiffs in *Marbury v. Madison* had been delivered.

Two weeks after Jefferson's inauguration, John Marshall conceded that he had neglected to have a number of the commissions delivered because of the weight of last-minute State Department business, but he did not think his oversight could affect the legitimacy of the appointments. He wrote his brother James that he considered the commissions legally binding once they had been signed by the president and sealed, even if they had not been delivered.

Soon after Jefferson was inaugurated, he learned that several of the commissions for Adams's justices of the peace remained on a table in the State Department. He instructed his attorney general, Levi Lincoln, who was also the acting secretary of state (James Madison would not take office until May), to withhold the commissions. Unlike life-tenured judicial appointees, justices of the peace served for five-year terms and were, in Jefferson's view, unprotected. In any case, the legal act of appointment would not be completed, Jefferson later maintained, until a commission was actually delivered.

After he ordered Lincoln to hold the commissions, the president swept aside Adams's list of forty-two justices of the peace, which he deemed too many, and substituted a reduced roster of thirty. In keeping with his inaugural theme of conciliation, Jefferson did not purge the entire Adams slate, retaining twenty-five of his predecessor's nominees and adding five later. But William Marbury and his three fellow plaintiffs in *Marbury v. Madison* were not among those on Jefferson's revised list.

Whether it was Marbury or someone higher up in the Federalist party who made the decision to bring suit demanding the delivery of the commissions has never been established. Certainly neither Marbury nor the other litigants sued because they were reliant on the office for their sustenance. Besides being a successful land speculator, Marbury was a principal in the Potomac Company, an ambitious venture led by George Washington that sought to build a canal linking the Potomac and Ohio rivers. A second litigant, Robert Hooe, speculated in land in the District of Columbia and elsewhere and owned more than a hundred thousand acres in the state of Kentucky. A third plaintiff, Dennis Ramsay, was the former mayor of Alexandria and had delivered the town's farewell address to George Washington. William Harper, the fourth plaintiff, was also a large landowner and had long-standing ties to George Washington, having served under him during the Revolutionary War.

It would be difficult to identify a Federalist who was better positioned or more highly motivated to embarrass the Jefferson administration than Charles Lee, the attorney for Marbury and his fellow plaintiffs. More than six months before he formally argued the Marbury case, Lee had bitterly accused Jefferson of destroying "stone by stone" the magnificent national edifice erected by the first Federalist president, George Washington.

Lee's opposition to Jefferson was only one of the views he shared with his close friend John Marshall. A moderate Federalist from Virginia, Lee was the younger brother of Henry "Light-Horse Harry" Lee, who, with Marshall, had answered Washington's call to run for Congress in 1798. Charles Lee had served as attorney general in the administrations of both Washington and Adams. During the Adams presidency, he was a resolute opponent of reconciliation with the French, had vigorously enforced the Alien and Sedition Acts, and had published *Defence,* a rebuttal to critics of the statutes. Like Marshall, he remained an Adams loyalist during the waning days of the administration, when real and imagined cabals by the High Federalists were rampant. Adams rewarded Lee with a "midnight" judicial appointment to one of the newly created federal circuit courts, which Lee declined, preferring to resume his private law practice in Richmond.

Lee combined passionate political belief in moderate Federalism with a finely honed legal mind. At Princeton, Lee had distinguished himself as a public speaker and delivered the Latin salutatory address at commencement. Austere in appearance and undemonstrative in court, Lee was an excellent and successful litigator. When Lee asked the Marshall Court on December 16, 1801, to issue a judicial order to Secretary of State Madison to show cause for his failure to deliver the commissions to Marbury and his co-complainants, the Republican press did not view the request as a cause for concern. The idea that the Supreme Court could pose a serious challenge to the new administration was almost laughable.

Whatever Lee's ultimate goal in pressing the Marbury suit, one unintended consequence quickly followed. After Jefferson had cautiously suggested in his first State of the Union address in December 1801 that the Republican Congress ought to consider repeal of the Judiciary Act of 1801, some moderates in his party expressed concern about the constitutional consequences of such a measure. But after the Court announced its show-cause order, opposition within the Republican congressional majority to the repeal noticeably softened. And the Court's action emboldened the Republican leadership in its determination to succeed in the repeal.

"What think you of the rule entered upon the federal court last week against the Secretary of State to show cause?" asked one of Jefferson's Senate leaders, John Breckinridge. "I think it the most daring attack which the annals of Federalism have yet exhibited. I wish the subject of the courts to be brought forward in the Senate next week." The reaction of Breckinridge's coleader, Senator Stevens Thomson Mason of Virginia, combined resentment with a realization that the Court's order would help their repeal movement. "An attempt has been made by the judiciary to assail the President (through the sides of Mr. Madison)," Mason wrote Monroe. "The conduct of the judges on this occasion has excited a very general indignation and will secure the repeal of the judiciary law of the last session, about the propriety of which some of our Republican friends were hesitating."

Mason was correct in forecasting the success of the Republicans' repeal effort. But the Court's order in *Marbury* did much more, providing one of the reasons for the irate Republican majority simply to erase the next two sessions of the Court. It was just that sharp punch of retribution that deepened Charles Lee's fears about the Jefferson administration and caused him to worry about the independence of the judiciary. By the time Lee appeared before the Court to make his case in *Marbury v. Madison,* he and other leading Federalists, including Chief Justice Marshall, had much more to fear than the loss of two Court terms. In the week before Lee made his opening argument in *Marbury,* the Republican Congress initiated the first impeachment proceedings against a sitting federal judge, District Judge John Pickering of New Hampshire, who was widely believed to be both alcoholic and insane. Republican Washington was already buzzing about further impeachments, beginning with Justice Samuel Chase. Could Chief Justice Marshall be far behind?

The Jefferson administration viewed the Marbury case as a political attack, not a genuine legal controversy. Every member of the administration called to account, from Attorney General Levi Lincoln down to the lowliest State Department clerk, bobbed and weaved around Charles Lee's persistent inquiries. And the target of the suit, Secretary of State Madison, ignored the proceeding altogether. Even though Madison was the named defendant, he never appeared before the Supreme Court. Nor was there any effort to defend his failure to deliver the judicial commissions when Charles Lee made his request for a show-cause order. At the preliminary hearing in December 1801, when the justices asked whether there had been any instruction from Madison, Attorney General Lincoln offered no response or explanation from Madison. At the fact-finding stage of the litigation, Madison appeared to go out of his way to be uncooperative. He deflected a direct request from Marbury and Dennis Ramsay that they be provided with written evidence of their appointments. Marbury and Ramsay were referred to the State Department's chief clerk, Jacob Wagner, who would say only that the commissions were not then in the department.

The Republican-controlled Senate was no more helpful to the plaintiffs. They were initially assisted by a sympathetic Federalist senator who introduced a motion asking the secretary of the Senate to provide the record of the Senate's Executive Committee session in which Marbury et al. had been appointed. But the Republican majority challenged and ultimately defeated the motion, because, as one Republican senator exclaimed, it was an "audacious attempt to pry into executive secrets, by a tribunal which had no authority to do any such thing."

This left Charles Lee, on the eve of his appearance before the Supreme Court, in a very awkward position. Before he could even make the argument that his clients' commissions had the force of law when signed and sealed, he faced the elementary forensic task of proving that his clients had actually been appointed in the first place. Lee decided to use the Republicans' recalcitrance to his advantage.

On the morning of February 10, 1803, Lee announced to the Supreme Court that both the secretary of state and the Senate had been uncooperative in that they had refused his clients' reasonable requests for information on their appointments. Lee ruefully reported to the justices that his clients had been deprived of "simple justice."

Lee then called the two State Department clerks, Brent and Wagner. Again, before the justices, Lee was rebuffed in his request for information. Undoubtedly on the instruction of their superiors, Brent and Wagner refused to answer Lee's questions voluntarily, stating that information on official State Department business was privileged and could not be shared in a court of law, even in the highest court in the land.

Responding immediately, Lee launched into one of his crucial legal arguments. The attorney began innocently enough, making "a few remarks on the nature of the office of the Secretary of State." The responsibilities of a secretary of state, Lee asserted, were of two kinds: "In the first he is the public ministerial officer of the United States; in the second he is the agent of the President." As a public officer, the secretary was obligated to perform legal duties independent of the president. In his second role, as the president's agent, the secretary served as confidential adviser and could pass along any political information or foreign correspondence to the president without fear that such information could be demanded in a court of law. Lee elaborated on the distinction. "In the one [role] he is an independent and accountable officer; in the other, he is dependent upon the President, is his agent and is accountable to him alone." Then Lee tightened the legal knot. "In the first, he is compellable by mandamus* to do his duty, and in the second he is not."

---

*A writ of mandamus is a judicial order to a government official directing him to do his legal duty. In the Marbury case, it was the judicial order directed at Madison.

No one in the Supreme Court's committee room that day could doubt on which side of the carefully delineated line of duty Marbury's attorney was going to place Madison and the State Department clerks. To clinch his argument that Madison's clerks were acting as public ministerial officers and therefore must testify, Lee referred to the 1789 statute that established the Department of State, noting that recording and sealing civil commissions were among the responsibilities of officers of the Department of State laid out in the statute. State Department employees Daniel Brent and Jacob Wagner must do their legal duty and give testimony under oath to the Court on the circumstances surrounding the commissions of Marbury and his fellow plaintiffs.

The Court agreed with Lee and ordered that Brent and Wagner be sworn and their answers taken down in writing, though the justices permitted them to state their objections to any questions asked. But the clerks' testimony was an anticlimax. Neither exhibited a particularly good memory for the details Lee sought. Brent said he "did not remember certainly" the names of any of the individuals whose commissions were signed by President Adams, though he was "almost certain" that William Marbury's and Robert Hooe's commissions were made out and that Dennis Ramsay's was not. He could not recall whether any of the commissions were actually delivered. Wagner remembered that some of the commissions were recorded, but he did not know if those included the commissions of the plaintiffs.

Lee's next witness, Attorney General Levi Lincoln, was even more resistant to Lee's inquiries. Lincoln asked that all questions be submitted to him in writing and said he hoped the Court appreciated his dilemma: He felt himself "delicately situated" between his duty to the Court and the duty he believed he owed to the executive department. Lee pressed Lincoln to provide information on what he had done with the commissions when he was Jefferson's acting secretary of state, arguing that he must divulge that information in his official capacity as a public officer of the United States. Lincoln resisted. "It was going a great way," he replied, "to say that every Secretary of State should at all times be liable to be called upon to appear as a witness in a court of justice and testify to facts which came to his knowledge officially." That was an opinion, Lincoln said, that was shared by others he "highly respected," presumably Jefferson and Madison.

Finally, the justices had enough of the minuet between Lee and Lincoln. They forced the issue on Lee's terms. The four justices on the bench that day–Marshall, Chase, Paterson, and Washington–told Lincoln they had no doubt that he should answer Lee's questions, since there was no information sought that could be deemed confidential. The Court implicitly accepted Lee's argument that only confidential political information exchanged between the president and his Cabinet officers was beyond their evidentiary reach. Whether the commissions were in Lincoln's State Department office was not, the Court declared, a confidential fact. It was, rather, "a fact which all the world have a right to know."

The next morning, Lincoln provided written answers to all but the last question submitted by Lee; his answers, however, were not enlightening. When he had been acting secretary of state, Lincoln testified, he had seen certain commissions that were signed and sealed, but he did not know whether they were the particular commissions in question. He could not say if any of the commissions at issue had been delivered to the plaintiffs. He could state unequivocally that he had no knowledge that the commissions were present when Madison took office, or that Madison was ever in possession of the commissions. On the last, crucial question–did Lincoln know what had happened to the commissions?–Lincoln requested that the Court not compel him to say what had been done with the commissions. The justices granted Lincoln's request, concluding that, if the commissions were not in Madison's possession, their whereabouts was immaterial. More to the point, perhaps, than the justices' technical reason for granting Lincoln's request was their wish not to force a stark confrontation with the Jefferson administration.

With the further assistance of an affidavit entered into the trial record from the chief justice's brother James Marshall and the testimony of another State Department clerk, Lee was able to identify the location of the signed and sealed commissions of three of the plaintiffs (no one had vouched for Ramsay's). Lee then announced that he had "proved the existence of the commissions" and was ready to move to the merits of his case.

Lee suggested that the justices should focus on three basic questions. First, did the Court have the authority to award the writ of mandamus that Lee had asked for his clients? If so, could the mandamus be directed against a secretary of state? And, finally, if the answers to the first two questions were in the affirmative, could the Court compel the present secretary of state to deliver the commissions that Lee's clients sought?

The answer to his first question, Lee asserted, was self-evident. If the Supreme Court was in fact the supreme judicial tribunal, it must have the authority to superintend inferior courts and governmental officers that withheld vested legal rights. The concept of a superior court's having that authority, through the legal instrument of a mandamus, dated back several centuries in English common law, to the king's bench, and was supported by the commentaries of Blackstone, the most respected interpreter of the common law. That same authority had been recognized by the original United States Congress, which enacted the Judiciary Act of 1789 providing original jurisdiction for the Supreme Court to issue a mandamus. Lee noted that the Court had recognized the practice in two earlier cases—the only major point in his presentation that Chief Justice Marshall would later dispute or, more to the point, simply ignore.

Given its authority to use the mandamus, could the Court direct it against any high government official? Lee conceded that the writ could not issue against the president, because the Constitution provided that impeachment was the only means of disciplining the chief executive. He also admitted that the secretary of state could disregard such an order as long as he was acting in his capacity as the president's agent. But if the secretary was serving as a public official and had deprived a U.S. citizen of a vested right, such as a land patent or, as in this case, a judicial commission, then, Lee argued, the Court could order him to do his legal duty. Lee reminded the justices of the statute that gave officers of the State Department the responsibility to record and seal civil commissions. What could be plainer than the secretary's duty to deliver these commissions? The secretary is "a high officer," Lee acknowledged, "but he is not above the law."

Justice Paterson interrupted: Was it the duty of the secretary of state to deliver commissions unless expressly directed by the president not to do so?

Once the president has signed the commissions, Lee replied, he "has done with it." And after the secretary of state has sealed the commission, he continued, the appointment is complete. A secretary of state who purposely refuses to deliver the commission, Lee declared, "does wrong."

The answer to Lee's third question, whether a mandamus could issue against *this* secretary of state, flowed from the attorney's previous arguments: Madison must be held accountable by the Court. Although Lee recognized that "the emoluments" of the office of justice of the peace were meager, he insisted that the principle at stake—the independence of the federal judiciary—was important. Citing Hamilton's article no. 78 in *The Federalist,* for the proposition that the judiciary must be independent, Lee argued that the Court should not allow a high officer of the executive branch of government, in this case Secretary Madison, to deprive the citizens of the District of Columbia of their duly appointed judges. His clients had made their case, Lee asserted, and now the justices were bound to grant them their remedy—the delivery of the commissions. Lee concluded with a mild reminder to the justices that "they can refuse justice to no man."

Had Marshall wanted to avoid participating in the *Marbury* decision, he would have had excellent reasons for doing so. The chief justice easily could have excused himself by pleading conflict of interest, because he had been intimately involved with the judicial appointments he was now asked to judge. Even if the chief justice had not played such a major role in the appointments and circumstances leading to the lawsuit, his brother James certainly did. James Marshall had delivered some of Adams's last-minute judicial commissions, and he later testified in an affidavit for Charles Lee about the fateful circumstances that had led to the lawsuit. No one could have faulted the chief justice for recusing himself in a lawsuit in which his brother was a key witness, though the standards of judicial ethics at that time did not require him to do so.

Why did John Marshall refuse to disqualify himself? Although he never provided an explanation, there was a compelling reason for the chief justice to insist on participating in the trial. He knew the importance of the large constitutional issues raised, particularly that of the independence of the judiciary, and he did not want to miss his opportunity.

As he contemplated his decision in the Marbury case, Marshall must have realized that *any* opinion he wrote would be condemned, either by his Federalist allies or by the Jeffersonian Republicans. If he ruled against Marbury, denying that he had a legal right to his commission, he would defeat the Federalists' immediate cause and, more generally, undermine their plan to control the federal judiciary long after being turned out of office. But the consequences of a decision supporting Marbury would almost surely be worse. It would place the Court in the line of fire of the ruling Republicans in Congress and of President Jefferson, whose popularity appeared to be increasing by the day. No matter how erudite an opinion demanding that Jefferson's secretary of state deliver the commissions might be, the likelihood that the president and his secretary would bow to the Court's dictate was remote. Silence, or studied indifference to such a decision from the administration, might be the best outcome for the Marshall Court. A worse scenario, by no means unrealistic given the political tensions, would cast the Court as catalyst for Republican retribution, triggering a rash of judicial impeachments, and possibly a complete reformation of the federal judiciary.

On February 24, two weeks after completion of Lee's oral argument, Marshall delivered his long (eleven thousand words), sometimes rambling opinion for a unanimous Court. Marshall's opinion began cautiously, acknowledging that the "peculiar delicacy of this case, the novelty of its circumstances, and the real difficulty attending the points which occur in it" required a thorough discussion of the principles on which the opinion was based. If those first, tentative words appeared to signal that the chief justice had lost his nerve and bearings, what followed disabused the Republicans of any such notion. Soon Marshall declared that he was much impressed with the arguments of Charles Lee, so much so that his opinion would track closely to Lee's arguments in substance, though he would depart from the form of Lee's presentation.

Marshall framed his opinion with three questions that Lee had said the Court must answer. First, has Marbury a right to the commission he demands? If so, and that right has been violated, "do the laws of this country afford him a remedy?" Finally, if the laws do afford Marbury a remedy, is it a mandamus issuing from the Supreme Court?

In answering his first question, Marshall said he had no doubt that William Marbury was entitled to his commission, because, as he himself had insisted before Lee made the argument, an appointment that was signed and sealed was, for all legal purposes, complete. Once the commission was legally binding, Secretary of State Madison was obligated to do his legal duty and deliver the commission. Marshall reiterated Lee's key argument that Madison was acting as a legal officer of the United States, not as the agent of President Jefferson. "He acts, in this respect, as has been very properly stated at the bar [by Lee], under the authority of law, and not by the instructions of the President," Marshall wrote. In this regard, Marshall said, Madison's duty to deliver the commission was no different from that he owed to the grantee of a land patent (the legal analogy that had been made by Lee).

Since Marbury had a right to the commission, the chief justice continued, he must have a remedy in law. "The very essence of civil liberty," Marshall wrote, was "the right of every individual to claim protection of the laws, wherever he receives an injury." The chief justice drove his point home, asserting that "one of the first duties of government" was to afford its citizens the protection of the laws. "The government of the United States has been emphatically termed a government of laws and not of men," he wrote. "It will certainly cease to deserve this high appellation, if the laws furnish no remedy for the violation of a vested legal right."

To complete an answer to his second question, Marshall elaborated on Lee's distinction between Madison's *duty* as a legal officer of the United States and his *discretion* as a Cabinet member who owed exclusive allegiance to the president in all confidential political matters. He assured Jefferson and Madison that they need not worry that the Court would intrude in their purely political conversations and actions. He shuddered at the thought that the Court would attempt to supervise such discretionary political conduct. "It is scarcely necessary for the Court to disclaim all pretension to such jurisdiction," he wrote. "An extravagance, so absurd and excessive, could not have been entertained for a moment."

But at the same time that Marshall announced this judicial forbearance, he seized the opportunity to expand the Court's authority. It must be the Court's responsibility, he claimed, to decide what was political and what was not. And, alas, in Marbury's case, Secretary Madison was not acting as Jefferson's agent but as a public officer, "where specific duty is assigned by law, and individual rights depend on the performance of that duty." The chief justice further agreed with Lee that the mandamus was the correct legal instrument for seeking the justice that was due Marbury and his coclaimants.

At this point in his opinion, Marshall had answered two and a half of the three questions he had posed, and it seemed as if he was heading toward the collision with the Jefferson administration he had so skillfully avoided during the two years he had been in office.

At this critical juncture, as the narrator in a suspense novel pulls his hero from the cliff's edge, Marshall rescued his Court from imminent disaster. The chief justice began the delicate task of extricating the Court from the very tight vise of his own making by inquiring whether the mandamus could issue from the Supreme Court, as Lee had argued that it should. It was here that Marshall veered abruptly, and decisively, away from Lee's position. Lee had contended that the Court possessed ample authority to issue the mandamus, finding statutory support for his argument in the Judiciary Act of 1789, in which Congress conferred original jurisdiction on the Court to issue just such a mandamus, as well as in two earlier Supreme Court decisions acknowledging that authority.

Marshall did not dispute that Congress had granted the Court jurisdiction in cases such as Marbury's, but he declared that the Court owed allegiance to a higher authority than Congress. That authority was the Constitution, and its provisions contradicted the Judiciary Act of 1789. Under Article III of the Constitution, the Supreme Court was given original jurisdiction in all cases affecting ambassadors or other public ministers, and cases in which a state was a party. In all other cases that were properly before the Court, its jurisdiction was appellate. Nowhere under the original jurisdiction provided in the Constitution, Marshall noted, was there a category of cases that would include William Marbury's lawsuit. Unless the framers had indulged in useless phrase-making, Marshall reasoned, they must have meant what they wrote.

Finding no words in the Constitution that required the Court to accept Congress's judgment over that of the Constitution's framers, Marshall moved toward his conclusion. "The question whether an act repugnant to the Constitution can become the law of the land is a question deeply interesting to the United States but, happily, not of an intricacy proportioned to its interest. It seems only necessary to recognize certain principles, supposed to have been long and well established, to decide it." Those principles could best be understood, he suggested, by asking a single question: Did the Court owe its primary allegiance to the fundamental law contained in the Constitution or to an ordinary act of legislation? Marshall answered this question by posing an alternative to his position that appeared intolerable. "The Constitution is either a superior paramount law, unchangeable by ordinary means, or it is on a level with ordinary legislative acts, and, like other acts, is alterable when the legislature shall be pleased to alter it." Surely the framers did not intend for the legislature, only one of three coequal branches of the federal government, to change the rules governing our constitutional democracy as it pleased. They must, therefore, have intended for the Constitution to be supreme.

Marshall then fit the final piece in his elaborate Marbury puzzle, insisting that the Court was the institution responsible for interpreting the Constitution. "It is emphatically the province and duty of the judicial department to say what the law is," he proclaimed. Otherwise, he would be "reduced to the necessity of maintaining that courts must close their eyes on the Constitution, and see only the law." The justices, who had taken an oath to uphold the Constitution, could not permit that to happen without untoward consequences. "Must the court condemn to death those victims [of a bill of attainder] whom the Constitution endeavors to preserve?" Or convict a citizen of treason on the basis of a confession made out of court when the Constitution explicitly requires that there be "no conviction of treason unless on the testimony of two witnesses"? Certainly not.

Applying these principles to the case at hand, the chief justice announced that, although Marbury's cause was just and Secretary Madison should not have deprived him of his legal right, the Supreme Court could not remedy this obvious wrong. For the Constitution, the paramount law, did not give the Court jurisdiction in the case. Marshall was duty-bound to declare, therefore, that the portion of the Judiciary Act of 1789 erroneously conferring original jurisdiction on the Court was unconstitutional.

With the extraordinary display of his judicial craft in *Marbury,* the chief justice had solved his, and the Court's, looming political problem with the Jefferson administration. He had managed to lecture Jefferson and Madison on their executive responsibilities without giving them or the Republican Congress serious cause to attack him or his institution. The Federalist appointee William Marbury lost his case before the Supreme Court. The reason he lost had nothing to do with the merit of his claim against Madison, which Marshall firmly supported, but with the cumbersome restrictions imposed by the Constitution on the Court's jurisdiction.

But although Marshall had satisfied the Republicans' short-term interests by rejecting Marbury's claim, he had purchased an enormous piece of constitutional real estate for the Court. *Marbury v. Madison* established the Court's authority to declare an act of Congress unconstitutional, a power that would prove to be of historic significance in securing the institution's parity with Congress. Marshall's opinion also served notice that the Court, not the president, would be the ultimate judge of claims of executive privilege, an authority of seismic proportions.

In performing this miracle of judicial ingenuity, Marshall put his rhetorical skills on full display. With his penetrating logic, simple but compelling command of the English language, and indestructible conviction that he was right, Marshall had marched toward his conclusions. But were those conclusions as inescapable as the chief justice had, in his inimitable way, made them appear?

Consider an alternative judicial interpretation that could, reasonably, have led the Court to a very different conclusion from Marshall's. The *Marbury* opinion hinged, critically, on Marshall's contention that the Constitution did not give the Court the original jurisdiction required to hear the case. If Marshall had taken up that jurisdictional issue first, instead of last, and decided that the Court lacked jurisdiction, there would have been no need to reach the merits of the case.

That cautious approach became an article of constitutional faith among proponents of judicial restraint in the twentieth century. Under this theory of constitutional interpretation, justices should make every effort not to decide a case on the merits if other grounds for decision are available.

Another judge, without Marshall's ambitions, might have avoided the large constitutional questions that the chief justice addressed. An alternative reading of Article III, for example, could have found the language consistent with the provisions of the Judiciary Act of 1789 that the chief justice had declared unconstitutional. Under this interpretation, the Court could have reasonably concluded that those cases set out for its original jurisdiction in the Constitution were the minimum required, not the unalterable number suggested by Marshall, and that Congress was free to add classes of cases, as it chose to do in the Judiciary Act of 1789. Support for that interpretation can be found in the same Article III, which, after setting out cases for the Court's original and appellate jurisdiction, adds, "with such Exceptions and under such Regulations as the Congress shall make." A plausible purpose of the "Exceptions" clause, it could be argued, was not only to guarantee immediate access to the Supreme Court for important cases, such as those involving ambassadors, but also to give Congress the flexibility to add to those cases of original jurisdiction, as it later considered necessary.

But if the chief justice had chosen that interpretation of Article III, he would have lost his chance to declare an act of Congress unconstitutional, and to expound on the Court's role in interpreting the Constitution. *Marbury* would have been a footnote in constitutional history.

There was no suggestion in Marshall's opinion that there might be a reasonable interpretation of the constitutional language that differed from his own. He did not even discuss the "Exceptions" clause, or the earlier decisions cited by Charles Lee in support of his argument that the Court had recognized its original jurisdiction in such mandamus cases. That skewed approach to legal argument was characteristic of Marshall, as both attorney and judge. Recall his brilliant performance before the House of Representatives in the Jonathan Robbins case, in which he argued his side of the issue with such authority, and such absolute certainty that he was correct, that he saw no need to discuss alternative possibilities. In *Marbury* he demonstrated, once again, that he was a consummate legal tactician.

Marshall's lecturing on executive responsibility may have been momentarily infuriating to Jefferson, but the president apparently concluded that it was prudent to let the decision pass without comment. He did not utter a word about the opinion, so far as his public statements or private correspondence show, for the remainder of the year. He offered his own views on judicial review to Abigail Adams the following year: "The opinion which gives to the judges the right to decide what laws are constitutional, and what not, not only for themselves in their own sphere of action, but for the legislature & executive also, in their spheres, would make the judiciary a despotic branch." It was Jefferson's opinion that each coequal branch of the government stood as its own unchallenged judge of what was constitutional. The president and members of Congress, after all, took an oath to uphold the same Constitution as had the chief justice. Jefferson did not criticize Marshall's *Marbury* opinion in his letter to the former president's wife, apparently because he was satisfied that the Court had acted within its legitimate constitutional sphere in determining that it did not have the jurisdiction to hear the case.

Many years after *Marbury*, however, Jefferson did denounce the decision. His primary objection was that Marshall had incorrectly decided that Marbury's commission had vested when it was signed and sealed; Jefferson contended that delivery of a commission, like that of a bond or deed, was essential to its validity. He later complained, "This practice of Judge Marshall of traveling out of his case to prescribe what the law would be in a moot case not before the court, is very irregular and very censurable." Advocating judicial restraint, Jefferson insisted that the chief justice should not have pronounced judgment on the merits of the Marbury case when the Court's lack of jurisdiction made it unnecessary. "The object was clearly to instruct any other court having the jurisdiction, what they should do, if Marbury should apply to them," Jefferson wrote. "Besides the impropriety of this gratuitous interference, could anything exceed this perversion of the law?"

But in 1803, Jefferson had more important business to consider. Midway through his first presidential term, Jefferson and the Republican Congress had accomplished most of their legislative goals. They had reduced the size of the federal government, slashed the military budget, eliminated internal taxes, and repealed the hated Judiciary Act of 1801.

The president was enjoying unprecedented popularity in 1803 and, forward-looking politician that he was, he did not wish to jeopardize his reelection chances by engaging in a noisy public quarrel with Chief Justice Marshall over what then appeared to be the relatively unimportant issues raised in the *Marbury* decision. The Republican press in 1803 followed Jefferson's example and did not denounce the *Marbury* decision, choosing in most instances merely to report the Court's holding without editorial comment.

Only decades later was Marshall's momentous achievement in *Marbury* fully appreciated. With his *Marbury* opinion, the chief justice had embarked on his ambitious quest to establish the Supreme Court as an independent and truly coequal branch of the federal government, a result that was inconceivable when he took the oath of office in the tiny Senate committee room in February 1801.

[9]

A "Bungling Way" to Remove Judges

SHORTLY AFTER HIS ELECTION, President Jefferson predicted that his Republican ship of state would experience a deservedly smoother voyage than the tumultuous journey of his Federalist predecessor. Midway through his first term, he could take pride in the seaworthiness of his Republican vessel. Jefferson and the Republican Congress had succeeded impressively with their domestic agenda. And in the field of foreign affairs, Jefferson had achieved the greatest triumph of his presidency, the purchase from France of the Louisiana Territory, which more than doubled the size of the United States.

He had accomplished his objectives by a blend of ideology and pragmatism, exalting Republican principles but working within practical political limits. The finest example of Jefferson's technique was the Louisiana Purchase. Had he adhered to rigid Republican principles, it would have been impossible to complete negotiations without a constitutional amendment.

Jefferson had long insisted on a narrow reading of federal constitutional powers, maintaining that no branch was authorized to take action not explicitly provided for in the Constitution. Recall that in 1791, Jefferson, as Washington's secretary of state, contended that no provision in the Constitution allowed Congress to establish a national bank. He lost the debate with Alexander Hamilton, who argued that Article I of the Constitution must be interpreted broadly to permit

Congress to take all necessary and proper steps to accomplish legitimate ends.

In 1803, the acquisition of the Louisiana Territory posed an uncomfortable problem for the president: under a strict constitutional view of federal authority, the government could not take the action required to purchase the territory; no provision in the Constitution allowed it. Jefferson drafted a constitutional amendment that would authorize the purchase. But he received word from his negotiators in Paris that Napoleon was increasingly nervous about the sale. Whatever his reservations, Jefferson quickly overcame them and urged his supporters in Congress to ratify the purchase "in silence" and "with as little debate as possible, and particularly so far as respects the constitutional difficulty."

But during that same year, Jefferson's judgment failed him when he was considering another issue with constitutional implications, and, in the process, caused a rift between radical and moderate Republicans. The miscalculation occurred over what more should be done about the Federalist-dominated judiciary, after the successful repeal of the Judiciary Act of 1801. Radical Republicans such as William Branch Giles urged severing the Federalist judicial branch. "No remedy is competent to redress the evil system," he wrote Jefferson in June 1801, "but an absolute repeal of the whole judiciary and terminating the present offices and creating a new system." Other radical Republicans, particularly the florid orator of the House, John Randolph of Roanoke, were ready to make good on Giles's threat, with or without the president's instruction.

Although Jefferson never supported the most radical measures advocated by Giles and Randolph, he approved the removal of Federalist judges who had demonstrated blatant partisanship on the bench. Jefferson's bitter memory of the active role that members of the Federalist judiciary had played in defending the Sedition Act (and, in many cases, aiding prosecutions under the law) was still vivid. He believed that there was more work to be done to eliminate the last vestiges of Federalist tyranny. "My opinion is that two or three years more will bring back to the fold of Republicanism all our wandering brethren whom the cry of 'Wolf' scattered in 1798," he wrote New York Governor George Clinton. "Till that is done, let every man stand to his post, and hazard nothing by change."

The first Republican attacks on the Federalist judiciary came far from Washington, in what was then the Pennsylvania state capital, Lancaster, where the Republicans controlling the legislature sought to remove the most partisan Federalist judicial holdovers. They began with the chief judge of the state's western judicial district, Alexander Addison, an outspoken defender of the Sedition Act. In 1798, Addison had published a spirited defense of the legislation that impressed George Washington, who, in turn, sent a copy of the judge's essay to John Marshall.

As presiding judge, Addison became the master of the political polemic, disguised as an instruction to the grand jury, regularly lambasting the perceived low tricks of the Republicans and, with equal verve, praising the high-mindedness of the Federalists. Using the grand-jury instruction as bully pulpit, Addison had denounced the Kentucky and Virginia Resolutions and championed Adams's candidacy in 1800. The judge was such an aggressive, uncompromising advocate of Federalist causes that he was known as "the transmontane Goliath of federalism."

Addison appeared oblivious to the Republican sweep of both the national and Pennsylvania executive and legislative offices in 1800. Spurred by a diatribe by Addison against the new Republican governor, the Republican-controlled legislature passed articles of impeachment against the judge. In January 1803, the most prominent Republican lawyer in the state, Alexander Dallas, who had been appointed federal district attorney by Jefferson, prosecuted. Following a nine-day trial, in which Addison acted as his own counsel, the judge was convicted and removed from office. Later, the radical Republicans in Pennsylvania attempted to impeach all three Federalist judges on the state supreme court, but the drastic action so appalled moderates in the party, including Dallas and the single Republican member of the state's highest court, that they successfully came to the Federalist judges' defense.

There is no evidence that Jefferson played an active role in Addison's impeachment. But only a week after the Pennsylvania Senate convicted Addison, the president showed that impeachment was very much on his mind when he formally initiated the first impeachment of a federal judge, New Hampshire's District Judge John Pickering. On

February 4, 1803, Jefferson forwarded materials on Pickering with a message "to the House of Representatives, to whom the Constitution has confided a power of instituting proceedings of redress if they shall be of opinion that the case calls for them." Jefferson's message was the small flame the House radical Republicans had been looking for to start a bonfire of the Federalist judiciary.

John Pickering had drafted New Hampshire's constitution and was generally regarded as one of the finest lawyers in the state; in 1791, he was appointed New Hampshire's chief justice, overseeing the unwieldy state judicial system. But illness and a nervous disorder affected Pickering's judicial performance, so much so that, within three years of his appointment, he persistently ignored many of his duties and became a source of embarrassment to the state's bar and legislature. An effort to remove Pickering from office failed by only one vote in the New Hampshire House of Representatives, a result that satisfied no one, not even Pickering's Federalist supporters. They transferred the state's Pickering problem to the federal judiciary by prevailing upon President Washington to appoint the judge to the federal district court.

Soon after he began his duties in the federal court, Pickering's health problems became worse, leading the poor man to insanity and alcoholism. Finally, his Federalist colleagues realized that saving Pickering's judgeship was a hopeless cause and invoked a provision of the Judiciary Act of 1801 that permitted one of the new circuit-court judges to assume the duties of an incapacitated district-court judge. But the Republicans inadvertently squelched the Federalists' solution to the problem by passing the Repeal Act of 1802, which eliminated the new circuit courts and forced Pickering to resume his federal district-court duties.

Impeachment was not Jefferson's first choice of remedies for the Pickering problem. Two months before he sent the Pickering materials to the House, Jefferson had written his friend Thomas Cooper expressing satisfaction in the tranquil course that his administration had taken in realizing Republican goals. Soon after Jefferson wrote to Cooper, Secretary of the Treasury Albert Gallatin was dispatched to speak directly to Pickering's friend, New Hampshire's Federalist Senator William Plumer, on the necessity of finding a discreet way to relieve Pickering. If Pickering was not removed voluntarily, Gallatin warned, sterner measures would be taken.

But neither Pickering's family nor Senator Plumer wanted to make Jefferson's task easy. Despite the judge's poor health, no member of his family was willing to ask him to step down. And Senator Plumer had many reasons to resist the administration's entreaties. Asking Pickering to leave the bench was, for Plumer, tantamount to surrendering to Jefferson's design to destroy the independence of the federal judiciary. Besides, if Pickering were removed, his most obvious replacement would be Plumer's arch political enemy, Republican District Attorney John Sherburne.

According to Senator Plumer, Jefferson complained to him that the impeachment process was too cumbersome and slow; he told Plumer that he would have much preferred the system in place in several states whereby the chief executive could remove a judge with a majority vote of both houses of the legislature. But neither Jefferson nor any other leader of his party attempted to sponsor a constitutional amendment that would have provided such a procedure for removal at the federal level. Shortly before Pickering's impeachment trial began in the Senate, Jefferson admitted to Plumer, "This business of removing judges by impeachment is a bungling way."

Pickering's impeachment proved Jefferson's point. The Constitution's grounds for removing a federal judge, applied to Pickering's case, were conspicuously inadequate. A judge may only be impeached for "Treason, Bribery, or other high Crimes and Misdemeanors," an awkward constitutional match for Pickering's insanity and alcoholism.

The Republicans faced a dilemma. If they conceded Pickering's insanity, they would have to argue that a mental incompetent was responsible for his actions and, therefore, impeachable. But to make that argument would call into question the constitutional concept of high crimes and misdemeanors. Rather than entering that interpretative morass, the Republican leadership in the House—which first had to issue articles of impeachment that would go to the Senate for trial—chose to suppress discussion of the insanity issue entirely. All the while, they pushed for articles of impeachment, which, if passed, would be sent to the Senate for Pickering's trial. House leaders John Randolph and Joseph Nicholson concentrated exclusively on Pickering's rulings and his habitual drunkenness. When asked by New Hampshire's Senator Plumer if Pickering's insanity rose to the level of a high crime or misdemeanor, Jefferson replied, "If the facts of his denying an appeal &

of his intoxication, as stated in the impeachment are proven, that will be sufficient cause of removal without further inquiry."

The House committee that considered the impeachment was packed with Republican loyalists. They did not question the statements of the Republican district attorney who insisted that Pickering's rulings and antics—in one case the judge refused to hear the federal government's witnesses and shouted obscenities at the prosecutor—were due solely to drunkenness. Not a word was said about the judge's derangement. The Republican floor managers forced the vote of the full House without permitting evidence of Pickering's insanity to be heard; their charges voted overwhelmingly in favor of impeachment.

The House vote was taken in such haste that there was not time to draw up formal written articles of impeachment. Instead, Randolph and Nicholson personally delivered an oral impeachment to the Senate chamber. The four articles of impeachment that were later drafted did not refer to the possibility that Pickering was insane.

At the Senate trial, the Republican prosecutors called seven witnesses, all members of their party, five appointed to office by Jefferson and two who stood to gain promotion in the federal judicial system if Pickering were impeached. Their testimony was of a piece: Pickering's misconduct could be traced directly and exclusively to his alcoholism. There was no lawyer representing Pickering to cross-examine. (Robert Goodloe Harper had been asked to defend Pickering, but he refused on the grounds that he could not represent an insane man in a criminal proceeding.) After a meager effort by both of New Hampshire's Federalist senators to defend the judge based on his insanity, the vote on impeachment was set for the next congressional business day. Senator Plumer, who had testified in Pickering's behalf, harbored no illusions about the outcome. "Tomorrow, no doubt, an insane man will be convicted of high crimes & misdemeanors," Plumer wrote; "& probably the next day John Samuel Sherburne [his Republican rival who had testified against the judge] will be announced as his successor."

The stench of the impeachment proceeding was so strong that it nauseated even a number of Republican senators. On the final roll call, eight senators, including three Republicans, did not vote. The remaining twenty-six convicted Pickering by a strict party vote, with nineteen Republicans voting yea and all seven Federalists opposed. Senator

Plumer's second prediction, that John Sherburne would succeed Pickering on the federal bench, also proved accurate: Jefferson appointed the Republican district attorney to the judicial vacancy ten days after Pickering's removal.

The Pickering impeachment was a partisan brawl. The Republican leadership manipulated the system, willfully stretching the constitutional language for impeachment to ensnare the judge. The impeachment stood, at its worst, for the proposition that an insane man could be found guilty of high crimes and misdemeanors. But if there was no honor on the Republicans' side, the Federalists hardly displayed more. After all, the Federalists were perfectly willing to keep an obviously deranged and thoroughly incompetent man on the federal bench indefinitely to foil Republican designs.

There is no record that Jefferson orchestrated the Pickering impeachment. Still, it is inconceivable that the president was indifferent. The kindest view of Jefferson's role was that he reluctantly initiated the Pickering impeachment, and did so only because there was no less drastic method for removing Pickering after his own family and friends refused overtures from the administration to negotiate the judge's resignation.

Fortunately, the Pickering impeachment was an anomaly that set no important precedent. It did, however, encourage the most radical Republicans to set their sights on loftier judicial game: members of the U.S. Supreme Court. On the very day the Senate voted the New Hampshire judge guilty of impeachable offenses, the House passed a resolution, introduced by John Randolph, for the impeachment of Supreme Court Justice Samuel Chase. And with the Chase impeachment, Jefferson did more than simply transmit materials about the judge to the House. There is no doubt that the idea of impeaching Chase was initiated by the president.

In the spring of 1800, as a presidential candidate, Jefferson assured James Monroe that no slander by Justice Chase against the Republicans or himself personally would provoke in him the slightest tremor of indignation. As if to prove his point, Jefferson made no comment about Chase's handling of the Sedition Act trial of James T. Callender, even at the height of Chase's withering attacks on Republican counsel. And when Chase, from the bench, took a thinly disguised swipe at Jefferson's suspected atheism, Jefferson's only response was to say that no personal attack caused him less concern than that of Justice Chase.

President Jefferson made considerable efforts to overlook the excesses of the Federalist judiciary in the interest of national unity. In 1802, he went so far as to congratulate Cyrus Griffin, the federal district-court judge who had served with Chase at the Callender trial, for no longer being among those who "have lent their influence to the promotion of a certain set of principles disapproved . . . by the great majority of our citizens."

But Chase continued to test the president's resolve. The justice's transgressions dated back to early Federalist prosecutions under the Sedition Act and had wounded personal friends of Jefferson's. It was Chase who had stampeded a jury into returning a guilty verdict in the sedition trial of Jefferson's friend Thomas Cooper and then slapped Cooper with the largest fine and prison term of anyone convicted under the statute. After Jefferson was elected president and the Republicans won control of Congress, Chase, unlike most other Federalist members of the judiciary, made no attempt to hide his hostility to the Republicans. Alone among the members of the Supreme Court, Chase advised Chief Justice Marshall that the justices should directly challenge the legitimacy of the Republicans' Judicial Repeal Act of 1802.

Increasingly bitter, Chase rejected any accommodation with the political enemy. Finally, he abandoned caution. In a harangue that would precipitate impeachment proceedings against him, Chase reiterated his apocalyptic vision of government under the Republicans. The charge occurred in his instruction to a federal grand jury in Baltimore on May 2, 1803. The justice began with the charge that the Republican-sponsored 1802 Judicial Repeal Act (which had been upheld as constitutional by Chase's colleagues on the Supreme Court) shook the foundation of an independent national judiciary. He condemned universal suffrage and equal rights, which, Chase predicted, would soon sink Maryland's constitutional government "into a mobocracy." Taking dead aim at Jefferson, the justice complained that "the modern doctrines by our late reformers, that all men in a state of society are entitled to enjoy equal liberty and equal rights, have brought this mighty mischief upon us; and I fear that it will rapidly progress until peace and order, freedom and property, shall be destroyed."

Chase's instruction to the grand jury was published in a Baltimore newspaper, and a copy was sent to Jefferson by a Republican member of the Maryland legislature. At the time, Jefferson certainly had more important matters of state to consider than the wild accusations of Justice Chase. In Paris, negotiations with Napoleon's government for the Louisiana Purchase had reached a critical stage.

Until Chase's attack, no Federalist judge had seriously disturbed President Jefferson's determined equanimity. Chief Justice Marshall's stern lecture to the president and his secretary of state on their duties in *Marbury v. Madison* may have grated, but at the time, Jefferson made no recorded criticism. Judge Pickering's aberrant behavior on the bench provoked the president, but he gave every indication that he would have preferred a negotiated settlement and a discreet exit for the judge. But with Justice Chase's grand-jury tirade, the president snapped.

Jefferson reacted immediately, sending a letter to one of the Republican leaders of the House, Maryland's Joseph Nicholson, asking, "Ought the seditious and official attack on the principles of our Constitution and of a state to go unpunished? And to whom so pointedly as yourself will the public look for the necessary measures?" Since Nicholson had been one of the managers of Pickering's impeachment, there could be no doubt of Jefferson's meaning: Justice Chase should be impeached. Having planted the idea in his lieutenant's mind, Jefferson promptly backed away from taking responsibility for the suggestion (a familiar Jefferson stratagem when he anticipated a nasty political fight). He advised Nicholson not to draw him into the certain controversy. "For myself," he wrote, "it is better that I should not interfere."

But Nicholson was not so quick to take up the president's cause. He first sought the counsel of the Speaker of the House, Nathaniel Macon, who expressed serious reservations about Nicholson's role and questioned the idea of impeachment. In a letter to Nicholson, Macon conceded his dislike for Justice Chase but pointed out that Nicholson might not be in the best position to prosecute the case, because he would probably be in line to succeed the justice should the impeachment succeed. In a second letter, Macon questioned the rationale for an impeachment of Chase, listing a number of worrisome questions that needed to be answered before the serious step of constitutional removal should be undertaken. Macon wondered whether political opinions expressed by judges, Federalist or Republican, were grounds for impeachment. "Change the scene," Macon wrote, "and suppose Chase had stretched as far on the other side, and had praised where no praise was deserving; would it be proper to impeach because, by such conduct, he might lull the people to sleep while their interest was destroyed?" Macon was clearly suggesting that taking on the cantankerous Justice Chase in an impeachment trial was not a good idea.

One of the open secrets to Jefferson's enormous success during his first term was his ability to impose his will on Congress without leaving a presidential fingerprint. He was the master of indirection, often speaking elliptically to influential Republican congressmen at his frequent dinner parties or in his correspondence. He usually showed keen judgment about which congressional leaders he could trust to carry out his wishes. In the hands of capable and loyal lieutenants, Jefferson's wishes became their commands and were effectively translated into Republican legislation. The challenging assignment of moving the controversial Judicial Repeal Act of 1802 through a closely divided Senate, for example, was given to Senators John Breckinridge and Stevens Thomson Mason, both trusted allies of the president. They did not disappoint him.

Jefferson was not so well served with the Chase impeachment. Congressman Joseph Nicholson, on the advice of Speaker of the House Nathaniel Macon, had declined the president's invitation. The vacuum was eagerly filled by Nicholson's friend and colleague John Randolph. But Randolph's impetuousness and ignorance of the law made him unqualified to manage the impeachment.

Not that John Randolph lacked talent. The son of a prosperous southern-Virginia planter, Randolph was elected to the House of Representatives at the age of twenty-six and quickly established himself as a shrewd parliamentarian and potent orator. Speaker Macon made him chairman of the powerful Ways and Means Committee. Despite his youth and eccentricities (he brandished a horse whip while patrolling the House chamber wearing boots and spurs), Randolph became the Republicans' majority leader only two years after his first election.

From his first days in Congress, it was obvious that Randolph was no favorite of Jefferson, who never personally tapped him for any leadership role. Randolph was too moralistic, vain, and resistant to party discipline to suit Jefferson's presidential purposes. He possessed a pure vision of Republicanism that rejected all compromise. For Randolph, the bedrock Republican ideals were states' rights and agrarianism. He supported Jefferson in the presidential election of 1800, but his loyalty was to party principle, not to the man. Once Randolph had developed a power base in the House, he openly pursued an independent course from that of the administration.

The president's initiative to impeach Justice Chase languished during the summer and fall of 1803. Randolph, apparently without Jefferson's approval, resuscitated the idea in January 1804, when he rose on the House floor to demand an inquiry into Justice Chase's continued suitability to serve on the Supreme Court. A House committee headed by Randolph then recommended impeachment proceedings. On March 26, 1804, Randolph placed seven articles of impeachment before the full House. Only one of the seven articles concerned Chase's instruction to the Baltimore grand jury, which had so infuriated Jefferson and been the original impetus for the impeachment drive.

Randolph's first two articles focused on Chase's conduct of the second trial of John Fries, a minor militia officer who had led a small group of angry Pennsylvania German farmers protesting a federal property tax passed by the Federalist Congress in 1798 to support an anticipated war with France. Fries and his band of armed men attempted to intimidate tax assessors and succeeded in frightening one federal marshal into releasing prisoners in Bethlehem, Pennsylvania. No shots were fired, and no one was hurt. Fries, nonetheless, was arrested, convicted of treason, and sentenced to death. The defendant was granted a new trial when it was discovered that one of the jurors had expressed a bias in the case.

In 1800, Chase presided at the second Fries trial, and his rulings from the bench antagonized the defendant's lawyers, both prominent Republicans. They conceded the facts of the case but announced their intention to argue that Fries's conduct did not fit within the legal definition of treason. After the jury was impaneled, Chase denied Fries's lawyers' request to argue the law rather than the facts of the case. Outraged, the attorneys withdrew from the trial. The next day, Chase, in a rare display of contrition, offered to rescind his ruling. But Fries's counsel refused to reenter the case, contending that the jury was irrevocably prejudiced because it had heard the judge's opinion. Without counsel, the defendant was convicted and again sentenced to death. Later that year, President Adams, against the advice of his entire Cabinet, pardoned Fries.

Given the rich trove of Justice Chase's aberrant behavior on the bench, particularly his patently unfair handling of the Sedition Act trials of Thomas Cooper and James T. Callender, his conduct of the Fries trial was unexceptional. He would have shown better judgment to have allowed Fries's lawyers to make their argument that the applicable law of treason did not cover the defendant's conduct. On the merits, however, Chase's instruction to the jury on the law was technically correct. Besides, Chase had offered to withdraw his ruling. Randolph's first two articles of impeachment, nonetheless, charged that the judge had conducted himself "in a manner highly arbitrary, oppressive, and unjust," which resulted "in manifest violation of law and justice."

Selecting Chase's conduct of the Fries trial as the subject of his first two impeachment articles was Randolph's first mistake. Under the most critical reading of the Fries trial record, Chase's rulings could hardly be considered high crimes, as contemplated by the framers of the Constitution's impeachment clause. Randolph had set an unnecessarily difficult task for himself.

Randolph was on firmer ground with his next three articles of impeachment, all directed at Chase's conduct of the Callender sedition trial. Article three condemned Chase's failure to excuse a juror who, before the trial, had expressed an opinion on the defendant's conduct. The fourth article accused the judge of improperly rejecting the testimony of a key defense witness, Colonel John Taylor. In article five, Randolph charged Chase with general misconduct by demonstrating "manifest injustice, partiality, and intemperance" in his bullying of defense counsel.

Chase's blatant partisanship during the Callender trial was unacceptable by any reasonable standard of judicial conduct. But did such conduct constitute an impeachable offense? Convincing the jury of the U.S. Senate of that proposition would be a challenge for a superb prosecutor.

Randolph continued his impeachment articles by citing Chase's actions before two grand juries. The first occurred shortly after the Callender trial, when Chase traveled to New Castle, Delaware, where a grand jury had failed to return indictments under the Sedition Act. The jurors, most of them farmers, were eager to return to their chores during the wheat harvest, but Chase refused to release them. Instead, he declared that there was a treasonable paper being published at Wilmington and ordered the U.S. attorney to investigate. The next day, he was forced to release the jurors after the federal prosecutor reported that his investigation had uncovered nothing seditious.

To succeed, the sixth article, like the previous five, would require the most astute legal argument. Chase's motive in refusing to dismiss the New Castle grand jury, his defenders would surely contend, was only to assure that no illegal seditious conduct within the jurors' jurisdiction was overlooked. To make matters worse for Randolph, the first six articles suffered from yet another problem: if Chase's conduct, as outlined in these articles of impeachment, was so serious as to be impeachable, why had the majority leader and his fellow Republicans waited four years to prosecute?

Randolph's seventh article centered on Chase's controversial instruction to the Baltimore grand jury. Even Speaker of the House Macon had suggested that making Chase's rant to the grand jury the subject of impeachment would be problematic. It would be difficult to show that Chase's charge differed in nature from scores of political instructions delivered from the bench by Federalist judges, including other members of the Supreme Court, over the course of the Adams presidency.

The full House did not immediately act on Randolph's articles of impeachment, which allowed the majority leader later in the year to revise the charges slightly. He consolidated the articles concerning the Fries trial and added two more charges stemming from the Callender trial, contending that Chase had made gross errors in his rulings on the relevant law of trial procedure. With the addition of the two articles on procedure, Randolph was making the statement, in effect, that any judge who committed technical errors of judgment could be removed by the same impeachment method as one guilty of treason, bribery, or other high crimes and misdemeanors.

Randolph's expanded articles (now officially numbering eight) were approved by the House in December 1804 and lent credence to earlier charges from the Federalist press that the purpose of the Republicans' impeachment efforts was to purge all Federalists from the judiciary. "Our Courts are filled by federal [Federalist] Judges," the *New York Evening Post* stated. "Here is the mighty crime, here the high misdemeanor. . . . The bench in short is to be cleared of its present incumbents, no matter by what means, and filled with men subservient to the views of the powers that be . . . at the expense of all that renders a court of justice respectable."

As if the problems inherent in Randolph's articles of impeachment did not pose enough difficulties for the majority leader, he would have to face a defense team consisting of the best legal talent the Federalists could muster. Justice Chase appointed Robert Goodloe Harper to be his chief counsel. Harper solicited the services (without fee) of the elite of the Federalist bar, including Alexander Hamilton, James Bayard, Charles Lee, and Luther Martin. Bayard and Hamilton declined Harper's invitation to join Chase's defense team; Bayard contended that Chase could ably defend himself.

Chase called upon Chief Justice Marshall for assistance in his defense. Marshall, of course, could not join Chase's legal-defense team, but he could contribute in other valuable ways. Specifically, Chase asked Marshall to gather recollections of those who had attended the Callender trial, with particular attention to the testimony of Colonel John Taylor, the subject of one of Randolph's articles of impeachment. Marshall replied that he had asked his brother William (who was the court clerk at the Callender trial) and John Wickham, a good friend and leader of the Richmond bar, to put their recollections of Colonel Taylor's testimony in writing. The chief justice also offered his opinion of the judge's ruling on Taylor's testimony, emphasizing the distinction between an inadvertent judicial error and an impeachable offense. "Admitting it to be true that on legal principles Colonel Taylor's testimony was admissible," Marshall wrote Chase, "it certainly constitutes a very extraordinary ground for an impeachment."

Marshall had no confidence that Chase's jury, the Republican-controlled Senate, would make his distinction between judicial error and impeachable offense. In fact, he believed that the intricacies of the law would be sacrificed at Chase's impeachment trial, and that the Republicans would succeed.

Marshall's anxiety about the deleterious effect that the Chase trial would have on an independent judiciary led him to make the surprising suggestion that a federal judge's controversial rulings could best be taken care of by the legislature acting in the capacity of an appellate court, thereby bypassing an impeachment proceeding entirely. "I think the modern doctrine of impeachment should yield to an appellate jurisdiction in the legislature," Marshall wrote Chase. "A reversal of those legal opinions deemed unsound by the legislature would certainly better comport with the mildness of our character than a removal of the judge who has rendered them unknowing of his fault."

Marshall's letter to Chase showed an uncharacteristic willingness to make broad concessions to Jefferson's Republicans. His suddenly compliant posture was undoubtedly influenced by his apprehension that Justice Chase made too ripe a target for the Republicans. Even if Randolph's legal arguments were weak, the majority leader might find the requisite votes to make bad judgment an impeachable offense. If Chase were removed, no member of the Court, including the chief justice, would be safe. Better to give the responsibility for correcting judicial error to the legislature, acting as an appellate court.

Would the Republicans, as Marshall suspected, convert the Constitution's impeachment clause into a blunt political instrument? They had succeeded in removing John Pickering, and now Chase was in their sights. Certainly John Randolph had signaled his willingness to make impeachment a weapon that could be aimed at any Federalist judge.

But at precisely the moment when Randolph began his effort to force Chase from office, the political winds blew in the direction of the justice's Federalist defenders. Whereas Randolph should have been building consensus among radical and moderate Republicans for his impeachment drive, the majority leader split irrevocably with the Jefferson administration over a proposed land settlement known as Yazoo, in the distant Indian territory of western Georgia. That disagreement with the administration imperiled Randolph's impeachment ambitions.

The Yazoo controversy dated back to 1795, when Georgia legislators filled their pockets with bribes from land speculators who coveted the thirty-five million acres of land known as the Yazoo Territory (in what is now Alabama and Mississippi). In exchange for the bribes, the Georgia legislators passed a law that granted the speculators title to the Yazoo lands for the sum of a penny and a half an acre. When the state's voters learned of the scandal, they turned the crooked legislators out of office and replaced them with reformers, who immediately repealed the law. But the cleansing legislation did not solve the complicated legal problems created by the corrupt transaction. After the first speculators had taken title to the Yazoo lands, they quickly sold the property for handsome profits, often to Northern speculators who had no knowledge of the corruption that had made the land available.

Three years after the original sale, the federal government became involved in the dispute, challenging Georgia's jurisdiction of the Yazoo Territory. In 1802, Georgia agreed to cede the land to the federal government on the condition that it assume responsibility for all outstanding claims of innocent third-party purchasers. Jefferson appointed a high-level commission, which included his three most trusted Cabinet members—Madison, Gallatin, and Levi Lincoln—to make recommendations for the final settlement of the Yazoo Territory.

The president was well aware that many of the third-party purchasers of the Yazoo lands resided in Northern states, where he hoped to make significant gains in his 1804 reelection bid. Yazoo, therefore, became not just a legal tangle but one with serious political consequences for Jefferson's moderate Republicans. When the commission submitted its recommendations in February 1804, it took no official position on the 1795 Georgia law. It recommended, nonetheless, that five million acres of the Yazoo territory be dedicated to innocent third-party purchasers of land that had been sold as a result of the original legislation. It was a pragmatic, politically astute solution that satisfied Jefferson's purposes.

Randolph was outraged when he learned of the commission's recommendations. He denounced the commission's compromise. By granting even five million acres under the terms of the original land deal, Randolph charged, the commission had implicitly sanctioned public corruption. He claimed that the proposed settlement was an unforgivable blow to states' rights, because the commission had refused to recognize Georgia's sovereign authority to repeal the 1795 act and nullify all of the land purchases. Randolph also questioned the motives of those who supported it. He viciously attacked Jefferson's postmaster general, Gideon Granger, for his lobbying activities on behalf of Northern speculators who stood to gain from the settlement. And though he did not mention Madison, Gallatin, and Lincoln by name, no one in the House chamber could mistake his disdain for their handiwork.

With the commission's recommended settlement of outstanding Yazoo claims, Jefferson had hoped to put the controversy behind him and at the same time offer moderate Federalists in the Northern states a tangible reason to support him in the upcoming election. But Randolph's public denunciation of the commission's proposal guaranteed that no permanent resolution of the Yazoo dispute would be reached during the election year. His assault on the proposal and its sponsors, moreover, widened his estrangement from Jefferson and the moderate wing of his party. By his actions, Randolph narrowed his margin for error in the impending impeachment trial. Assuming the opposition of all nine Federalist senators, Randolph would need to persuade twenty-three of the twenty-five Republican senators, including several Northern-state moderates who favored the Yazoo compromise, that Justice Chase should be removed from the U.S. Supreme Court.

Despite the embarrassment of the Yazoo controversy, Jefferson's reelection was a singular triumph. As the president had hoped and planned, his policies appealed to moderates in both parties. When all ballots were counted, Jefferson carried all but two states (only Delaware and Connecticut eluded him) and could justifiably claim that his second election was a true mandate. And this time, he did it without Vice President Aaron Burr, whom the Republicans had unceremoniously dumped from the ticket in favor of New York Governor George Clinton.

After being dropped by the Republicans, Burr entered New York's gubernatorial race. But moderate Republican forces put up their own candidate, undercutting Burr's chances. Meanwhile, Alexander Hamilton resumed his attacks, warning that Burr was "a dangerous man and one who ought not to be trusted with the reins of government." After his defeat, Burr directed his fury at Hamilton, demanding that Hamilton retract reported aspersions that he had cast on Burr's character. When Hamilton refused, Burr challenged him to a duel by pistols on the bluffs of Weehawken, New Jersey. On July 11, 1804, after the two men took their measured paces and faced each other, Burr shot and mortally wounded Hamilton.

Burr was indicted for the murder of Hamilton in both New York and New Jersey. But he was still the vice president and, in that capacity, was scheduled to preside at the Chase trial, expected to begin the first week in February 1805. Anticipating that incongruous scene, one Federalist newspaper observed caustically that usually "it was the practice in courts of justice to arraign the *murderer* before the *judge,* but now we behold the *judge* arraigned before the *murderer.*"

Jefferson surely recognized the awkwardness of a proceeding in which the indicted Burr would preside at the first impeachment trial of a member of the nation's highest court. That did not prevent the president or members of his Cabinet from showering the lame-duck vice president with attention and political favors shortly before the trial began. Admirable qualities of the man who had been demoted to pariah status within the administration were rediscovered. Burr was invited to the President's House for dinner, and his company was sought by Madison and Gallatin. Two of Burr's relatives as well as one of his closest friends were appointed to high administrative positions in the Louisiana Territory. And Republican Senator William Branch Giles, who would work closely with Randolph to secure Chase's impeachment, circulated a petition, signed by many moderate Republican members of the Senate, requesting that the indictment against Burr in New Jersey be dropped. The avid courting of Burr suggested that, despite their deep reservations about the radical Randolph's judgment and ambition, the Republicans hoped the Chase impeachment would succeed.

Burr ignored the Republicans' blandishments and made the trial his grand public finale, managing the proceeding down to the most minute detail. At the beginning of the Chase trial, on February 4, 1805, the trim, immaculately dressed Burr placed his chair at the center of the Senate chamber. The thirty-four senators who would decide Chase's fate were seated on either side of him. By Burr's order, the senators' desks were festooned with bright-crimson cloth. The defendant, Justice Chase, and his five lawyers were directed to a partitioned area in front and to the left of Burr, the stall and their desks covered with lustrous blue cloth. The House managers, led by Randolph, sat in a designated box opposite the defense team, in front and to the right of Burr. Their desks were also decorated with blue fabric. Three galleries, with benches adorned in handsome green cloth, were arranged in tiers to accommodate the more than one thousand spectators who crowded into the Senate chamber for the trial. The gallery closest to Burr and Chase was filled by members of the House of Representatives, the second by visiting dignitaries (including Chief Justice Marshall and the associate justices of the Supreme Court) as well as selected ladies of Washington society, and the third, the permanent Senate gallery, was open to the public.

Burr immediately asserted his authority over the proceeding by denying the request of Justice Chase to sit rather than stand during the proceeding. But the vice president quickly relented, mindful that Chase was sixty-four years old, overweight, and suffering from a painful inflammation of gout.

Chase proved to be vital in mind and spirit, if not in body. For the next two and a half hours, he laid out in elaborate detail his response to the articles of impeachment, substantiating the view of many of his Federalist supporters, including Senator Bayard, that the justice was his own best lawyer. Chase quickly unveiled his legal strategy: under a proper reading of the impeachment clause of the Constitution, he could be impeached only if he were found guilty of an indictable offense within the strictures of the criminal law. And not one of the articles of impeachment, he argued, approximated such an offense.

In discussing Randolph's impeachment articles in meticulous detail, Chase demonstrated his command of the technicalities of the law. He insisted that all of his rulings from the bench that were the subject of Randolph's articles of impeachment, including the two procedural rul-

ings that had been added to Randolph's original articles, were technically correct and fully within the parameters of accepted judicial practice. As to his instruction to the Baltimore grand jury, Chase, the
zealous advocate of Sedition Act prosecutions, reveled in the protection
of free speech under the First Amendment. In delivering his grand-jury
instruction, the justice claimed, he had proudly exercised the precious
right of every citizen, including a Supreme Court justice, to express his
political opinions.

When the time came for John Randolph to begin the prosecution,
the majority leader, sickly and teetering on nervous exhaustion, desperately attempted to turn the senators' focus away from the technicalities of criminal law that had been emphasized by Chase. Impeachment
could not be confined to indictable criminal offenses, Randolph
argued, but must include the sustained dereliction of official duty by a
member of the nation's highest court. He intended to prove that Justice
Chase had repeatedly, and with malevolent political intent, perverted
the federal judiciary with his overbearing manner and biased rulings.

Randolph, even in his weakened physical state, was still capable of
producing first-rate public drama, and he treated the spectators to one
such high moment when he contrasted the judicial conduct of Justice
Chase at the Sedition Act trial of James T. Callender with that of
Chase's Federalist colleague Chief Justice Marshall. The comparison
was suggested to Randolph by an 1804 trial in Richmond at which
Marshall had presided. Acting in his capacity as a circuit judge, Marshall had conducted the trial of Thomas Logwood, who had been
indicted for counterfeiting. Randolph praised the chief justice's
admirably unbiased handling of the trial, even though "the government was as deeply interested in arresting the career of this dangerous
and atrocious criminal [Logwood], who had aimed his blow against the
property of every man in society, as it could be in bringing to punishment a weak and worthless scribbler [Callender]." Unlike Chase in the
Callender trial, Randolph noted, Marshall had refused to declare any
testimony on behalf of Logwood inadmissible or force a witness to put
his testimony in writing (as Chase had required of a principal witness,
Colonel Taylor, for the defendant Callender).

"No, Sir!" Randolph shouted. "The enlightened man who presided
in Logwood's case knew that, although the basest and vilest of crimi-
nals, he was entitled to justice equally with the most honorable mem-

ber of society." Chief Justice Marshall "never thought it his right or his duty to require questions to be reduced to writing," Randolph observed. The worthy Marshall "gave the accused a fair trial according to law and usage, without any innovation or departure from the established rules of criminal jurisprudence in his country."

Randolph then moved to his major theme, that the senators were not required to find Chase guilty of an indictable offense to impeach him. It was a "monstrous pretension," he declared, "that an act to be impeachable must be indictable." Without mentioning the fallen Judge Pickering by name, Randolph reminded the senators that nowhere in the criminal laws was it stated that conducting a "national court while drunk" was an indictable offense. But who, asked Randolph, could deny that such conduct was grounds for impeachment? "It is indictable nowhere for him [a judge] to omit to do his duty, to refuse to hold a court," Randolph conceded. "But who can doubt that both are impeachable offenses, and ought to subject the offender to removal from office?"

In all, fifty-two witnesses were sworn to testify at the trial, but, unfortunately for Randolph, none gave effective testimony to corroborate Randolph's argument that Justice Chase was repeatedly guilty of impeachable behavior. John Fries's Republican attorneys defended their actions in Chase's courtroom but refused Randolph's invitation to support his broad charges against the judge. A leading Philadelphia lawyer, Edward Tilghman, upon cross-examination by Chase's attorneys, conceded that Chase's issuing written instruction to the Fries jury without hearing arguments from the defendant's attorneys was not illegal. Attorneys and witnesses for James T. Callender in his Sedition Act trial substantiated the acknowledged fact that Chase had intimidated them with his bullying tactics, but none could give persuasive testimony that the judge had violated the law. John Marshall's brother William Marshall, the court clerk at the Callender trial, did the most damage to Randolph's case against Chase's conduct in that trial, when he delivered a devastating rejoinder to Randolph's accusation that Chase had attempted to exclude all potential jurors who might be sympathetic to the defendant. "Nay," said William Marshall emphatically, "he [Chase] wished that Callender might be tried by a jury of his own politics."

Randolph was more successful with his examination of Chief Justice

Marshall, who appeared nervous and exhibited extreme caution in his responses to questions about Chase's conduct of the Callender trial. Marshall was asked whether it was the practice for federal judges to hear counsel argue the law as well as the facts of a case, as Callender's attorneys had attempted to do in challenging the constitutionality of the Sedition Act. "If counsel have not been already heard," Marshall replied, "it is usual to hear them in order that they may change or confirm the opinion of the court, when there is any doubt entertained." Marshall attempted to throw a judicial blanket over Chase's rulings by adding, "Where the judge believes that the point is perfectly clear and settled, he will scarcely permit the question to be agitated." But then he quickly pulled the protective cover away, admitting that "it is considered as decorous on the part of the judge to listen while the counsel abstain from urging unimportant arguments." Counsel challenging the constitutionality of the statute on which his client was charged could hardly be considered "unimportant."

At this point, Aaron Burr interrupted to ask a question of the chief justice that cut to the core of Randolph's argument. "Do you recollect whether the conduct of the judge at this trial was tyrannical, overbearing, and oppressive?"

"I will state the facts," Marshall replied. He then described the persistent demand of Callender's counsel, George Hay, that he be allowed to challenge the constitutionality of the Sedition Act, and Judge Chase's determination to exclude the argument. "If this is not considered tyrannical, oppressive, and overbearing," Marshall continued, "I know nothing else that was."

Senator William Plumer wrote in his diary that the chief justice "really discovered too much caution—too much fear—too much cunning," adding, "He ought to have been more bold, frank, & explicit than he was." Plumer detected in Marshall's manner "an evident disposition to accommodate the managers."

The chief justice's carefully considered replies to Randolph's and Burr's questions certainly exhibited none of William Marshall's outspoken conviction of Chase's innocence that so impressed Plumer. But John Marshall's goals were both more modest and more ambitious than his brother's. As a superb lawyer, he had been trained to respond tactically to the aggressive thrusts of his adversaries. At Chase's impeachment trial he was aware that his lawyerly caution would appeal to moderate Republican senators, who would, ultimately, decide Chase's fate. If they accepted his statements as impartial, they might conclude, as Marshall himself had, that Chase's judicial conduct, though objectionable, did not rise to an impeachable offense.

Whatever the shortcomings of John Marshall's testimony in the minds of Chase's Federalist defenders, it did not appear to bolster the struggling Randolph's case. And when Randolph dealt with the final charges against Chase, those relating to his grand-jury instructions, he again failed to make a persuasive case that the justice had committed an impeachable offense. No witness substantially undermined Chase's contention that his conduct was within acceptable judicial standards.

Pitted against Randolph and the other House managers were the superior talents of five of the Federalist party's most illustrious attorneys. "We appear for an ancient and infirm man whose better days have been worn out in the service of that country which now degrades him," began thirty-four-year-old Joseph Hopkinson for the defense. Justice Chase, Hopkinson continued, had been maligned and persecuted by partisans bent on distorting his judicial opinions for unfair political advantage. Surely the Constitution demanded more of the Senate than judgment based on "opinion, whim, and caprice." High crimes and misdemeanors were well understood by the framers, Hopkinson insisted, and they were narrow legal and technical terms. Was a senatorial court created "to scan and punish paltry errors and indiscretions, too insignificant to have a name in the penal code, too paltry for the notice of a court of quarter sessions?" an indignant Hopkinson asked. "This is indeed employing an elephant to remove an atom too minute for the grasp of an insect."

Others on Chase's team filled in the technical details of the justice's defense. Philip Barton Key (brother of Francis Scott Key, the future composer of "The Star-Spangled Banner") and Charles Lee divided the impeachment articles pertaining to the Callender trial, offering erudite explanations of Chase's rulings that exonerated the justice. But for sheer legal pyrotechnics, no member of Chase's defense team could compare to Luther Martin, generally regarded as the best trial lawyer of his generation.

Martin had represented Maryland at the Constitutional Convention and later served as his state's attorney general. An indefatigable Federalist warrior, Martin had been attacking Jefferson for years. Jefferson labeled him "the unprincipled and impudent Federalist bulldog." Martin was also an old and devoted friend of Justice Chase.

Balding, poorly dressed, Martin was uncouth in appearance and often ungrammatical in speech. He was also an alcoholic, but his frequent drunkenness in court did not diminish his extraordinary ability to explain the law and the reasonableness of his client's position to lay jurors. He cited precedent prodigiously, but his legal narrative was sprinkled with humor, often aimed with devastating effect at his adversary.

Given Martin's celebrity, it was no wonder that the public gallery at the Chase trial swelled on February 23, 1805, when he was scheduled to speak. For five hours that Friday and two and a half the following Monday, a sober Martin (steadied only by two glasses of red wine) confidently suggested to the senators that his cause was just and their duty (to acquit Chase) obvious.

Martin began by establishing a bond between himself and key members of his jury. "I see two honorable members of this court [Senators Jonathan Dayton and Simeon Baldwin] who were with me in the convention in 1787." These veterans of the Philadelphia convention, Martin observed, "perfectly know why this power [to try impeachments] was invested in the Senate. It was because among all our speculated systems, it was thought this power could no where be more properly placed, or where it would be less likely to be abused."

Having professed his faith in the Senate, Martin first argued that there was no legitimate basis for convicting Chase. Like Hopkinson before him, Martin argued that Chase could only be impeached for an indictable offense such as treason or bribery. The attorney then turned his sardonic wit on Chase's accusers, who had charged him with overbearing conduct at the Callender trial. Even if his client had "used unusual, rude, and contemptuous expressions towards the prisoner's counsel," Martin said, such behavior was "rather a violation of the principles of politeness, than the principles of law; rather the want of decorum, than the commission of a high crime and misdemeanor." Later, Martin noted that the justice was accused of using the word "damned" in conversation with a potential juror at the Callender trial.

Admitting that his client may have used the word, he suggested that such vulgarity, if that it be, was commonly employed to good purpose as a substitute for the adverb "very." Martin illustrated his point mischievously: "We say indiscriminately a very good or a damned good bottle of wine."

Logical and humorous, scholarly and charming, Martin wove his spell, finally reminding the senators of what was ultimately at stake: the independence of the federal judiciary. "Our property, our liberty, our lives can only be protected and secured by such [independent] judges," he said. "With this honorable court it remains, whether we shall have such judges!"

After the relentless legal volleys of Luther Martin and his colleagues, no one could envy John Randolph, who was scheduled to sum up the case for the House managers. To make matters worse, Randolph's physical and mental condition had deteriorated during the three weeks of the Senate trial. Exhausted and flustered by the loss of his notes, Randolph delivered a peroration that combined invective (toward his opponents) with a few well-considered arguments, all accompanied by tears, groans, and sobs. One moment he was contorted in pain, the next swathed in self-pity ("It is the last day of my suffering and yours").

But throughout his ordeal, Randolph never lost his ability to make reasoned argument or dazzle his audience with his considerable rhetorical powers. If the framers meant to confine impeachment to indictable offenses, as Chase and his lawyers claimed, why had they not put that simple thought in writing, instead of inserting the more general phrase "high crimes and misdemeanors"? The answer, Randolph submitted, was that the framers intended to include abuse of authority by public officials. Suppose the president subverted the legislative process during a short congressional session by purposely withholding his signature from bills until it was too late for Congress to override his veto. The president could not be indicted for his conduct, Randolph conceded, but no one could doubt that he could be impeached and removed from office. And that very constitutional remedy must be available to the Senate when a high officer of the federal judiciary, with comparable disrespect for his oath of office, subverts justice.

Randolph implored the senators "to say whether he [Justice Chase] shall again become the scourge of an exasperated people, or whether he shall stand as a landmark and a beacon to the present generation and a warning to the future that no talents, however great, no age, however venerable, no character, however sacred, no connection, however influential, shall save that man from the justice of his country who prostitutes the best gifts of nature and of God and the power, with which he is invested for the general good, to the low purposes of an electioneering partisan." Randolph ended his two-and-a-half-hour speech with a call to the senators to do their constitutional duty. "In the name of the nation," Randolph exhorted, "I demand at your hands the award of justice and of law."

On the morning of March 1, 1805, a pale and bedridden Uriah Tracy, a veteran Federalist senator from Connecticut, was carried into the Senate chamber on a couch so that he might join his thirty-three colleagues in judgment of Justice Samuel Chase. The galleries were filled and hushed as Vice President Burr sternly warned the gathered throng that "the Sergeant-at-Arms will face the spectators and seize and commit to prison the first person who makes the smallest noise or disturbance." With the chamber silent, Burr read the first article of impeachment against Chase and ordered the calling of the Senate roll.

"Senator Adams of Massachusetts. How say you? Is Samuel Chase, the respondent, guilty of high crimes and misdemeanors as charged in the article just read?"

"Not guilty," was the firm, predictable response of the Federalist senator from Massachusetts, John Quincy Adams.

The real drama began when the name of the first Republican senator was called. After his name was announced, moderate Republican Senator Stephen Bradley of Vermont rose.

"Not guilty."

Moments later, Bradley was joined by Republican colleague, John Gaillard of South Carolina, who voted not guilty. Only one more Republican defection was needed to defeat the first article of impeachment. And that defection came quickly, in the surprising person of Virginia's William Branch Giles. If the influential and stalwart Republican Giles would not support Randolph on the first impeachment article, Chase's acquittal was virtually assured.

Each senator rose eight times that day to record his vote, and on each article of impeachment Justice Chase was found not guilty. All nine Federalist senators voted for acquittal on each of the eight articles, as expected. But six Republican senators joined them each time, exceeding even the most optimistic estimates of Chase's defenders. The Republican votes of guilty varied with the articles, reflecting an admirable scrutiny of Randolph's broad-based charges. On the first article, involving charges stemming from the trial of John Fries, only sixteen Republicans recorded a vote of guilty, seven short of the required two-thirds. On the fifth article, which charged Chase with procedural errors at the Callender trial, not a single Republican voted in favor. The last article, dealing with Chase's instruction to the Baltimore grand jury, drew the most votes of guilty, nineteen, but fell four votes short. The relatively large number of guilty votes by Republicans on this article was probably cast in deference to Jefferson, who had suggested Chase's impeachment after learning of his grand-jury instruction.

"It appears that there is not a constitutional majority of votes finding Samuel Chase, Esq. guilty of any one article," Burr solemnly announced. "It therefore becomes my duty to declare that Samuel Chase, Esq. stands acquitted of all the articles exhibited by the House of Representatives against him."

To the end, Randolph was convinced that his cause was righteous and that he would succeed with the impeachment. Immediately after the result was announced in the Senate chamber, Randolph rushed over to the House in a fury. After denouncing Chase and the Senate, Randolph introduced a constitutional amendment providing for the removal of any federal judge by the president upon a majority vote of both houses of Congress. But that, too, failed.

Why did Randolph's impeachment effort fail so miserably? Republican politics, as much as law and legal strategy, were responsible for the disastrous result. From the moment Randolph broke with the Jefferson administration over the Yazoo compromise, his chances of convicting Chase were seriously jeopardized. With his tirade against the Yazoo settlement, Randolph openly defied Jefferson as well as key moderate Senate Republicans, whose votes were essential to success of his impeachment efforts. Randolph later bitterly complained that Jefferson and the moderate Senate Republicans had abandoned him in his crusade against Chase.

Randolph's tempestuous and erratic management of the Chase prosecution also contributed to the justice's acquittal. Untrained in the law, he was poorly matched against Chase and his lawyers, who succeeded in focusing the Senate's attention on their technical legal analysis, and away from Randolph's broad-brush charges. Credit must be given to those Republicans who voted their conscience. Although disgusted with Chase's conduct, they concluded that the charges against him did not rise to the level of high crimes and misdemeanors required by the Constitution. As one of the Republicans, Senator Samuel Mitchill of New York, explained his and the other dissidents' votes: "We did so on full conviction that the evidence, our oaths, the Constitution, and our conscience required us to act as we have done."

Quite aside from Randolph's mismanagement of the trial, Chase benefited from the fact that an independent federal judiciary was important not only to John Marshall and the Federalists, but to many Republicans as well. By 1805, partisan outbursts on the bench, so common among Federalist judges during the Adams administration, had become increasingly rare. Had Chase been convicted, moderates in both parties realized, there might be no limit to prosecutions of politically unpopular judges.

Both Marshall *and* Jefferson encouraged the spirit of moderation that saved Justice Chase. From his first days as chief justice, Marshall was determined to separate the Court from partisan politics. His efforts impressed both Federalists and Republicans, as Randolph's praise of the chief justice at the Chase trial had demonstrated.

To be sure, Jefferson had initiated the idea of impeaching Chase and only reluctantly refrained from providing behind-the-scenes encouragement of the drive to get rid of the justice. But Randolph's split with the Jefferson administration over Yazoo, as well as his poorly managed prosecution of Chase, caused Jefferson to lose enthusiasm for the effort. As an old man, Jefferson would scorn the impeachment clause as "a mere scarecrow." But when he was president, his desires to rid the federal bench of Pickering and Chase were aberrations from his generally moderate policies. When he finally was given the opportunity to make his first appointment to the Supreme Court, in 1804, he chose

Republican William Johnson, a distinguished lawyer and state judge from South Carolina, who was a judicial moderate.

Even Samuel Chase eventually accepted the prevailing mood of moderation. After he escaped impeachment, Chase served another six years on the Supreme Court. He never returned to the fiery partisanship of his earlier days that had so incensed Jefferson. Shortly after his trial, the Republican *National Intelligencer* noted approvingly that the justice had "delivered a short and pertinent charge to the grand jury—his remarks were pointed, modest, and well applied."

[10]

Treason Against the United States

Shortly before noon on March 4, 1805, President Thomas Jefferson, accompanied by his private secretary and groom, boarded a carriage in front of the President's House and was driven to the still-unfinished Capitol building to deliver his second inaugural address. The Senate chamber that had churned with anticipation of a new political era four years earlier was relatively bare and lifeless; many senators, exhausted by the Chase impeachment trial just completed, chose to skip the presidential ceremony altogether in favor of returning to their home states.

The three men who had shared the inaugural stage in 1801—President Jefferson, Chief Justice John Marshall, and Vice President Aaron Burr—were again present. But Burr was now relegated to a seat in the public gallery. His precipitous drop in status in official Washington (he had been the presiding officer in this same Senate chamber only three days earlier) was the least of his problems. He was desperately in debt and shorn of influence in Jefferson's administration. And now Burr's once-thriving New York City law practice was closed to him, for he was under indictment in both New York and New Jersey for the murder of Alexander Hamilton.

Burr's dire circumstances would have crushed a less ambitious and resourceful man. But even before he had vacated the office of vice president, Burr had begun to plan a Western adventure that contemplated fortune, fame, and, if entirely successful, possibly a throne for himself in Mexico City. Unfortunately for Burr, the plan would fail miserably. Worse, he would be forced to stand trial in 1807 on charges of treason in the courtroom of Chief Justice Marshall. Marshall's rulings during the Burr trial chagrined and enraged President Jefferson, who, in a prior address to Congress, had preemptively announced Burr's guilt. The chief justice's decisions not only were instrumental in leading to Burr's acquittal but set the standards for executive privilege and treason that are the starting points for modern constitutional doctrine. The Burr trial, moreover, irrevocably embittered Jefferson toward the chief justice, a feeling that was reciprocated by Marshall and that deepened in their old age.

Ten months before Jefferson's second inauguration, Burr had met with Brigadier General James Wilkinson, the stout, hard-drinking, and shrewd commander-in-chief of the U.S. Army. Throughout his career, Wilkinson had demonstrated a flair for intrigue, and a genius for wriggling in and out of tight situations. As a young military man, he had been dismissed from the Continental Army for "gross irregularities in his accounts." He nonetheless succeeded General Anthony Wayne as commander of the U.S. Army in 1796. Even then he was the paid double agent of the Spanish government, having already collected $26,000 from Spain for his services.

When Wilkinson called at Vice President Burr's Richmond Hill country estate, on the northern outskirts of New York City, in May 1804, the two men studied manuscript maps of Texas, New Mexico, and Spain's other American possessions, anticipating a military expedition to conquer those colonies. But when Burr later met with Anthony Merry, the British minister to the United States, the avowed purpose of his Western expedition had changed. The vice president told Merry that he planned to lead a secessionist movement of the Western states against the union, and asked for His Majesty's government's financial and military help. Whether Burr intended to lead a secessionist movement, as he told Merry, or only to wheedle funds from the British with the promise of treachery against his own country is a question that historians continue to debate.

Whatever his purpose, Burr headed west by stagecoach from Philadelphia in late April 1805, rented a flatboat at Pittsburgh, and floated down the Ohio River, making stops in Ohio and Kentucky before traveling by horseback to the interior of Kentucky and Tennessee. Along the way, he conferred with four men. Three were well-known public figures, Senator John Smith of Ohio, former Senator Jonathan Dayton of New Jersey, and Major General Andrew Jackson of Tennessee; the fourth man was Harman Blennerhassett, a wealthy Irish émigré who had built a splendid mansion on a 179-acre island below Marietta, Ohio.

When he reached Nashville, Burr was treated to a flag-waving parade, a vivid demonstration of his popularity among Western frontiersmen, who shared his ambition to conquer Spanish America, presumably with the tacit support of the Jefferson administration. Later, Burr conferred for four days with General Wilkinson at Fort Massac, an isolated military outpost on the northern bank of the Ohio, before sailing on a large barge, furnished by Wilkinson, to New Orleans, where he met with prominent private citizens who were interested in the conquest of Spain's American colonies.

By the time Burr had completed his Western trip, some had begun to assign conspiratorial motives to the former vice president. "How long will it be before we shall hear of Col. Burr being at the head of a revolution party on the stern waters?" asked the anonymous author in the leading Federalist newspaper, the *Gazette of the United States*. That question was followed by a barrage of accusations that Burr had plans to form a separate government of the Western states, seize the port of New Orleans and other military installations on the Mississippi, revolutionize Mexico, and confiscate its treasure, all with military help from Great Britain.

President Jefferson was undoubtedly aware of Burr's Western trip and probably read the accusations in the *Gazette* (and reprinted in the Republican *Aurora*). But he apparently gave Burr's mysterious adventure little serious thought, since he was preoccupied with more pressing matters, particularly the nation's deteriorating relations with Spain and the ominous movement of Spanish troops on the United States' southwestern border. In December 1805, Jefferson received two anonymous letters accusing Burr of attempting to overthrow the administration and conspiring against the state. Shortly afterward, U.S. Attorney Joseph Daveiss of Kentucky began to write to the president charging that General Wilkinson, Burr, and others were plotting against the union.

By midsummer 1806, Burr had recruited a cadre of trusted deputies, including former Senator Dayton and two young men, Samuel Swartwout and Dr. Erick Bollman, who were dispatched from Philadelphia with separate copies of a coded letter for General Wilkinson. In the letter, presumed to be from Burr,* the author reported that he had secured naval protection from Great Britain and that Burr and his second in command, Wilkinson, would lead a force of five hundred to a thousand men in light boats down the Mississippi, possibly seizing the Spanish possession of Baton Rouge along the way. "The people of the country to which we are going are prepared to receive us," the letter continued. "The gods invite us to glory and fortune."

Burr added to the mystery by suggesting to Secretary of the Treasury Albert Gallatin, among others, that he was primarily interested in the peaceful settlement of the Bastrop lands, a vast tract on the Washita River, in the Louisiana Territory. In August, Burr embarked on his second trip to the West, meeting with Colonel George Morgan at Morgan's country estate outside of Pittsburgh before stopping at Harman Blennerhassett's island near Marietta, Ohio. Burr and Blennerhassett purchased a hundred barrels of pork and arranged to have constructed fifteen boats large enough to transport five hundred men, to be delivered on December 9. Burr stayed with Blennerhassett two days before sailing down the Ohio River and meeting with Senator Smith at Cincinnati and Major General Jackson in Nashville. At Burr's request, Jackson filled an order for the construction of five large boats, paid for by Burr with $3,500 in Kentucky bank notes.

But even as Burr moved back and forth across Tennessee and Kentucky, consulting with friends, acquiring provisions, rallying young recruits, all was not well. A new wave of accusations against Burr had spread across the West. U.S. Attorney Daveiss had intensified his investigation, and a new publication, *The Western World,* unleashed a relentless attack on Burr and Wilkinson, accusing them of treason. Blennerhassett made matters worse by writing a series of articles in the *Ohio Gazette* recommending the eventual disengagement of the Western states from the union. Blennerhassett's articles and actions drew the attention of citizens

---

*At the Burr treason trial, the author of the cipher letter was assumed to be Burr, but modern historians have concluded, based on both the information presented and the style of the letter, that the writer was probably Jonathan Dayton.

of nearby Wood County (now in West Virginia), who called a protest meeting, adopted a resolution accusing Burr and Blennerhassett of treason, and authorized a muster of the county militia to halt the conspirators' preparations.

Meanwhile, General Wilkinson, on the orders of Secretary of War Dearborn, had left his headquarters at St. Louis in August and sailed down the Mississippi to command U.S. troops at Natchitoches. His mission was to force the retreat of Spanish troops that had crossed the Sabine River to occupy territory the United States claimed. Wilkinson wrote Dearborn that he planned to achieve the administration's goal by diplomacy if possible, but would unsheathe his sword if necessary, and "drive the enemy back on the side of Mexico." While the general awaited an answer to his demand from the Spanish governor of Texas, the commanding officer of Spanish troops that had crossed the Sabine withdrew his troops. His iron diplomacy appeared to have achieved the Jefferson administration's goal without a shot being fired. Despite published reports of Wilkinson's traitorous collaboration with Burr, the general, for the moment, had served his president.

A little more than a week after the retreat of the Spanish troops, Samuel Swartwout arrived at Natchitoches and presented Wilkinson with a copy of the cipher letter. On October 10, the day after he had decoded the cipher letter, Wilkinson called his adjutant, Colonel Thomas Cushing, to his quarters to declare that he had evidence of a treasonable plot, led by Burr, to overthrow the U.S. government.

Wilkinson had several reasons to betray Burr at this time. With his agile handling of the border crisis with Spain, Wilkinson's standing with the Jefferson administration appeared secure. If peaceful relations between the U.S. and Spain continued, moreover, the general could look forward to profitable public service for both countries, since he was a paid agent of the Spanish government. And despite the outlandish claims for success in the cipher letter, Burr's publicly reported conspiracy did not seem very promising. There was nothing to support the letter's assertion that Great Britain was allied with Burr; the general was much too shrewd to rely on bold declarations that could not be confirmed by his own network of intelligence sources.

Having declared a treasonous plot afoot, Wilkinson nonetheless waited two weeks before he wrote the president. In the first of two letters to Jefferson, Wilkinson reported that eight to ten thousand men planned to meet in New Orleans and sail to Vera Cruz with the intent of overthrowing the Spanish government in Mexico. The general's second letter, inconsistent with the first, described the conspirators' purpose as to revolutionize the Louisiana Territory before turning "to the main design of attacking Mexico." Although he had told Cushing that Burr was the chief conspirator, he wrote Jefferson that he did not know the enterprise's leader. The general assured Jefferson that he knew his duty: to "throw myself with my little band into New Orleans, to be ready to defend that capital against usurpation and violence."

Jefferson had been given numerous warnings of a Burr conspiracy long before he received Wilkinson's letters. His most persistent informer was U.S. Attorney Daveiss, who had written him eight letters over a ten-month period. In September 1806, the president received a letter from Colonel George Morgan, who reported that during Burr's visit to his estate Burr had spoken disparagingly of the federal government and the inevitable split of the Western states from the union. In October, Jefferson received a further warning from his postmaster general, Gideon Granger, that finally persuaded him to take action. According to Granger, Burr had offered General William Eaton the second military command under Wilkinson in a conspiracy to separate the Western states from the union.

Shortly after receiving Granger's letter, Jefferson met with his Cabinet and agreed that confidential letters would be written to governors and district attorneys in the West to have Burr "strictly watched and on his committing an overt act unequivocally, to have him tried for treason, misdemeanor, or whatever offence" the evidence justified. General Wilkinson was also to be placed under "very general suspicion of infidelity." But, given the general's position as the army's commander-in-chief at a time of crisis on the nation's southwestern border, Jefferson decided not to take any action against him. After his Cabinet meeting, Jefferson instructed John Graham, secretary of the Orleans Territory, to stalk Burr, consult with territorial governors, and, if evidence merited, to arrest the former vice president.

On November 25, two days after receiving Wilkinson's letters, Jefferson issued a proclamation announcing that "sundry persons" were illegally conspiring to make war with Spain. Jefferson did not name

Burr as the leader or raise the charge that Burr and his collaborators planned to lead a secession of the Western states, though he believed both to be true. Jefferson's conspicuous omissions were grounded in legal and diplomatic strategy. There was not yet evidence that Burr had committed an overt act of treason. Jefferson was mindful, moreover, that he and his Cabinet had decided to pursue a negotiated settlement with Spain over the nation's southwestern border. His proclamation alerted Spain to the U.S.'s peaceful intentions.

When Jefferson delivered his sixth annual address to Congress a week later, he downplayed the danger of the conspiracy, saying only that his proclamation and some special orders were necessary so that "the criminal attempts of private individuals to decide for their country the question of peace or war . . . should be promptly and efficaciously suppressed." In private, Jefferson expressed confidence that the Burr conspiracy would be thwarted once his proclamation reached the Western states.

In fact, Burr had become a hunted man long before Jefferson's proclamation had circulated in the West. In early November, Daveiss had Burr arrested and convened a grand jury in Frankfort, Kentucky, charging him with the "high misdemeanor" of preparing a military expedition against Mexico. The proceeding ended abruptly when Daveiss told the presiding judge that his key witness was no longer in the state, and requested that the grand jury be discharged. But that minor embarrassment did not deter Daveiss, who two weeks later again had Burr arrested and convened a second grand jury in Frankfort, bringing forward identical charges. This time, the grand jury refused to return a true bill, and Burr was again released from custody.

In Ohio, Governor Edward Tiffin ordered the state militia to seize the supplies and boats gathered by the conspirators on the Muskingum River, just above Marietta, and to arrest Burr's agents. And on December 9, the Ohio militia intercepted fifteen boats on the river and confiscated two hundred barrels of supplies. The next night, a few boats escaped from Blennerhassett Island, carrying the owner among others. Three weeks later, Blennerhassett caught up with Burr and other members of his bedraggled group of recruits at a little island opposite the mouth of the Cumberland River. Despite the capture of most of his boats and supplies by the Ohio militia, Burr and his men continued to sail down the Mississippi in a tiny flotilla.

On January 3, 1807, Jefferson wrote General Wilkinson, who had arrived in New Orleans in late November and imposed martial law on the port city, that he believed Burr's "projected enterprise may be considered as crushed." Three weeks later, the president, at the insistent request of House majority leader John Randolph, sent the House a lengthy message on the conspiracy accompanied by a host of documents, including Wilkinson's translation of the cipher letter. He commended Wilkinson for acting "with the honor of a soldier and fidelity of a good citizen" in sending him the incriminating materials. The conspiracy, the president declared, had two main objectives: "One of these was the severance of the union of these states by the Allegheny Mountains; the other an attack on Mexico." For the first time, Jefferson publicly identified Burr as "the principal actor, whose guilt is placed beyond question."

Jefferson also informed Congress that two of Burr's principal emissaries, Dr. Erick Bollman and Samuel Swartwout, had been captured by General Wilkinson and sent east to stand trial. The president did not mention that Bollman and Swartwout had petitioned the supreme court of the Orleans Territory for writs of habeas corpus to force government authorities to justify their incarceration, and that the petitions had been granted. General Wilkinson, in defiance of the court orders, had hustled the two men off on separate ships to face treason charges thousands of miles from the scene of their alleged crime, a violation of the Sixth Amendment to the U.S. Constitution.*

Wilkinson arrested three other suspected conspirators, who were eventually released for lack of evidence of any crime. Jefferson was well aware of Wilkinson's capacity for excess in the performance of his military duties and had admonished him not to deport suspected conspirators on mere suspicion (a warning that came too late for Bollman and Swartwout). Even so, Jefferson resolutely supported the actions of the army's commander-in-chief.

Jefferson appeared unconcerned that basic liberties continued to be violated, even after any realistic threat to the nation's security had vanished. When Bollman and Swartwout arrived in Charleston, South

---

*The Constitution's Sixth Amendment provides, "In all criminal prosecutions, the accused shall enjoy the right to a speedy and public trial, by an impartial jury of the State and district wherein the crime shall have been committed. . . ."

Carolina, a U.S. district judge issued another writ of habeas corpus on their behalf, which was again disregarded by military authorities, who shipped the prisoners north. On January 23, 1807, one day after Jefferson's message to Congress, Bollman and Swartwout reached Washington and were placed in marine barracks under heavy guard. That day, the president personally delivered Wilkinson's affidavits describing the conspiracy to U.S. Attorney Walter Jones and instructed him to seek an indictment against the two prisoners on the charge of treason. At the same time, William Branch Giles, the Republican majority leader in the Senate, introduced a bill to suspend habeas corpus for three months in all cases of persons charged with treason.

While under marine guard, Bollman requested a meeting with the president, which was promptly granted. According to Bollman, Jefferson promised that anything he said would be held in confidence and his later written statement, given at the president's request, would not leave Jefferson's hands. What Bollman said and later committed to writing confirmed Jefferson's view that the Burr-led conspirators had as one of their main objectives to conquer Spanish America (with the presumed support of the Jefferson administration). But Bollman refused to confirm Jefferson's other deeply held conviction, that the conspirators intended to commit treason by separating the Western states from the union. He also told the president that Wilkinson had been an integral member of the conspiracy until he betrayed Burr.

Resentment of Wilkinson's high-handed ways began to permeate official Washington shortly after the Senate passed the bill suspending habeas corpus. Three days later, the House, in a blunt bipartisan rebuke to the Senate, overwhelmingly defeated the bill. "It not infrequently happens," observed Republican Congressman James Hughes of Kentucky, "that, transported by the indignation arising from an attempt to destroy a free government, its friends, by the measures they take to defend and support it, sap those principles on which it is founded."

Adding to the already tense political atmosphere, the two Republican judges on the circuit court voted to arraign Bollman and Swartwout on charges of treason and commit them without bail, while the lone Federalist jurist, Chief Judge William Cranch, dissented.

Up to this point, John Marshall had not been involved in the controversy surrounding the Burr conspiracy or the legal actions taken against the suspected conspirators. But one week after Bollman and Swartwout were arraigned, the fate of the defendants was placed squarely in the hands of Marshall and the other members of the Supreme Court. On February 5, attorney Charles Lee, who had been retained by Swartwout, appeared before the Court to request that the justices issue a writ of habeas corpus to free the prisoners.

The arguments made over the next two weeks by Lee and the other Federalist lawyers representing the defendants (including Luther Martin and Robert Goodloe Harper) addressed the Court with three critical legal questions. First, did the Court have the authority to issue a writ of habeas corpus? Second, did the evidence against Bollman and Swartwout support the charge of treason? Finally, could a federal court in Washington decide the case when the alleged crime had taken place thousands of miles from the nation's capital?

Marshall first delivered the opinion of the Court on the procedural issue, concluding that in the Judiciary Act of 1789 Congress had given the Court the authority to issue the writ of habeas corpus. The only question that remained, as it had in *Marbury v. Madison,* was whether the Constitution prohibited the Court from exercising the authority granted by Congress. Marshall drew a critical distinction between *Marbury,* where the Court was asked to decide a case of first impression, and Bollman and Swartwout's case, in which the justices were called upon to review a lower-court decision. "It is the revision of decision of an inferior court," Marshall emphasized, "by which a citizen has been committed to jail."

The chief justice then cautiously approached the issue of whether there was sufficient evidence to support the charge that the defendants were guilty of treason against the United States. He noted that the framers had set down the precise elements of the crime of treason in the Constitution,* to prevent the possibility that a zealous prosecutor might extend the crime to lesser offenses. The chief justice distinguished *conspiracy* to commit treason from the actual crime of treason,

---

*"Treason against the United States, shall consist only in levying war against them, or in adhering to their enemies, giving them aid and comfort."

and then insisted that there must be evidence that Bollman and Swartwout had participated in an assemblage of men for a treasonable purpose. Having demanded stringent proof of the crime of treason, Marshall then appeared to relax the standard to include what was known as constructive treason under British common law. "If war be actually levied, that is, if a body of men be actually assembled for the purpose of effecting by force a treasonable purpose, *all those who perform any part, however minute, or however removed from the scene of action,* and who actually leagued in the general conspiracy, are to be considered traitors" (italics added). With that expansive qualification, Marshall provided the Jefferson administration with an additional legal tool for its future prosecution of the lead conspirator, Burr. But nothing, the chief justice immediately made clear, convinced the Court that there was sufficient evidence under his articulated legal standard to prosecute Bollman and Swartwout for treason.

Neither General Wilkinson's copy of the cipher letter nor his affidavit of his recollected conversations with Swartwout at Natchitoches, Marshall wrote, established the defendants' requisite treasonous purpose. The evidence did not suggest that any territory of the United States was the objective of the conspirators. The cipher letter spoke of a plan for five hundred to a thousand men to sail down the Mississippi toward Natchez, possibly seizing the Spanish possession of Baton Rouge en route. Statements in the letter, if true, supported the charge that the defendants were "engaged in a most culpable enterprise (making war with a nation at peace with the United States)," Marshall conceded. But Bollman and Swartwout had been arrested for another crime, treason, for which they had been in custody for two months.

Finally, Marshall dealt with the issue of whether the Jefferson administration had unconstitutionally prosecuted the defendants in Washington, since their alleged crime of making war against Spain had not taken place in the District of Columbia. Both defendants, Marshall declared on February 21, must be released, though he anticipated that the government might "institute fresh proceedings against them" in the proper legal venue and on the basis of more persuasive evidence.

On January 10, 1807, as Bollman and Swartwout were being transported to Washington for trial, Burr and his men landed on the shores of the

Mississippi Territory, just north of Natchez. Burr arranged to spend the night with an old friend, Peter Bruin, one of the judges of the territorial supreme court. That night, Bruin showed Burr a copy of the January 6 edition of the Natchez *Mississippi Messenger,* which carried Jefferson's proclamation announcing the conspiracy, the text of Wilkinson's cipher letter, and Louisiana Governor William Claiborne's proclamation calling for Burr's arrest. Burr knew at once that his plans for glory and conquest lay in shards. All that remained was for him to surrender. But he sensibly refused to turn himself over to his betrayer, General Wilkinson, who had already sent out army regulars to capture him. Rather than submit to military custody, Burr insisted that he would only surrender to the civil authorities in the Mississippi Territory. He then gave himself up to the territorial governor's aides and was escorted to Washington— the small capital of the territory, seven miles inland from Natchez— where he was bound over on $5,000 bail to a grand jury.

While the U.S. Supreme Court heard arguments in Bollman and Swartwout's case, Burr was brought before the federal territorial court in Washington to determine, in presiding Judge Thomas Rodney's words, whether "this once illustrious Citizen . . . was guilty of the Nefarious design to Separate the Western Country of the United States from the Union, and to combine it with a part of the whole of Mexico, and erect them into a New and Independent Empire for himself Or for Some Rich Patron under whom he acts." Despite that loaded instruction from Judge Rodney (who was the father of Jefferson's attorney general, Caesar Rodney), the grand jury refused to return a true bill against Burr, concluding that there was no evidence that he had committed any crime.

Having escaped a third grand-jury indictment, Burr expected to be free. But Judge Rodney had other ideas. Although there was no legal reason for Rodney to continue to hold the defendant, the judge ordered the sheriff to find Burr and bring him to the courtroom. Burr did not respond to Rodney's directive, but instead fled into the woods of western Mississippi. Two weeks later, when Burr stopped to ask for directions in the village of Wakefield, he was recognized by a local attorney who was alert to the $2,000 reward offered by the territorial governor for Burr's capture. Burr was soon in custody and, escorted by six armed civilians and two soldiers, made the long, arduous trip north on horseback. On March 26, the prisoner, wearing the same

floppy white hat and loose homespun suit in which he had been captured more than a month earlier, arrived at the Eagle Tavern in Richmond, where he would face federal charges of treason and the high
misdemeanor of making war against Spain.

When Burr stood before John Marshall on March 30, 1807, in a small
back room of the Eagle Tavern to hear the government's formal
charges against him, he was dressed in the black silks of a gentleman,
his hair powdered and properly coiffed. Two of Virginia's best attorneys, John Wickham and Edmund Randolph, represented him, but no
one doubted that the defendant, a man of superior legal skills and
extensive trial experience, would devise his own courtroom strategy.
Central to that strategy would be Burr's resolve to put the government—including General Wilkinson and President Jefferson—on trial.

Richmond bustled with excitement in anticipation of the Burr trial.
The city's population of five thousand swelled with ordinary curiosity-
seekers as well as fashionable ladies and gentlemen of New York,
Philadelphia, and Charleston society. Washington Irving, a young journalist on assignment with a New York newspaper, privately recorded
his first impressions. "I am absolutely enchanted with Richmond. . . .
The society is polished, sociable and extremely hospitable." Irving
believed in Burr's innocence and would happily have left the dashing
colonel's fate to the ladies he had met. "The ladies have been uniform
in their expressions of compassion for his [Burr's] misfortunes, and a
hope for his acquittal." The public's interest in the Burr trial was so
great that Marshall was forced to move the proceedings from the Eagle
Tavern to the large room in the State Capitol building normally
reserved for the House of Delegates. Yet even the legislative chamber
could not accommodate everyone who wanted to witness the treason
trial of a former vice president of the United States.

At ten o'clock on the morning of March 31, Marshall took his seat
on the bench in the temporary courtroom. Virginia's District Attorney
George Hay argued the government's case, asserting that Burr had
committed a treasonous act by his intention "to take the city of New
Orleans, make it the seat of his dominion and the capital of his empire."

The charge was proved, Hay contended, by the Eaton and Wilkinson affidavits, which the prosecutor discussed in minute detail. Burr should also be committed, Hay argued, for the high misdemeanor of leading an expedition against the American colonies of Spain. As further evidence of the defendant's guilt, the prosecutor commented "on the flight of Colonel Burr from justice."

Burr's attorneys, Wickham and Randolph, attacked the prosecutor's most dangerous assertion, that Burr was guilty of treason. No overt act of treason was committed, they argued, nor was there probable cause to believe that Burr was guilty of such a crime. Burr's intention to revolutionize Spanish America was not only "innocent, but meritorious," Wickham suggested.

The main argument for the defense was made by the defendant, Burr, who directed the court's attention to the actions of Wilkinson and Jefferson. "Alarms existed without cause," Burr declared. "Mr. Wilkinson alarmed the President, and the President alarmed the people of Ohio." Burr reminded the court that he had been honorably discharged by three grand juries and that the third, in the Mississippi Territory, had censured the conduct of the government. He noted that more than three months had elapsed since the government had issued the orders to seize him, and yet that same government had contended that it had not had sufficient time to collect testimony in support of its prosecution. As to his flight in the Mississippi Territory after his exoneration by the grand jury, Burr said that Wilkinson's pursuing troops had threatened his life, and therefore, on the advice of friends, he had "abandoned a country where the laws ceased to be the sovereign power." He concluded by stating that he must be acquitted, because there was no proof to support either the charge of treason or high misdemeanor but only the affidavits of Wilkinson and Eaton, "abounding in crudities and absurdities."

The arguments were completed in a single day, and Marshall announced his decision on the government's motions the next morning. Marshall first distinguished between the standard of proof necessary to commit Burr (probable cause) and to convict him at trial (guilt beyond a reasonable doubt). This gave him the opportunity, according to the Republican press, to condemn the Jefferson administration's aggressive pursuit of Burr. Referring to Blackstone's definition of probable cause, Marshall observed, "I do not understand him as meaning to say that the hand of malignity may grasp any individual against whom its hate may be directed, or whom it may capriciously seize, charge him with some secret crime, and put him on the proof of his innocence." Having offered that observation, Marshall gave the government its only victory of the day, declaring that he was persuaded by the Eaton and Wilkinson affidavits that there was probable cause to bring Burr to trial on the high-misdemeanor charge of making war on Spain's American colonies.

But treason demanded a more exacting standard of proof, wrote Marshall. The framers well knew the dangers inherent in such a quintessentially political crime, and therefore had set out the precise requirements for proof of the offense in the Constitution itself.

Eaton's and Wilkinson's affidavits, sufficient to hold Burr on the high-misdemeanor charge, fell short of the constitutional standards for treason, Marshall declared. The affidavits, at most, established probable cause that Burr had harbored treasonous designs. But intentions alone are not enough to try a man for treason. "War can only be levied by the employment of actual force," Marshall wrote. All that Wilkinson's rendition of the cipher letter and Eaton's affidavit had shown was Burr's *intention* to assemble troops.

Marshall chided the government for not making a better effort to prove its case. "The fact to be proved in this case is an act of public notoriety. It must exist in the view of the world, or it cannot exist at all." Surely, if Burr had assembled troops at Blennerhassett Island, witnesses could be produced to swear to it. So where was proof of that assembly of troops? Making the same point Burr had raised, Marshall asked why, more than three months after the president himself had publicly announced the conspiracy and called for the arrest of all participants, and five weeks after the chief justice had issued his evidentiary demands in *Bollman,* the government had not collected the necessary proof to hold Burr on the charge of treason.

Even before Marshall issued his reprieve for Burr, Jefferson was convinced that only a sympathetic, politically motivated judiciary could save Burr and his fellow conspirators from being hanged. In a letter to a Virginia friend and neighbor, Joseph Cabell, he noted that the New Orleans Judge James Workman, who had released Peter Ogden (one of Burr's suspected coconspirators) on a writ of habeas corpus, was a member of the Mexican League, which shared the conspirators' eagerness for war with Spain. The president struck what would become a recurring Jeffersonian theme during the Burr prosecution: "This insurrection will probably show that the fault in our Constitution is not that the executive has too little power, but that the judiciary either has too much, or holds it under too little responsibility." A week later, the president was blunter in his criticism of politically motivated judges. Writing to his old friend Colonel George Morgan, Jefferson was certain that members of the Federalist party would try to manipulate the law in the Burr case to serve their political ends.

When Jefferson received the news of Marshall's opinion, he was convinced that the Federalist judiciary's meddling with justice in the Burr case had begun. "The fact is that the federalists shield him from punishment," he wrote James Bowdoin, the U.S. minister to Spain.

Marshall's complaint that the government had been given ample time to produce the necessary affidavits did not seem unreasonable. Jefferson's investigator, John Graham, had been stalking Burr since the previous October. The president also could have called upon others with knowledge of the activities of Burr and his collaborators, including Governor Tiffin of Ohio, who had made the first arrests of the suspected conspirators in early December. Besides Tiffin, Jefferson had been in close communication with Governor William Claiborne of the Orleans Territory, who, presumably, could collect affidavits from those in the lower-Louisiana region with firsthand knowledge of the conspiracy. And the president was aware, at least since Marshall's February opinion in *Bollman,* of the standard of proof required by the chief justice.

But the problem for the administration, as Jefferson pointed out in a letter to Senate Republican leader William Branch Giles, was that transportation of legal papers and witnesses from the Western states was exceedingly slow. "As if an express could go to Natchez, or the mouth of the Cumberland, and return in five weeks, to do what has never taken place in twelve," Jefferson angrily retorted. And the destination of the documents was not known until Burr's final capture and the subsequent designation of Richmond as the location for the trial.

When Giles warned the president that the administration had best attend to the proof of treason that Marshall demanded or suffer serious political consequences, Jefferson admitted, "That there should be anxiety & doubt in the public mind, in the present defective state of the proof, is not wonderful." Nonetheless, he again accused the Federalists of making Burr's cause their own. But the president remained firm in his belief that the people would ultimately learn the truth as he understood it. "The nation will judge both the offender & judges for themselves," he told Giles. If Federalist judges were so foolish as to continue their protection of Burr, Jefferson predicted, the people would pass a constitutional amendment to bring the entire federal judiciary under popular control. "If their protection of Burr produces this amendment," he concluded, "it will do more good than his condemnation would have done."

Here we see Jefferson at his emotional worst, hurling wild charges and threats at his political enemies. Yet the president had good cause to want to see Burr punished. His former vice president had possibly jeopardized the United States' shaky relations with Spain. One can also understand Jefferson's frustrations in reading one Marshall opinion after another in which the chief justice carefully weighed each critical legal issue and usually ruled against the position Jefferson supported. Even outside the courtroom, Marshall did not do much to discourage Jefferson's mistrust. Shortly before the Burr trial began, he accepted an invitation to dine at the residence of Burr's lead counsel, John Wickham, where Burr was the guest of honor.

But Jefferson had become a man possessed, determined to see that Burr and his fellow conspirators went to the gallows. Jefferson besieged District Attorney Hay with advice on tactics and law that he hoped would lead to the successful prosecution of Burr. In his zeal, he did not always observe common standards. He sent Hay the statement that Dr. Erick Bollman had provided him and Madison after Jefferson had promised that the statement would be kept confidential.

If Marshall's decision in *Marbury v. Madison* was cited, as it was in the chief justice's *Bollman* opinion, Jefferson urged Hay to challenge it as bad law. Marshall's opinion affirming the Court's authority to declare an act of Congress unconstitutional was extraneous to the decision, Jefferson asserted, since the Court did not have the original jurisdiction to hear Marbury's case.

Despite his railing against the chief justice's demands for evidence, Jefferson asked his attorney general to create a special fund to cover the costs of gathering affidavits and witnesses to satisfy Marshall's evidentiary standard. By committing substantial financial resources to bring evidence against Burr, as well as by his constant flow of written instructions to Hay, Jefferson sought to present the strongest case for Burr's guilt on the treason charge. But the president could not count on Marshall's ruling in his favor. From the outset, Jefferson's strategy was to portray Burr as guilty before the larger court of public opinion, even if he was acquitted in Richmond. Thus, regardless of the verdict in court, he instructed Hay "to provide that full testimony shall be laid before the legislature &, through them, the public." If Marshall allowed the testimony of government witnesses to be introduced into the judicial record, fine. If not, Jefferson told Hay, "I must beseech you to have every man privately examined by way of affidavit, and to furnish me with the whole testimony." Cost was no obstacle. "Go into any expense necessary for this purpose & meet it from the funds provided by the Attorney General for the other expenses."

The prosecution of Burr began ominously in mid-May, according to Jefferson, when Marshall (now joined by District Judge Cyrus Griffin) allowed Burr to challenge successfully two grand jurors who were "as far above all exception as any two persons in the U.S." The first was William Branch Giles, the Republican Senate leader, and the second, former Republican Senator Wilson Cary Nicholas, Jefferson's neighbor and confidant. Even with John Randolph, no friend of Burr's, chosen as the grand-jury foreman, and thirteen other Republicans on the panel, Jefferson was not satisfied.

At Hay's request, Marshall delayed formal proceedings until the government's star witness, Wilkinson, could make his way from New Orleans to Richmond. Much to the prosecutor's embarrassment, many days passed as the grand jurors, lawyers, and judges waited. Burr, however, was not idle. On June 9, with General Wilkinson still unaccounted for, the defendant brought the president directly into the case in spectacular fashion. Addressing the court, Burr said that it was necessary for his defense that he see Wilkinson's letter to Jefferson that the president had referred to in his January congressional message announcing Burr's guilt. He also demanded copies of military orders from the War and Navy Departments that, he claimed, had threatened his life and property while he was in the Mississippi Territory. Burr may have hoped that the president would voluntarily supply the requested documents, but in case he did not, Burr asked that Marshall issue a subpoena *duces tecum* to force the president to come to court with the documents or give the reasons why he refused to produce them.

Burr's request put the executive and judicial branches on a collision course. Marshall had avoided just such a confrontation four years earlier, in *Marbury v. Madison,* when he managed to criticize the conduct of the Jefferson administration without provoking the president to retaliate. But this time Jefferson was inextricably identified with the government's case, and, if directly challenged, was unlikely to accept Marshall's judgment as placidly as he had in *Marbury.*

Marshall said he would grant Burr's request, but only if there was no objection from the government. When Hay protested, Marshall had little choice but to call for argument on the issue from the impressive legal talent arrayed on both sides. By this time, Burr's team had more than doubled in size and included the redoubtable Luther Martin. The government's team had also been strengthened, most notably by William Wirt, a combative young Virginia lawyer.

Luther Martin had rushed to the side of his friend Burr two weeks earlier, donating his services without charge. Until now, Martin had been silent. With Burr's motion to subpoena the president, Martin lashed out at Jefferson. "This is a peculiar case, sir," Martin began. "The President has undertaken to prejudice my client by declaring that 'of his guilt there can be no doubt.' He has assumed to himself the knowledge of the Supreme Being . . . and pretended to search the heart of my highly respected friend. . . . He has let slip the dogs of war, the hell-hounds of persecution. . . . And would this President of the United States, who has raised all this absurd clamor, pretend to keep back the papers which are wanted for this trial, where life itself is at stake? It is a sacred principle that in all such cases the accused has a right to all the evidence which is necessary for his defense. And whoever withholds, wilfully, information that would save the life of a person charged with a capital offence is substantially a murderer, and so recorded in the register of heaven."

Wirt was determined to turn Martin's vitriol to the government's advantage. He asked a series of rhetorical questions: What is to be gained by the defense's "perpetual philippics against the government? Do they flatter themselves that this court feel political prejudices which will supply the place of argument and innocence on the part of the prisoner? Do they use the court merely as a canal through which they may pour upon the world their undeserved invectives against the government?"

Wirt then directed his anger at the chief justice. It was bad enough that a foreign visitor might hear the government referred to in a court of law as "blood hounds, hunting this man with a keen and savage thirst for blood." But what made it intolerable was the spectacle of a supposedly detached judiciary receiving this language "with all complacency."

Wirt's attack embarrassed Marshall, who felt compelled to respond. He had not approved of the heated exchanges between counsel, Marshall told the attorneys after the day's proceeding had adjourned, but had not wanted to interrupt "in the heat of debate." But since Wirt had called upon the judges "to support their own dignity, by preventing the government from being abused," Marshall wished to express his views on the rancorous arguments. "Gentlemen on both sides had acted improperly in the style and spirit of their remarks," said Marshall, distributing blame evenly between opposing counsel. He hoped, therefore, that they would not continue "to excite the prejudices of the people."

But neither Martin nor the government's counsel heeded Marshall's mild reprimand. For days, opposing attorneys exchanged insults and partisan declamations that had little bearing on the pressing constitutional issue at stake: whether a federal judge could order the president of the United States, the head of a coequal branch of government, to produce evidence for a criminal trial.

Jefferson instructed George Hay to gather information from a flour merchant in Baltimore who, the president had been informed, had knowledge of Martin's complicity with Burr. "Shall we move to commit Luther Martin, as *particeps criminis* with Burr?" asked Jefferson. "Graybell [the merchant] will fix upon him misprision of treason at least," he added. "And at any rate, his evidence will put down this unprincipled and impudent federal bulldog, and add another proof that the most clamorous defenders of Burr are all his accomplices." On the same day, Jefferson wrote his attorney general, Caesar Rodney, asking him to contact another Baltimore man, John Gordon, to learn more about Martin's relationship with Burr. Rodney was to visit Gordon "as secretly as possible" and promise him confidentiality. Such surreptitious efforts carried obvious risks for the president, but these were clearly outweighed by the information he hoped to gather against Martin.

After four days of furious arguments by Martin and the other lawyers over Burr's demand to subpoena Jefferson, Marshall delivered his opinion. Calmly and with understated confidence, the chief justice ruled that Burr had the right to examine documents relevant to his defense, even if they were in the possession of the president and his Cabinet officers. The Constitution, Marshall noted, entitled a defendant in a criminal case in the federal courts to a speedy and public trial. That must mean that the accused should have the opportunity to prepare his defense expeditiously. Burr, therefore, had the right, before as well as after indictment, to ask the court to subpoena witnesses and documents necessary for his defense.

Inching ever closer to the volatile issue of the court's authority to issue a subpoena *duces tecum* to the president, Marshall then asked if there was an exception to the law that he had just announced. The chief justice could think of only one exception in the common-law rules of evidence: the king of England was considered immune from legal process because under the British constitution he was incapable of doing wrong. But Marshall easily distinguished the position of the king from that of the president of the United States, who, under the U.S. Constitution, could be impeached and removed from office. Unlike the king, Marshall noted, the president of the United States is elected and returns to the mass of the people once his term is over. In the eyes of the law, the president is no different from any other American citizen. (What a delicious irony it must have been for Marshall, a committed Federalist whose party had repeatedly been accused by Jefferson of monarchial tendencies, to invoke the Republican principle of pure democratic rule.)

Having established his general premise that the president was not above the demands of the criminal law, Marshall proceeded systematically to reject every government argument in favor of a broad executive privilege. Anticipating Jefferson's later objection that his presidential duties required his full attention, Marshall said that he did not believe "that this demand was unremitting." Besides, if the president's official duties prevented him from responding to the subpoena, he could say so in his return of the court's order. But what if the subpoenaed documents contained confidential information vital to the national security, as prosecutor Hay had argued? There was no danger posed by the mere issuance of the subpoena, replied Marshall. If the requested documents contained government secrets, there would be time enough for the president to say so in his response to the subpoena. "If it [the document] does contain any matter which it would be imprudent to disclose, which it is not the wish of the executive to disclose, such matter, if it be not immediately and essentially applicable to the point, will, of course, be suppressed," Marshall assured. In an obvious reference to Jefferson's public denunciation of Burr, Marshall wrote, "It is not easy to conceive that so much of the [Wilkinson] letter as relates to the conduct of the accused can be a subject of delicacy with the president."

In his opinion on executive privilege, Marshall was, in effect, continuing the dialogue with Jefferson that he had begun in *Marbury,* where he had carefully distinguished between documents fully within the control of the executive branch, such as confidential political information exchanged between the president and a member of his Cabinet, and other written materials. Marbury's judicial commission, the chief justice had ruled, had the force of law independent of the president's political concerns.

The judiciary had no interest in confidential political information, Marshall wrote in *Marbury.* But who was to decide what was political? That was not an issue in *Marbury,* since the information sought was not of a political nature. The circumstances were different in *U.S. v. Burr.* The president's attorney had specifically claimed that the president had the constitutional right to keep the requested documents to himself. Marshall implicitly rejected the government's argument; the final authority to make that decision resided with the court.

Was Marshall's decision a humiliating judicial defeat for Jefferson? Not as far as Jefferson was concerned. The president had been willing to satisfy Burr's attorneys even before Marshall issued the subpoena. Immediately upon receiving word from Hay of Burr's request, Jefferson had instructed the prosecutor to ask his attorney general to furnish the Wilkinson letter with other documents relating to the Burr prosecution. Jefferson left it to Hay, however, to determine whether there was anything in Wilkinson's letter that should be kept confidential. Emphasizing that he would voluntarily furnish all materials "that the purposes of justice may require," Jefferson issued a broad caveat. He would reserve "the necessary right of the President of the United States to decide, independently of all other authority, what papers coming to him as President the public interests permit to be communicated and to whom." Jefferson drew the constitutional battle line between the president and the federal judiciary on the issue of executive privilege before Marshall had written his opinion.

Jefferson advised Hay in a personal note that his letter (which the prosecutor read into the court record) "is written in a spirit of conciliation & with the desire to avoid conflicts of authority between the high branches of the government which would discredit it equally at home & abroad." Behind Jefferson's words of conciliation lay his determination to respond to the judiciary's commands only so long as he thought they served the national interests. Marshall may not have thought that the president's duties prevented him from responding to all of the court's demands, but Jefferson was of a different view.

Although Jefferson's letters to Hay gave assurances that his administration would cooperate fully with the court, the president privately expressed anxiety that he and Marshall might be headed toward a constitutional showdown. The president believed that Burr wished to "divert the public attention from him to this battle of giants," a reference to himself and Marshall. Later, he struck that phrase and wrote that Burr wanted to "convert his trial into a contest between the judiciary and executive authorities." The court's subpoena was "the first step to bring it on." Although Jefferson still held out hope that Marshall would not be lured into such a confrontation, he was not prepared to rely on Marshall's "good sense" alone, and instructed Hay to alert him immediately at the first indication that Marshall was pursuing confrontation. If confrontation could not be avoided, the president was confident "that the powers given to the executive by the Constitution are sufficient to protect the other branches from judiciary usurpation."

Jefferson's worst fears proved unfounded. After his offered pledges of cooperation, Burr's attorneys did not press Marshall on the issue, though the subpoena, technically, called for the president's personal appearance in court. The constitutional parameters of the president's responsibility to respond to a subpoena were left largely unresolved, because Jefferson had agreed to produce the requested documents before Marshall ordered him to do so. Marshall's opinion would later be interpreted by the Supreme Court to give the federal judiciary the authority to make the final decision on the issue. But in 1807, even after Marshall had written his opinion, Jefferson was convinced that he still possessed the constitutional authority to respond to the court's demands on his terms.

When Jefferson read Marshall's opinion, he was furious. Confident in his constitutional position, Jefferson was predictably critical of Marshall's opinion. Marshall's error, according to Jefferson, was in slavishly applying general principles that admitted "no exception unless it can be produced in his law books." Would the chief justice, Jefferson wrote Hay, be so insistent on his general rule that every citizen must answer a court's subpoena if it prevented Marshall himself from performing his important judicial duties? What if the sheriff of Henrico County, Virginia, summoned Marshall from the bench to quell a riot. "The federal judge is, by the general law, a part of the posse of the state sheriff," Jefferson noted. "Would the judge abandon major duties to perform lesser ones?"

Jefferson believed that the Constitution provided incontrovertible proof that each branch of the federal government was independent of the other two. It was inconceivable to him that the judiciary "could bandy him from pillar to post, keep him constantly trudging from North to South and East to West, and withdraw him entirely from his constitutional duties." Such judicial commands would undermine the constitutional concept of separation of powers.

Marshall had not pushed his judicial interpretation to the extreme limits conjured up by Jefferson. He never said that a president must obey every command of the judiciary, only that a subpoena *duces tecum* could be issued for vital evidence in a criminal trial. The chief justice left sufficient room for the president to argue that the subpoenaed document either was not relevant to the case or contained confidential information that the executive branch must protect in the interests of national security.

General Wilkinson finally arrived in Richmond on Friday, June 13, the day that Marshall issued his subpoena to Jefferson. The following Monday, the general "strutted into the court," wrote Washington Irving, and "stood for a moment swelling like a turkey cock." Burr, sitting at his counsel's table, showed not the slightest interest in the man primarily responsible for his legal predicament. According to Irving, when the clerk administered the oath to Wilkinson, the defendant "turned his head, looked him full in the face with one of his piercing regards," and quickly returned to his conversation with his lawyers.

Once he had been sworn in, the general was pummeled with embarrassing questions by the grand jurors, led by the foreman, John Randolph. Wilkinson's troubles began when he submitted to the court a copy of the famous cipher letter. Randolph and the other grand jurors examined it and quickly realized that the general had doctored the document by eliminating passages that suggested Wilkinson's prior knowledge of and possible participation in Burr's plans. For example, the first sentence of the letter, which stated, "Your letter postmarked 13th May is received," had been omitted. Such revelations destroyed whatever credibility the general had.

Wilkinson may have expected that he would be treated with the respect and admiration that were his due as the army's commander-in-chief who had revealed Burr's treasonous plot. Instead, he became a target of the grand jury's investigation. Before the jurors finished their business, the general, the government's presumptive prize witness against Burr, barely escaped indictment himself, by a nine-to-seven vote.

If Jefferson was discouraged by the disintegration of Wilkinson's reputation, he did not record it. From his perspective, the grand jury's handling of the general appeared to be a momentary setback in what turned out to be an essentially good result. Earlier, Marshall had agreed to defer to the grand jury on the question of whether Burr should be indicted on the charge of treason, as prosecutor Hay had urged in resubmitting his original motion. After a parade of forty-eight witnesses before the grand jury, many of them summoned at the urging of the administration, Burr was indicted on charges of treason and high misdemeanor. The jurors' true bill accusing Burr of treason was taken verbatim from prosecutor Hay's charge:

> Aaron Burr . . . being . . . under the protection of the laws of the United States, and owing allegiance . . . [thereto], not having the fear of God before his eyes . . . but being moved and seduced by the instigation of the devil, wickedly desiring and intending the peace and tranquillity for the said United States to disturb and foster, move and excite insurrection, rebellion and war against the said United States, on the tenth day of December [1806] . . . at a certain place called and known by the name of Blennerhassett's Island in the county of Wood, district of Virginia . . . with force and arms unlawfully, falsely, maliciously and traitorously did compass, imagine and intend to raise and levy war, insurrection and rebellion against the said United States. . . .

Marshall immediately understood that the grand jurors had applied the definition of constructive treason that he had given in his Supreme Court opinion in *Bollman*. In that opinion he wrote that a defendant could be charged with treason even if his participation in the assembling of troops was minute, or he was actually removed from the scene. Burr had left Blennerhassett Island two days before there was any assembling of troops. Yet, under Marshall's definition of constructive treason, Burr's absence from the island did not prevent him from being charged with treason. And that was precisely the grand jury's conclusion.

After reading the indictment, Marshall had second thoughts about how he had defined treason. Anticipating that he would have to rule on the issue when Burr stood trial in early August, he decided to explore the implications of his earlier opinion with his Supreme Court colleagues. Among the issues Marshall raised with his brethren was the extent to which American courts were obligated to follow the British law of constructive treason. "How far is this doctrine to be carried in the United States?" Marshall asked Associate Justice Cushing. "If a body of men assemble for a treasonable purpose, does this implicate all those who are concerned in the conspiracy, whether acquainted with the assemblage or not? Does it implicate those who advised, directed, or approved of it?" If Marshall and his colleagues continued to apply the doctrine of constructive treason in the August trial, the government's case against Burr would be significantly strengthened. "Ought the expressions in that opinion be revised?" Marshall asked Cushing.

On August 10, Marshall convened the federal circuit court in the state legislative chamber to decide whether Aaron Burr was guilty of treason against the United States. Neither the excitement nor the partisanship surrounding the trial had abated. The first task was to find twelve eligible citizens who could render an impartial verdict. Feelings ran so high that, after two days of screening potential jurors for prejudice, the lawyers had exhausted an entire panel of forty-eight and found only four men who had not pronounced Burr guilty as charged. Although Burr's attorneys hinted that it might be impossible for their client to receive a fair trial, Burr himself solved the problem by promising to take eight jurors from the second panel of forty-eight men, regardless of their opinions.

Burr was true to his word. One prospective juror, Richard Parker, a staunch Republican, declared, "If these newspaper statements were true, Colonel Burr had been guilty of some design contrary to the interest and laws of the United States."

"I have no objection to Mr. Parker," said Burr. "He is, therefore, elected."

It would seem that the defendant was unnecessarily generous, perhaps fatally so, in agreeing to accept jurors who had formed preliminary opinions of his guilt. But Burr was not the first, or last, shrewd defense lawyer to show potential jurors that he was supremely confident that the evidence would persuade them to decide the case in his favor.

There was a second reason why Burr was willing to accept jurors with preconceived opinions on his guilt. In the end, he did not think the jury would decide his fate. That responsibility would be John Marshall's. Burr knew that the decisions on what evidence would be admissible and, more crucially, the standard necessary to prove treason were in the hands of the judge. From the outset of his trial, Burr would argue that most of the government's case was irrelevant to the crucial issue of whether he had committed an overt act of treason. He would contend that the government must first prove that a specific overt act of treason had occurred before it could introduce other witnesses to testify to Burr's participation in the act. If he prevailed with that argument, Burr and his attorneys could undercut the government's case by contending that he was physically incapable of committing treason, as the crime was defined in the Constitution, because he was not present on Blennerhassett Island on the night in question. To succeed, Burr would have to persuade the chief justice that the expansive words in his *Bollman* opinion, which appeared to accept the common-law understanding of constructive treason (and would cover Burr), were not binding.

On Monday, August 17, George Hay opened the case for the prosecution. He admitted at the outset that the defendant was not on Blennerhassett Island on the night of the treasonous assembly charged in the indictment. But Burr was nonetheless legally accountable, said Hay, because he had "procured" and "advised" the assembly, and that made him a part of the overt act. As his legal authority, Hay cited Marshall's opinion in *Bollman*. A man may commit an overt act of treason, he argued, even if he was not physically present.

Having established what he considered to be the law for the case, Hay described the expedition down the Ohio River that began on Blennerhassett Island and ended with Burr's capture in the Mississippi Territory. The district attorney alerted the jurors that they would hear crucial testimony about the plot from a true national hero, General James Wilkinson, who, though "much censured, abused, and calumniated, as if he had joined in it," had rendered essential service to the people and government of the United States "by counteracting and defeating the project."

The government's first witness, General William Eaton, was prepared to give elaborate testimony on his conversations with Burr in the winter of 1806, when the two men met in Washington and, according to Eaton, Burr had proposed making him second-in-command of his revolutionary expedition. Eaton had barely begun his testimony when Burr was on his feet with an objection. The government must first prove the overt act of treason charged in the indictment, Burr asserted, before Eaton or any other government witness could offer collateral evidence of the crime. Eaton could only speak of Burr's general intentions, the defendant argued, not of the assembly on Blennerhassett Island, and therefore his testimony could not be admitted into evidence at that time.

Prosecutor William Wirt responded that the jury could not fully understand the case against the defendant unless the government presented testimony about the sequence of events that led to Burr's treasonous act. "Would you begin to narrate a tale at the end of it?" he asked. "If you were to write a history of the late revolution, would you begin at the siege of Yorktown?"

Marshall was confronted with his first critical decision of the trial. The next morning, he read his opinion, which appeared to split the difference between the two sides but effectively favored the defendant. Both intention and the overt act were necessary to prove treason, and it did not matter in what sequence the government presented its case. The government could continue to question Eaton about Burr's treasonous intentions, but Marshall warned that he would keep the prosecution on a tight leash: the testimony of every government witness must be relevant to the overt act of treason, as stated in the indictment. When Eaton resumed his testimony, he was forced to admit that he knew nothing about Burr's role in assembling men on Blennerhassett Island.

Eaton was followed on the witness stand by Commodore Thomas Truxtun, who testified that he had known the defendant for many years and was aware of his ambitions to revolutionize Spanish America. But Truxtun said he had no knowledge of Burr's plan to separate the Western states from the union. Next, Peter Taylor, Blennerhassett's young gardener, spoke at length about his trip to Kentucky in search of his master and Burr to tell them of the threatened Wood County militia's raid on Blennerhassett Island. Under cross-examination, Taylor admitted that he had never seen Burr on Blennerhassett Island. After Taylor, the government called Colonel George Morgan and his two sons to the witness stand to tell about Burr's visit in August 1806 to Morgan's estate outside Pittsburgh, and the defendant's grandiose talk of conquest. But none of the Morgans could speak about the assembly on Blennerhassett Island.

Finally, two days after Hay had opened the government's case, the prosecutor called the first witness who had been on Blennerhassett Island on December 10 and, presumably, could testify about the overt act of treason. Jacob Allbright, a laborer assigned by Blennerhassett to build a kiln for drying corn, recalled that four boats were hastily loaded to sail downriver. Allbright recounted a confrontation between General Edward Tupper, the leader of the militia, and the men on the island. His testimony was not corroborated by any other witness and was directly contradicted by an affidavit that Tupper had given to the grand jury. Another witness, William Love, who was Blennerhassett's groom, said that the men assembled on the island hoped to leave without incident, but if confronted by militiamen, Love supposed, "they did not mean to be killed, without some return of the shot."

The government had called twelve witnesses, but the most important testimony—by those witnesses who had been on Blennerhassett Island on the fateful night—was confusing and sometimes contradictory. At best, the jury could envision vaguely a small band of frontiersmen embarking on a mysterious expedition down the Ohio River, with the defendant nowhere in sight. The prosecution's remaining hope was that the cumulative effect of the testimony of all 140 proposed government witnesses would persuade the jury of the existence of a vast, treasonous scheme that was set in motion by the assembly on Blennerhassett Island.

Burr, however, was determined to frustrate the government's strategy. After the prosecution's twelfth witness had stepped down, he and the other defense lawyers approached Marshall at the bench to demand that the government's testimony be halted. They argued that the Constitution was very clear on the law of treason: there must be proof of an overt act, as attested to by two witnesses. The government had not made its case. Not one witness had testified that Burr had committed the overt act of treason charged in the indictment. Without proof of that critical point, the defense argued, the collateral testimony of the scores of prosecution witnesses still to be heard was not only superfluous but inappropriate.

This was the defining moment of the trial, and the judge and lawyers knew it. Marshall called for oral argument on the issue. John Wickham opened for the defense, delivering a superb argument that was both erudite and plainspoken, offering a withering critique of the prosecution's case. The government had erroneously assumed that the defendant could be found guilty of the crime of treason for "procuring" a treasonous assembly from a distance. That might be true under the British common law of constructive treason, whereby all participants—principals and accessories—were considered equally culpable. But there was no common law of treason in the United States, only the crime defined by the Constitution and punishable through the statutes of Congress. That part of Marshall's *Bollman* decision discussing constructive treason was "extrajudicial," Wickham asserted, and could not be considered binding in the Burr case.

Marshall interrupted to ask Wickham whether he knew of cases where the court had advised a jury on the legal requirements for proving an overt act of treason. The defense attorney responded that it was "the right and duty" of the court to instruct the jury on the issue. That was particularly crucial in this case, because the defense and the prosecution interpreted the law so differently. The prosecution had argued that the mere assembly of men for a treasonous purpose satisfied the law of treason, but Wickham insisted that there must be a showing of force by the men before they could be found guilty.

Wickham directed Marshall's attention to the indictment, which charged Burr with a crime that the prosecution knew he had not committed. Instead of accusing Burr of actually assembling the men on Blennerhassett Island, the government should have charged him with procuring an assembly, as the prosecution had argued he had done. The indictment, besides having nothing to do with the facts as both prosecution and defense knew them, did not give Burr fair notice of the actual charge the government intended to prove.

When Wickham turned from a discussion of the applicable law to the testimony of the prosecution's witnesses, he cut even more deeply into the government's already vulnerable case. Where was the dreaded act of treason? Only one witness, Jacob Allbright, had even suggested that there was a drawing of arms. And his testimony was not supported by a single other witness.

Only William Wirt among the government's legal team was a match for Wickham, and the young Virginian readily accepted the challenge. The court could not ignore the opinion of Chief Justice Marshall in *Bollman,* he argued, and that opinion served as sturdy precedent for convicting Burr. Like Burr, neither Bollman nor Swartwout had been present at the treasonous assembly on Blennerhassett Island. "The question then of presence or absence was a question really presented by the case of Bollman and Swartwout," Wirt insisted. "It was one important to the decision of the case, and the Court, thinking it so, did consider and decide it in direct opposition to the principle contended for on the other side."

The defense's claim, Wirt continued, would lead to absurd results. By their reasoning, Harman Blennerhassett could be hanged as the arch-traitor* while Burr, the mastermind of the plot, would be set free. "Sir, neither the human heart nor the human understanding will bear a perversion so monstrous and absurd," declared Wirt. "Let Aaron Burr then not shrink from the high destination which he has courted, and having already ruined Blennerhassett in fortune, character, and happiness forever, let him not attempt to finish the tragedy by thrusting that ill-fated man between himself and punishment."

After Wirt's exhortation, the government's chief counsel, George Hay, would have been well advised to rest the government's case. Instead, Hay, dispirited and weak from influenza, spoke for two days and made what turned out to be a colossal blunder. He reminded Marshall that the ruling of another judge in the recent past had taken an important decision away from the jury. The judge's name was Samuel Chase, and Hay did not need to elaborate on the consequence for Marshall's colleague. Hay quickly added that he had not meant to threaten Marshall with impeachment if he ruled against the government, and Marshall responded that he had not understood the prosecutor to convey such a threat.

Luther Martin then spoke for the defense for fourteen hours, assisted by piles of law books and a steady supply of strong liquor. No man at the bar could top Martin for sarcasm in belittling his oppo-

*The grand jury had also indicted five other suspected conspirators, including Harman Blennerhassett, Jonathan Dayton, and Senator John Smith.

nent's argument. He referred to the government's case as "will o' the wisp treason" because "it is said to be here and there and everywhere, yet it is nowhere. It exists only in the newspapers and in the mouths of the enemies of the gentleman for whom I appear." Marshall's opinion in *Bollman* was mere *"gratis dictum,"* Martin asserted, and should be given "no more weight than the ballad or song of Chevy Chase."

On Saturday, August 29, after eight days of argument, the issue of whether the law prohibited the prosecution from continuing to present its case against Burr was submitted to Marshall for decision. The chief justice began working on his opinion with quill pen and paper that evening, labored throughout the next day, and put the finishing touches on his opinion in the predawn hours of the 31st. Running to twenty-five thousand words, the opinion was the longest in Marshall's thirty-four-year judicial tenure and contained extensive citations from both American and British law. By opinion's end, Marshall had accepted virtually every argument made by Burr's defense team, though he eschewed Luther Martin's florid rhetoric in favor of John Wickham's craftsmanlike demolition of the prosecution's case.

Early in his opinion, Marshall confronted the major obstacle to his ruling for Burr–his opinion in *Bollman*. Though he did not accept Wickham's claim that his discussion of constructive treason in that opinion was "extrajudicial," Marshall did the next-best thing from the defense's point of view: the chief justice said that his opinion in *Bollman* had been misunderstood and did not decide the issues of fact and law before him in the Burr case. Marshall then considered the specific charge in the Burr indictment, and the evidence that the government had presented to prove the charge. The overt act of levying war specified in the Constitution required more than a peaceable assembly, wrote Marshall, adopting Wickham's position that the assembly "must appear in force or military form." That hostile act must be proved by two witnesses, Marshall reminded the government, but the prosecution had not proved it "by a single witness."

Marshall went on to condemn the government's indictment of Burr as disingenuous, just as Wickham had argued earlier. Nobody believed Burr was present on Blennerhassett Island on December 10, so it was wrong for the prosecution to insist that, legally, he was. If Burr's crime was to "procure" and "advise" the assembly, then the indictment should have said so. By such misrepresentation, the government had violated the Sixth Amendment to the Constitution, which provided that a defendant must know the nature and cause of the charge against him. But even if the government had drafted the proper indictment, it would still have failed to sustain its charge. For the prosecution had offered no proof that Burr had "procured" or "advised" the assembly, which, Marshall wrote, required two witnesses (in addition to the two necessary to prove the overt act of levying war). If the government objected "that the advising or procurement of treason is a secret trans-action, which can scarcely ever be proved in the manner required by this opinion," Marshall wrote, "the answer which will readily suggest itself is that the difficulty of proving a fact will not justify conviction without proof."

In his opinion in *Bollman,* Marshall had written that the framers of the Constitution intended that the law of treason, so susceptible to manipulation by the dominant political party, demanded the very high-est standard of proof. In his opinion in the Burr case, he backed his earlier declaration with extensive citation and a detailed analysis of the government's charge and evidence to demonstrate the stringent requirements necessary to convict a man of treason. The prosecution had failed on all counts: its charge was imprecise, and its witnesses had not proved the crucial overt act of treason.

At the end of his opinion, Marshall addressed prosecutor Hay's veiled threat of impeachment: "That this court dares not usurp power is most true," he wrote. "That this court dares not shrink from its duty is not less true." If a man is faced with the choice between performing his duty and shrinking from that duty to avoid the slander and scorn of his critics, he asked, "who can hesitate which to embrace?"

His defiant words were unnecessary. That Marshall would not be intimidated by the prosecution or the president was clear enough from the decision itself. For the chief justice had cut the ground out from under the government's case in precisely the manner that Burr had hoped. There would be no parade of government witnesses testifying to the defendant's "general evil disposition," as Marshall had put it. With no more witnesses able to describe the requisite overt act of levy-ing war on Blennerhassett Island or Burr's role in procuring it, the gov-ernment's case was effectively closed down by Marshall's order. A distraught Hay recognized that depressing reality and consented reluctantly to send the case to the jury.

The next morning, the jurors entered the courtroom to announce the inevitable verdict of not guilty. But the wording of their judgment suggested that the jurors had come to their decision reluctantly. "We of the jury say that Aaron Burr is not proved to be guilty under this indictment *by any evidence submitted to us*. We, therefore, find him not guilty" (italics added). After Burr objected to the exceptional language of the verdict, jury foreman Edward Carrington, who was Polly Marshall's brother-in-law, offered to change it. But another juror, Richard Parker, said that he would not consent to changing a single word. Marshall declared that the verdict would be reported as "not guilty," although the jury's wording would stand.

On June 22, two days before Burr was indicted on charges of treason and high misdemeanor, Jefferson had received word that the unarmed American frigate *Chesapeake* had been fired on by the British man-of-war *Leopard* off the Virginia coast. The shelling had destroyed the American ship's masts and rigging, killed three sailors, and injured eighteen others. Members of the *Leopard*'s crew had boarded the *Chesapeake* and removed four sailors that they claimed were British citizens (three were American citizens).

Jefferson called an emergency Cabinet meeting to decide how to respond to this daring challenge to American sovereignty. The crisis deepened through the remainder of the summer and into the fall, as the British government refused to offer an apology or explanation for the attack.

With relations between the United States and Great Britain rapidly worsening, Jefferson did not devote much time to the Burr prosecution, though he followed the events in the newspapers and through Hay's periodic reports to him. What he learned did not please him. Even before the government had begun to present its case, Hay wrote the president that only Marshall's bias in Burr's favor could save him. "There is but one chance for the accused," Hay wrote, "and that is a good one because it rests with the chief justice." Specifically, Hay continued, "it is already hinted, but not by himself [that] the decision of the Supreme Court [in *Bollman*] will not [be] deemed binding."

Hay's letter confirmed Jefferson's worst suspicions, which had been festering for six months. From the moment of Burr's arraignment, Jefferson had believed that the chief justice would manipulate the law to protect the defendant. When informed of the jury's verdict, Jefferson responded with controlled outrage. "The event had been what was evidently intended from the beginning of the trial," he wrote Hay, "that is to say, not only to clear Burr, but to prevent the evidence from ever going before the world." The verdict, Jefferson lamented, will show that "the criminal is preserved to become the rallying point of all the disaffected and the worthless of the United States, and to be the pivot on which the intrigues and the conspiracies which foreign governments may wish to disturb us with may turn."

Jefferson was more determined than ever to prosecute Burr. He overruled Hay, who was ready to concede defeat on the government's pending high-misdemeanor charge against Burr of making war against Spain. "If he is convicted of the misdemeanor, the judge must in decency give us respite by some short confinement of him," wrote Jefferson, "but we must expect it to be very short." If Marshall further frustrated the president with his rulings, Jefferson stood ready to expose what he believed to be the chief justice's partisanship. He repeated his earlier instruction to Hay to make a complete record of the evidence against Burr, requesting that the prosecutor preserve every affidavit of the 140 government witnesses. Jefferson promised to lay the government's case before Congress for its judgment as to whether the "defect" had been "in the evidence of guilt, or in the law, or in the application of the law."

While Hay prepared the government's misdemeanor case against Burr, the defendant counterattacked, demanding that Marshall issue another subpoena *duces tecum* to force the president to produce another letter from General Wilkinson. When Marshall issued the second subpoena, Jefferson bristled. "As I do not believe that the district courts have a power of commanding the executive government to abandon superior duties and attend on them, at whatever distance, I am unwilling, by any notice of the subpoena, to set a precedent which might sanction a proceeding so preposterous." The president nonetheless sent

Hay a copy of the Wilkinson letter, though he carefully deleted passages that he deemed exclusively within the executive's control. The limits of executive privilege were not further pressed by Marshall or the president, and there matters stood for the duration of the Burr prosecution. The president continued to urge Hay to prosecute Burr vigorously for high misdemeanor in Marshall's courtroom, telling his lawyer, "If defeated, it will heap coals of fire on the head of the judge; if successful, it will give time to see whether a prosecution for treason against him [Burr] can be instituted in any, and what other court."

Burr's misdemeanor trial began on September 9, with the government still under the legal strictures of evidence that Marshall had imposed in the earlier, treason trial. Because the misdemeanor indictment charged that Burr's crime took place on Blennerhassett Island on December 10, 1806, the government's witnesses were again obligated to give testimony that was relevant to the formal charge. Hay managed to question more than fifty witnesses on the charge that Burr had planned to revolutionize Spanish America. But, again, as in Burr's treason trial, the witnesses failed to offer persuasive proof that the defendant had committed the crime. Many of the witnesses who admitted to having been recruited by Burr corroborated the defendant's claim that he had planned to attack Spanish colonies only if the United States declared war on Spain. Others seemed totally oblivious to any criminal design by Burr; they said they had joined the expedition because of the offer of free land on the old Bastrop estate in the Louisiana Territory.

After a week of testimony, Hay, recognizing that his case was extremely weak, made a motion to drop the prosecution and dismiss the jury. Marshall replied that the motion could be granted only with the defendant's permission. Burr refused; he wanted the jurors to acquit him of the misdemeanor charge formally, which they did.

But Burr's ordeal was not over. For the next month, the opposing attorneys haggled over the prosecution's motion to commit Burr to custody for trial on both the treason and misdemeanor charges in Western jurisdictions, presumably more congenial to the government's case. This allowed General Wilkinson, finally, to have his day in court—five days, to be exact. But his testimony was full of evasions and contradictions, and his efforts to alter the cipher letter to hide his collaboration with Burr were publicly exposed. Even Hay, who had earlier praised the general's role in defeating the Burr conspiracy, was forced to reevaluate his opinion. He wrote Jefferson, "My confidence in him [Wilkinson] is shaken, if not destroyed."

In fact, nothing that Hay or anyone else revealed about Wilkinson changed Jefferson's opinion of the general. Whatever the reason—a perverse sense of loyalty?—the president refused to abandon the general or alter his opinion that their cause—to bring Burr to justice—was right.

Although he continued privately to denounce the outcome of the Burr trials, Jefferson remained confident that what he considered the judicial travesty in Richmond would ultimately produce a salutary result. He returned to his original plan to support a constitutional amendment to curb the independence of the judiciary. With the entire record of the government's case against Burr before Congress (and not just what Marshall had allowed into evidence), the president expected the legislature to take the necessary action.

In his annual message to Congress, on November 23, Jefferson announced that he would send the legislature the evidence that the government had accumulated against Burr. But months of congressional hearings did not produce a constitutional amendment or any lesser sanction against the federal judiciary. Meanwhile, the ardor of federal prosecutors to pursue Burr in the Western states slowly expired; after his acquittal in Richmond, Burr never again stood trial on charges of treason or high misdemeanor.

Aaron Burr should not have been convicted of treason. The government failed to demonstrate that Burr's ultimate objective was to betray his country. The failure was due partly to the poor management of the government's case by the lead prosecutor, George Hay. The administration's legal problems were compounded by Burr, who proved to be a superior litigator and trial strategist. But aside from forensic considerations, the prosecution's treason case collapsed under the weight of the facts as then known. If Burr had harbored treasonous intentions, he had shrewdly wrapped his plans in ambiguity. Even if one of his goals was to separate the Western states from the union, he almost certainly planned first to revolutionize Spanish America. And though his claim to the Washita lands may well have been a cover for his true intentions, as Jefferson suspected, Burr could offer both documentation and witnesses to swear to this benign goal.

The Burr prosecution produced an ironic reversal of roles for Jefferson and Marshall. The president, author of the Declaration of Independence and a supporter of many of the individual rights contained in the Bill of Rights, pursued Burr and his associates with a vengeance that ignored basic civil liberties. The chief justice, whose major libertarian concern was the protection of private property, became the vigilant defender of criminal suspects' constitutional rights.

Jefferson's and Marshall's roles in the Burr affair deserve scrutiny beyond such broad generalizations. Before condemning Jefferson, one must ask whether any other president would have stood idly by while his former vice president met with representatives of the nation's major adversaries, openly condemned the administration, and traversed the Western states twice to make plans for a mysterious expedition down the Mississippi. When he finally acted, the greatest potential for danger had passed, so that the national alarms he sounded appeared strident and unnecessary. Nothing excuses Jefferson's belated zealous pursuit of Burr, but viewing the Burr conspiracy from the president's perspective makes his conduct understandable.

With his rulings in the Burr trial, Chief Justice Marshall made proof of treason under the Constitution rigorously demanding, virtually eliminating the crime as a tool for political oppression. For those rulings, we as a nation should be forever grateful. But despite the thousands of words in his opinions, the usually lucid Marshall failed to explain clearly why his *Bollman* decision accepting the law of constructive treason was not applicable in Burr's case. In Marshall's letters to his colleagues after Burr's indictment for treason, the chief justice had conceded that he recognized the British common law of constructive treason and asked whether his opinion should be revised. But it wasn't, and yet Marshall never acknowledged in his *Burr* opinion that his *Bollman* decision was defective. This may not have been manipulation of the law, as Jefferson claimed, but it was not the finest example of the chief justice's judicial craftsmanship.

Neither Jefferson nor Marshall was satisfied with the result of the Burr trial. Jefferson continued to believe that Marshall had acquitted a traitor, thereby encouraging further intrigues against the United States. Marshall was no more sanguine about the spectacle in Richmond. He was disturbed by the news that he had been hanged in effigy in the streets of Baltimore. A month after the trial, the chief justice offered a melancholy reflection that well summed up the ordeal of the Burr trial, writing that he had been "fatigued & occupied with the most unpleasant case which has ever been brought before a judge in this or, perhaps, in any other country which affected to be government by laws."

[11]

Final Battles

In late June 1807, Jefferson received a letter from Governor William Claiborne of the Orleans Territory. Would the president intervene on behalf of the United States to prevent Edward Livingston, former Republican member of the House of Representatives and a New Orleans attorney, from developing a small beachfront on the Mississippi River? Considering the national and international crises he was confronting, the controversy did not seem worth Jefferson's attention. Yet the president responded to the governor's appeal, perhaps because Claiborne had been a loyal ally during the Burr conspiracy. Livingston, on the other hand, had gone to court to seek writs of habeas corpus for Bollman and Swartwout, the suspected Burr conspirators, after they had been jailed by General Wilkinson.

Claiborne's request came to the president with a special urgency. If Jefferson did not intervene, the free flow of navigation down the Mississippi could be jeopardized. If Livingston were allowed to build a dam and levee, he could divert the river's flow, with devastating effect. Claiborne told the president that Livingston's claim had so roiled local residents that bloodshed was likely. The sandbank was considered public property, and the local population had freely used it for their own purposes.

The major obstacle to the president's intervention was a recent decision by the Superior Court of the Orleans Territory supporting Livingston's claim. Because Louisiana was not a state, there was no way to appeal the territorial court's decision. Claiborne urged the president to ignore the court decision (and the city of New Orleans' claim), on the grounds that the United States were the legitimate "legal claimants of the land in question."

Acting on an opinion by the attorney general that the riverfront was the federal government's property, Jefferson directed Secretary of State Madison to protect the public interest. Claiming authority under a congressional statute providing for the forcible removal of squatters from federal property, Madison ordered the U.S. marshal in the Orleans Territory to expel Livingston and his laborers. When Livingston successfully obtained an injunction from the territorial court prohibiting trespass on *his* property, the legal order was simply ignored by the federal marshal. At the same time, the secretary of war issued an order to the territory's U.S. military commander to evict trespassers if the governor requested it.

Neither Jefferson nor Madison appeared to consider settling the *batture* (the French word for the riverbed in question) controversy in a court of law. Jefferson expressed no reservations about taking the extraordinary executive action, later declaring the territorial court's decision "a mere nullity" that could not bind the federal government. After the federal executive orders had been carried out, he referred the matter to Congress for any further official action. There the issue was debated without result for two years, until April 1810, when the House indefinitely postponed a bill dealing with the controversy.

Livingston offered to settle his dispute with the administration through arbitration or in the federal courts. Jefferson declined. Livingston requested a personal meeting with the president. Jefferson refused. Livingston lobbied members of Congress, to no avail. Finally, he brought two lawsuits. In the first, he sued the U.S. marshal for the Orleans Territory for the recovery of his property. In the second, filed in John Marshall's circuit court in Richmond in May 1810, and naming Thomas Jefferson, now the former president of the United States, as the defendant, Livingston accused Jefferson of trespass and demanded damages of $100,000.

When he first heard of Livingston's lawsuit, Jefferson had been retired from the presidency for fourteen months, luxuriating in the quiet of his Monticello estate. His mornings were devoted to correspondence, but the remainder of the day was spent "in my shops, my garden, or on horseback among my farms; from dinner to dark, I give to society and recreation with my neighbors and friends; and from candle light to early bedtime, I read." As Jefferson approached his sixty-seventh birthday, he proudly boasted of perfect health and relished the "talk of ploughs and harrows, of seeding and harvesting, with my neighbors, and of politics, too, if they choose, with as little reserve as the rest of my fellow citizens."

Jefferson's blissful *joie de vivre* was, unfortunately, interrupted by chronic bouts of anxiety over his deteriorating finances. His debts had mounted steadily over the past decade, and his presidency did nothing to ward off creditors. He later complained that during his years in office the President's House had been turned into "a general tavern" for the Washington community. But much of the spending, in and out of office, was the result of his indulgent lifestyle, which included dining well, drinking fine European wines, and purchasing rare books for his private library.

Jefferson had always kept meticulous accounts of his spending, but, tellingly, he was rather careless in recording his income. He still owned approximately ten thousand acres of land and two hundred slaves, with an estimated value of $200,000, but his debts in 1810 exceeded his revenues by more than $25,000. And the prospects for wiping out that debt were dim. His farms had deteriorated from neglect during his presidency. Markets for the crops had seriously diminished, primarily as a result of a persistent economic recession that had been triggered by the Embargo Acts,* among the last and most unpopular laws passed during his presidency.

It was in these circumstances of economic crisis that Jefferson learned from John Wickham that he was being sued for $100,000 by Edward Livingston. What made the suit particularly painful for Jefferson was the realization that he again would have to enter the judicial

---

*In 1808, Congress, on the recommendation of President Jefferson, had responded to the increased incidents of the capture of American ships by Great Britain and impressment of American seamen by passing a series of embargo acts prohibiting all foreign trade by the United States.

lair of John Marshall. Jefferson's enmity for Marshall was returned in full measure by the chief justice, the only difference being that Jefferson repeatedly described his feelings in his private correspondence, whereas the more discreet Marshall did not.

When Jefferson informed his successor, President James Madison, of the Livingston suit, he took the occasion to recommend John Tyler as a replacement for the seriously ill District Judge Cyrus Griffin, who had served with Marshall loyally and silently during the Burr trial and was scheduled to sit with the chief justice in the Livingston case. The timing of Jefferson's entreaty to Madison suggests judge-tampering in a case in which he had an immediate interest. In fact, Tyler had taken the initiative with Jefferson before the Livingston case had been formally filed. He was an old friend of Jefferson's and an ardent Republican who had served on the Virginia state court and was then governor of the commonwealth. He had asked Jefferson to endorse him for the next vacancy on the federal district court. Jefferson almost certainly would have sent the same letter of support for Tyler to Madison if the Livingston lawsuit did not exist. But the appointment of Tyler (who did replace Griffin) had an added virtue.

Five months after his endorsement of Tyler, Jefferson joyfully contemplated a second judicial appointment, this time to fill the vacancy left by the death of the veteran Federalist on the Supreme Court, Associate Justice William Cushing. A sound Republican replacement for Cushing, Jefferson wrote Madison, would create a Republican majority on the Marshall Court, accomplishing a complete reformation of the federal government. The Republican revolution of 1800 had put the people in charge of the executive and legislative branches of the federal government, Jefferson reminded the president. But the Marshall Court, "not depending [on the people's will], has so long bid defiance to their will, erecting themselves into a political body to correct what they deem the errors of the nation."

Jefferson's hope of an eventual appeal to the Supreme Court was not much comfort to him in the fall of 1810, as he helped his lawyers prepare his defense. He had asked John Wickham to defend him, but Burr's defense lawyer chose instead to represent Livingston. Jefferson then retained two veterans of the Burr trial, George Hay and William Wirt, and added a third, Norfolk attorney Littleton Tazewell.

The lawsuit excited great public interest in Virginia, where the loyal

Republican *Richmond Enquirer* immediately took Jefferson's side and condemned Livingston. Others were not so sure. "The subject is not understood," an uneasy George Hay wrote Jefferson. "In fact, it is greatly misunderstood: and it is, therefore, important to yourself as well as to the public interests that the defense should be coextensive with the charge."

Jefferson needed no further prodding from Hay to immerse himself thoroughly in the details of his defense. He spent many weeks researching the legal history of riverbed property, reading old legal treatises as well as materials provided by Madison and other government officials that traced claims of riparian rights back to Roman times. He concluded that the legal rights to the New Orleans riverbed had been retained by the kings of France and Spain and, with the Louisiana Purchase, were transferred to the United States, and that Livingston's only legal avenue to claim the property was an act of Congress. Despite the ample opportunity that he, as president, had given Congress to legitimize Livingston's claim of ownership of the *batture,* no action was taken. Jefferson's brief ran ninety-nine pages. Despite his prodigious efforts, Jefferson did not object when Hay suggested that his best chance for success might well be to challenge the circuit court's jurisdiction. It was a technical point, but the financially strapped former president was not inclined to reject any legal strategy that could win the case for him.

For three days during the first week of December 1811, Marshall and the new district-court judge, John Tyler, heard arguments in *Livingston v. Jefferson* on the jurisdictional issue of whether the federal circuit court in Virginia could rule on a dispute involving property in New Orleans. On December 5, both judges announced that the case must be dismissed for lack of jurisdiction. Later, Tyler wrote Jefferson that he had persuaded a reluctant Marshall to come to that conclusion. According to Tyler, the chief justice had wanted to refer the case to the Supreme Court without rendering a decision.

Marshall's reluctance to dismiss Livingston's suit was apparent throughout his opinion. He called attention more than once to the fact that dismissal of the lawsuit left the plaintiff in the unhappy position of possessing a legal right to sue for trespass without a realistic remedy, since Jefferson, a Virginia resident, could only be held accountable in the Orleans Territory, where the property in dispute was located. Marshall suggested that Jefferson was saved only by an exception to the law of trespass. For centuries, the chief justice noted, British courts had recognized a suit for trespass against the person in any county in England, but a suit for trespass against property, for reasons relating to the difficulty of tracing title, could only be brought in the jurisdiction where the property was located. The great Lord Mansfield had recognized that injustice often resulted from the exception, but he could not bring himself to overrule centuries of common-law decisions. Neither could Marshall.

The chief justice wrote that the British common-law decisions, though not binding on American courts, "are entitled to that respect which is due to the opinions of wise men who have maturely studied the subject they decide." Marshall expressed frustration with the legal rule, which, he noted, was also recognized in both state and federal law. "Other judges have felt the weight of this argument & have struggled ineffectually against the distinction, which produces the inconvenience of a clear right without a remedy. I must submit to it." Marshall's opinion suggested that the former president of the United States was little better than a scofflaw. Had the case been litigated on the merits, he implied, Jefferson might well have been adjudged a trespasser.

Livingston did not appeal Marshall's decision, but he eventually succeeded in his claim against the federal marshal who had expelled him from the riverfront. In 1813, the federal district court in New Orleans ruled that the riverfront was private property and belonged to the attorney.

Jefferson never conceded that Livingston held a legitimate claim. But Livingston's later work in codifying the penal and procedural laws of the Orleans Territory was greeted with universal acclaim by lawyers and scholars. The New Orleans attorney also forged an impressive second political career, serving as U.S. senator from Louisiana and as secretary of state under President Andrew Jackson.

When Marshall dismissed Livingston's suit against Jefferson, President Madison still had not filled the Supreme Court vacancy caused by the death of Associate Justice Cushing. Finding an outstanding Republican from Cushing's New England circuit was difficult, because there was an extremely small pool of qualified legal talent among Republicans in that region. Jefferson had first recommended his former attorney general, Levi Lincoln of Massachusetts, for the vacancy, and Madison had followed the former president's recommendation. But Lincoln, whose eyesight was failing, declined the offer after Madison had sent his name to the Senate for confirmation.

After Lincoln rejected the appointment, Jefferson's euphoria over the Republicans' opportunity to effect a genuine reformation in the judicial branch of the federal government quickly evaporated. The president's next nominee, Alexander Wolcott, the Republicans' chief political operative in Connecticut, was not well qualified for the Court, and the Senate refused to confirm him. Next, Madison asked the independent John Quincy Adams, then serving as American minister to Russia. Adams, however, preferred a career in diplomacy and politics.

Madison turned to the young Republican leader of the Massachusetts legislature, Joseph Story. Story's father, Elisha, had been that rare political specimen, a Republican stalwart drawn from New England's affluent and educated class. The Harvard-educated Joseph Story had earned a reputation as a scholar of the law and an outstanding advocate. Though he followed his father into the sparse New England ranks of Republicans and was elected to Congress, Story refused to adhere to a strict party discipline. Believing in a strong national government, he rejected many of his Republican colleagues' uncompromising devotion to states' rights. Story's independence received the quiet approval of many New England Federalist leaders, but did not please Jefferson. When Story's name was first mentioned for the vacancy, Jefferson opposed the nomination, remembering that Story, as a congressman, had abandoned his earlier support of the Republican-sponsored Embargo Acts by calling for their repeal. According to Jefferson, Story was a "pseudo-republican," a "tory" in disguise, and not to be trusted with a pivotal seat on the Supreme Court. Besides, the former congressman was only thirty-two years old—too young, thought Jefferson.

Jefferson may have also been aware that Story had an affection for John Marshall. Story became acquainted with the chief justice in 1808, when he was a young attorney in Washington on business. He delighted in Marshall's company. "I love his laugh," he wrote. "It is too hearty for an intriguer—and his good temper and unwearied patience are equally agreeable on the bench and in the study."

Much to Jefferson's chagrin, Madison ignored his old colleague's negative opinion of Story and nominated him. At the same time, the president sent the name of a second nominee, Gabriel Duvall, to replace Associate Justice Samuel Chase, who had died shortly after Cushing. Duvall appeared to be a solid Republican choice: he was the former chief justice of the Maryland Supreme Court, appointed by Jefferson in 1802 to be comptroller of the treasury. With the easy Senate confirmation of both Story and Duvall, Republicans constituted a firm majority of five on the Supreme Court.[*] The only Federalists remaining on the Court were Marshall and Bushrod Washington.

If the former president assumed a reformation of the judiciary was at hand, he seriously overestimated the Republican justices' dedication to what he considered essential republican principles, and, just as important, he underestimated the superb leadership qualities of John Marshall. Not a single Republican member of the Court shared Jefferson's aversion to strong national government. Like Madison, each saw the need for extensive federal authority, a view that was strengthened by the War of 1812 against Great Britain. The Republican justices were moderates in their constitutional perspectives, not so very different in outlook from the two Federalists on the bench, Washington and Marshall.

Under these congenial circumstances, the chief justice's towering intellect, softened by the "unwearied patience" that had so impressed young Joseph Story, commanded the respect of all the associate justices. Marshall leavened his formidable analytical arguments with a robust sense of humor. Still, he never lost sight of his overarching constitutional vision of a powerful federal government. The conditions were firmly in place for Marshall to lead the Court in dramatically increasing the federal government's constitutional authority and, correlatively, diminishing that of the states. In a series of seminal constitutional decisions, beginning with *Martin v. Hunter's Lessee* in 1816, the Marshall Court seized its historic opportunity.

---

[*]Story and Duvall joined three Jefferson appointees, William Johnson, Brockholst Livingston, and Thomas Todd.

John Marshall and his younger brother, James, had more than a passing interest in the property at issue in *Martin v. Hunter's Lessee*. In 1793, the Marshall brothers had formed a syndicate that purchased more than 160,000 acres of rich timber and tobacco lands in northern Virginia that had belonged to Lord Fairfax, including the property in dispute in the Martin lawsuit. The Marshalls had bought the property from Denny Martin, a nephew of Lord Fairfax, who claimed legal right to the land on the basis of the peace treaty that the United States had signed with Great Britain in 1783 to end the Revolutionary War.

Before the Marshalls' purchase, David Hunter had challenged Martin's title to the land by laying claim to the same Fairfax property under the confiscation statutes that Virginia had passed during the Revolutionary War. Prior to the 1783 peace treaty, Virginia had seized the Fairfax properties as lands belonging to British loyalists during the Revolution. The state had parceled out some of the land to its own citizens, including Hunter. According to Hunter, the Virginia confiscation laws gave him title to the property that could not be undermined by any federal treaty. Under a compromise worked out by the Marshall brothers in negotiations with the state of Virginia during the 1790s, they would own the property that was designated for Lord Fairfax's personal use; the state would retain the rest. The legal controversy concerned only 739 acres of the vast Fairfax estate claimed by both Hunter (under a grant from the state) and the Marshalls. Although the land in dispute was not great, the constitutional stakes were momentous: *Martin v. Hunter's Lessee* presented an irreconcilable conflict between the judicial authority of a sovereign state (to enforce its statutes) and that of the federal government (to enforce the terms of a treaty).

Although Hunter had initiated his action to establish his right to the land in 1791, the litigation was held in abeyance for almost two decades. It was not until 1810 that the Virginia Supreme Court of Appeals, the state's highest court, first ruled in the case, deciding that Hunter's claim under the state confiscation statutes was valid. But the U.S. Supreme Court reversed the state court's decision in 1813 in a forceful opinion by Justice Story that "instructed" and "commanded" the Virginia judges to enter judgment for Lord Fairfax's heirs on the basis of the peace treaty of 1783 and the Jay Treaty of 1794.

The Virginia court rejected the Supreme Court's mandate. In an opinion written by State Judge Spencer Roane, a close friend and ally of Jefferson's, the Virginia Supreme Court of Appeals ruled that the U.S. Supreme Court could no more tell the state court what to do than the state judges could dictate to the highest federal court. Although Roane conceded that section 25 of the Judiciary Act of 1789 authorized the Supreme Court to hear an appeal of the Virginia court's decision in the Martin case, he declared that that provision was in conflict with state sovereignty, and therefore unconstitutional. The two courts represented independent and equal sovereigns, according to Roane, echoing the arguments made more than a decade earlier by Jefferson in the Kentucky Resolutions. Roane reiterated Jefferson's contention that the states had entered into a compact to form the union but retained all authority not expressly delegated to the federal government by the Constitution. "No calamity would be more to be deplored by the American people," wrote Roane, "than a vortex in the general government, which would engulf and sweep away every vestige of the state constitutions."

John Marshall had recused himself from hearing the Martin case when it first came before the Court because he had an obvious financial stake in the outcome. But after the second Virginia-court opinion was announced in December 1815, Marshall took the highly unusual step of personally drafting the petition for the writ of error that brought the case, once again, before the Supreme Court. The chief justice arranged for his colleague Bushrod Washington to sign the writ, but the petition was drafted in Marshall's unmistakable upright handwriting.

Marshall's aggressive intrusion in the appeals process in the Martin case could have undermined the Court's reputation as a nonpartisan judicial institution, a reputation that the chief justice had assiduously cultivated since joining the Court. Had Hunter's counsel or the chief justice's states'-rights enemies discovered that Marshall had drafted the petition, it could have caused him much embarrassment. Why did Marshall leave himself open to exposure for his role in bringing the appeal?

It is doubtful that Marshall was motivated by financial gain. The dispute involved a relatively small tract of the Marshalls' property. Marshall had earlier instructed his brother James that it was better to have the dispute settled, regardless of the outcome, than to hold uncertain legal title. The more likely reason for Marshall's bold intervention was to make certain that a state supreme court did not have the final judicial word on a subject of singular constitutional importance: whether the U.S. Supreme Court was the final appellate authority on issues of federal law, treaties, and the Constitution. By drafting the petition for the writ of error almost immediately after the Virginia court's decision was announced in December, the chief justice made certain that the case would be argued during the next session of the Supreme Court, due to begin in six weeks.

The Supreme Court swiftly placed the Martin case on its 1816 term docket. The justices heard arguments for three days in February and announced their unanimous decision only weeks later. The Court's decision was written by Justice Story, but modern research suggests that Story relied heavily on a memorandum drafted by Chief Justice Marshall discussing the constitutional issues. Story's opinion proclaimed broad appellate authority for the Supreme Court. He used all of the judicial tools available to him—constitutional history, text and structure, judicial precedent, and public policy—to declare emphatically the Court's authority to overturn the Virginia Supreme Court of Appeals' decision.

Story began with a basic premise: "The Constitution of the United States was established not by the states . . . but, as the preamble declared, by 'the people of the United States.'" The people, rather than the state governments, were therefore the sovereign protectors of the Constitution's authority. During the constitutional debates, Story wrote, the framers had accepted the concept of limited state sovereignty. That acceptance was demonstrated throughout the Constitution, including the provision authorizing the Supreme Court to hear appeals on matters of federal law, treaties, and the Constitution. Congress had reinforced the Court's authority in section 25 of the Judiciary Act of 1789. Story noted that the states had recognized that appellate authority sixteen times prior to the Martin case, by accepting the Supreme Court's decisions on appeals from various state supreme courts without ever questioning the Court's jurisdiction.

Story concluded his opinion by observing that, if conflicting state-court decisions on federal issues could not be appealed to the U.S. Supreme Court, disparate rulings among the state judiciaries would create confusion and, worse, destructive rivalries among the states (as had happened under the Articles of Confederation). "If there were no revising authority to control these jarring and discordant judgments and harmonize them into uniformity, the laws, the treaties and the Constitution of the United States would be different in different states," Story wrote. "The public mischiefs that would attend such a state of things would be truly deplorable."

The Court's second decision in the Martin case was not openly challenged by Virginia or any of the other states, and served as the foundation block for expanding federal judicial authority. Three years later, the second great Marshall Court decision consolidating the constitutional power of the federal government was written by the chief justice, and it involved a controversial symbol of national power, the Second Bank of the United States. Marshall's decision in *McCulloch v. Maryland* would place him in the direct line of attack of the leading states'-rights ideologue, Judge Spencer Roane, with the active encouragement of former president Jefferson.

The precise constitutional issue before the Court in *McCulloch* had been raised twenty-seven years earlier, during the spirited debate between the two dominant members of George Washington's first Cabinet, Alexander Hamilton and Thomas Jefferson. Hamilton had successfully argued that Congress possessed the constitutional power under the "necessary and proper" clause to establish a national bank that would facilitate Congress's ability to collect taxes, spend for the general welfare, and raise and support armies, particularly in emergencies. Jefferson had countered that Congress could only do what was explicitly authorized by the Constitution, and nowhere in that document, he pointed out, was Congress given the authority to establish a national bank. He also argued that the bank was not absolutely "necessary" for the national legislature to exercise the powers granted under Article I of the Constitution.

President Washington supported Hamilton's position, and the Bank of the United States was created. The bank fulfilled Hamilton's expectation that it would provide an important financial base for building a strong federal government. But Jeffersonian Republicans attacked the bank as a bastion of federal authority that doubled as a political arm of the Federalists. In time, the usefulness of the bank became so well established among Republicans as well as Federalists that even Jefferson, after he became president, did not challenge the constitutionality of the institution. Jefferson's Republican successor, James Madison, eventually endorsed the establishment of a second national bank, after the charter for the first had expired in 1811.

By 1816, when Congress passed legislation to charter the Second Bank of the United States, the Federalist party was virtually extinct, its candidates the victims of the popularity of the Republicans. But the Republican party no longer was made up solely of adherents of Jefferson's original vision of an agrarian party responsive to the people's needs. The Industrial Revolution converted most Republicans to a belief in a national economy that melded agricultural production with urban banking, business, and manufacturing interests. The metamorphosis of the Republicans' position on a national bank was best illustrated by the fact that states'-rights advocate John C. Calhoun of South Carolina was the legislative leader who successfully steered the bank bill through the House of Representatives.

At first, the Second Bank of the United States thrived, and questions about its constitutionality were buried by the optimism and economic boom that followed the Treaty of Ghent, which ended the War of 1812. The bank helped fuel the sizzling economy by extending easy credit even for risky, unsecured financial ventures. By the fall of 1818, however, the bubble of national prosperity had burst, and financial panic swept the country. When the bank, short on reserves, abruptly called in its loans, farmers, businessmen, even state banks cursed the "monster" bank and its centralizing "monied power." Amid calls for repeal of the bank's charter, a congressional investigation revealed embarrassing mismanagement in the bank's eighteen branches. Although the repeal movement failed, heads did roll, beginning with the bank's first president, William Jones, who resigned.

James McCulloch was no minor functionary at the Baltimore

branch of the bank. As cashier, he was the bank's chief local agent and had served as the bank's main legislative lobbyist during the congressional investigation. Rumors abounded (later confirmed) that McCulloch and his accomplices had systematically looted the bank's reserves of more than a million dollars by authorizing unsecured loans and sanctioning unreported overdrafts.

Hard economic times and suspicions about the integrity of bank officials such as McCulloch led several states, including Maryland, to pass legislation to curb the power of the national bank. Maryland's antibank measure was a tax: banks doing business "without authority from the state" were required to issue bank notes only on stamped paper furnished by the state for a fee based on the denomination of the note. Any bank subject to the tax could "relieve itself" of the financial burden by paying a flat fee of $15,000 to the state. Under the statute, failure to abide by the law would result in a substantial and progressively heavy fine.

McCulloch ignored Maryland's law and continued to issue bank notes without either buying stamped paper from the state or paying the required $15,000 fee. The state at once brought suit against the cashier, setting up the constitutional confrontation that ultimately would be settled by the opinion of Chief Justice Marshall in *McCulloch v. Maryland*.

Both the Baltimore county court and the Maryland Court of Appeals ruled that the state law was a valid exercise of Maryland's sovereign authority, even though it brought a federal banking institution under the control of the state's revenue collectors. The issue of whether the Second Bank of the United States was obligated to submit to a state's tax laws was of great importance to the federal government. If Maryland (or any of the other states—including Georgia, Kentucky, and Ohio— that had passed laws taxing branches of the bank) could tax a federal institution at will, the power of the federal government to do business without obstruction from the states would be seriously jeopardized.

When *McCulloch v. Maryland* was appealed to the Supreme Court, the justices agreed that the constitutional issues raised by the case were of such importance that they allowed six lawyers to argue the case instead of the usual two allotted for each side. The roster of attorneys that appeared before the Court at oral argument read like a veritable who's who of the American bar and included Luther Martin, William Wirt, William Pinckney, and Daniel Webster.

The chief justice's masterly opinion for a unanimous Court in *McCulloch* offered further proof that the strength of Marshall's judicial opinions lay not in their originality. Marshall borrowed freely from the ideas of those who shared his view of federal power, such as Hamilton and Story, and from attorneys who appeared before the Court, such as Charles Lee in *Marbury*. In *McCulloch v. Maryland,* Marshall drew heavily on the arguments, and sometimes the very words, of Hamilton, Pinckney, and Webster. What made Marshall's opinion unique was the compelling way in which he presented his arguments, using logic, searing legal analysis, and the lucidity of his prose (often with a disarmingly simple turn of phrase) to march toward what appeared to be an inevitable conclusion.

In *McCulloch,* the chief justice wasted no time before challenging Jefferson's (and Roane's) basic constitutional assumption that the framers had ratified a compact among the states. Declaring that the Constitution emanated from the sovereign people, not the states, Marshall quoted from the preamble to provide textual support for his argument (as did Story in *Martin v. Hunter's Lessee*). He asserted that the people had made their national government supreme over the states within the sphere of its powers. If those powers were to be sufficient to meet "the various crises of human affairs," Marshall warned, they must be construed generously. "We must never forget," Marshall said, that "it is a constitution we are expounding." The framers did not intend the document to be read like a municipal code. Instead, the Constitution's general phrases, like the "necessary and proper" clause, were meant to be interpreted broadly, so that the federal government could effectively perform its constitutional obligations.

Having declared those basic premises, Marshall applied them to the facts in the banking case. He held that Congress possessed the authority to incorporate the national bank under the "necessary and proper" clause because the framers had anticipated that the federal legislature would need flexibility in choosing the means to implement its constitutional powers. The fact that the people's representatives in Congress had passed bills creating both the first and second banks indicated that this interpretation was no bald constitutional usurpation. For the Court to rule that the creation of the bank was unconstitutional would place the justices in the untenable position of defying the intention of the framers as well as the sustained will of the popularly elected national legislature.

Marshall then joined the epistemological debate over the meaning of "necessary" begun almost three decades earlier by Hamilton and Jefferson. Raising a point made at oral argument by Pinckney, the chief justice noted that the word "necessary" appeared more than once in the Constitution, first without a modifying adverb, later with one ("absolutely necessary"). How could anyone insist on a single definition for a word that the framers used differently within the same text? Any rigid textual interpretation of Congress's authority, Marshall continued, would lead to absurd results. For example, the Constitution gave Congress the power "to establish post offices and post roads." Marshall reasoned that Congress must have the *implied* authority to see that the mail was delivered along post roads from one post office to another and, further, to punish anyone who stole a letter at a post office or along a post road.

Like Hamilton before him, Marshall interpreted the words "necessary and proper" generously to mean "appropriate" and "plainly adapted" to achieve goals expressly provided under Article I. Adhering closely to Hamilton's 1791 opinion on the constitutionality of the bank, Marshall wrote: "Let the end be legitimate, let it be within the scope of the Constitution, and all means which are appropriate which are plainly adapted to that end, which are not prohibited, but consist with the letter and spirit of the Constitution, are constitutional."

Once he had established Congress's authority to create the Second Bank of the United States, Marshall quickly disposed of Maryland's claim that, as a sovereign state, it could tax the national bank. Repeating the argument made by Daniel Webster before the Court, Marshall said that the power to tax was the power to destroy. In the case at hand, concluded Marshall, such power would allow an inferior government to destroy its superior. If Maryland or other states could tax the national bank, "they may tax the mail; they may tax the mint; they may tax patent rights; they may tax the papers of the customhouse; they may tax judicial process; they may tax all the means employed by the government, to an excess which would defeat all the ends of government. This was not intended by the American people," Marshall asserted. "They did not design to make their government dependent of the states."

A week after Marshall delivered his *McCulloch* opinion, the Court adjourned and the chief justice returned to his Richmond home, where he learned that the *Richmond Enquirer,* the Republicans' impassioned voice for states' rights, was preparing a series of articles attacking the *McCulloch* decision. "Our opinion in the bank case has roused the sleeping spirit of Virginia—if indeed it ever sleeps," Marshall wrote Story. "It will, I understand, be attacked in the papers with some asperity; and, as those who favor it never write for the public, it will remain undefended &, of course, be considered as *damnably heretical.*" Three days later, Marshall told Bushrod Washington about his frustration in having to endure the anticipated attacks on *McCulloch.* "We shall be denounced bitterly in the papers &, as not a word will be said on the other side, we shall undoubtedly be condemned as a pack of consolidating aristocrats," he wrote Washington. "The legislature & executive who have enacted the law, but who have power & places to bestow, will escape with impunity, while the poor court, who have nothing to give & of whom nobody is afraid, bears all the obloquy of the measure."

On March 30, the first in a series of essays that the chief justice dreaded appeared in the *Enquirer.* It was introduced by Thomas Ritchie, the *Enquirer*'s editor (and Spencer Roane's cousin), who implored his readers to pay strict attention to the essayist's explanations of "the alarming errors" in the Court's *McCulloch* decision. The first two essays were signed "Amphictyon" and were written by Virginia Judge William Brockenbrough. With Roane and Ritchie, Brockenbrough was a member of the "Richmond Junto," the tight group of states'-rights advocates who then dominated Republican politics in Virginia. Brockenbrough was an orthodox Jeffersonian who rued every extension of federal authority.

According to "Amphictyon," the Supreme Court had made the inexcusable mistake of ignoring the elemental constitutional truth that the states and the federal government were equal sovereigns. Had the states known that the U.S. Supreme Court would attempt to intrude upon the sovereign power of the states, as it had done in *McCulloch,* they "never could have committed an act of such egregious folly as to agree that their umpire should be altogether appointed and paid by the other party." "Amphictyon" warned, "If the governments [state and federal] are to move on harmoniously, neither ought to attempt to pull down what the other has a *right* to build up."

To Marshall, the "Amphictyon" essays posed a threat to the Supreme Court, and perhaps, the union. If the charges against the Court's *McCulloch* decision were not answered quickly and decisively, he feared, the *Enquirer's* essays might become the inspiration for an overt insurrection by the states. The chief justice felt he could no longer endure criticism of the Court in silence. He would have to answer *McCulloch's* critics.

Using the *nom de plume* "A Friend to the Union," Marshall wrote two essays responding to "Amphictyon" and asked Bushrod Washington to arrange to have them published in the *Philadelphia Union,* a Federalist newspaper. But to Marshall's consternation, the essays, when printed, were garbled. Inexplicably, the *Union* editor had transposed the middle sections of Marshall's two essays, so that neither made any sense. Marshall quickly arranged for his essays to be published, correctly, in the *Alexandria Gazette.*

Meanwhile, reports were circulating in Richmond that critics of *McCulloch* planned to introduce resolutions in the next session of the Virginia legislature that, the chief justice wrote Story, were "not very unlike those which were called forth by the alien & sedition laws in 1799." If latter-day versions of the Virginia and Kentucky Resolutions were passed in the Virginia legislature, Marshall believed, a militant states'-rights movement could spread to other states, with disastrous results for the union.* Although Marshall dismissed the arguments of states'-rights advocates as "too palpably absurd for intelligent men," he conceded that "prejudice will swallow anything." Should the Jeffersonians win the national debate, Marshall concluded, "the Constitution would be converted into the old confederation."

Marshall also heard a rumor that "some other essays written by a very great man are now preparing & will soon appear." And soon enough, the rumored second series of essays attacking the Court appeared in the *Enquirer.* These were signed "Hampden," but Marshall

---

*The Virginia House of Delegates passed a series of resolutions denouncing *McCulloch* and proposing a constitutional amendment creating a new court to referee disputes between the states and the federal government. The measures did not become law, lacking a majority of votes in the Virginia Senate.

quickly identified the author as Judge Spencer Roane. Unlike "Amphic-tyon," Roane made no attempt to hide his contempt for Marshall's *McCulloch* opinion. He accused the chief justice of writing "a *general* let-ter of attorney to the future legislators of the union," inviting them to trample on the rights of the states at will. Under the guise of the "nec-essary and proper" clause, Roane charged, Marshall had granted Con-gress unlimited, and illegitimate, constitutional power. "I consider that opinion as the *Alpha* and *Omega,* the beginning and the *end,* the first and the last—of federal usurpations," Roane wrote.

Marshall did not cower before Roane's invective. Rather, the "Hampden" essays only hardened the chief justice's resolve to fight back. "I find myself more stimulated on this subject than on any other, because I believe the design to be to injure the judges & impair the Constitution," he wrote Bushrod Washington. Marshall informed his colleague that he would write a new set of essays to answer Roane, which he hoped Washington could place in the *Alexandria Gazette*. He cautioned Washington that his identity must not be revealed, and instructed him to have the manuscripts burned after they were printed.

Less than two weeks later, the *Alexandria Gazette* published the first of nine essays written by the chief justice. Signed "A Friend of the Consti-tution," the articles were a fervent restatement of the principles that Marshall announced in *McCulloch*. The Constitution did not create a league of independent states, Marshall wrote, rejecting Roane's major premise. The framers established legislative, executive, and judicial departments, he continued, "all of which act directly on the people, not through the medium of the state governments." In his last essay, he warned his readers that much more was at stake in his argument with Roane than scoring abstract debating points. "Let 'Hampden' succeed," the chief justice concluded, "and the Constitution will be radically changed. The government will be prostrate at the foot of its members, and that grand effort of wisdom, virtue, and patriotism which pro-duced it will be totally defeated."

Jefferson remained at Monticello during the Marshall-Roane debate, content to honor his long-standing vow to abstain from taking public positions on the political controversies of the day. That does not mean he kept his passionate views on states' rights and John Marshall's Supreme Court to himself. He wrote Judge Roane that he had read his essays "with great approbation" and, after a second careful reading, concluded, "I subscribe to every tittle of them." Under Marshall's leadership, "we find the judiciary on every occasion still driving us into consolidation." The former president complained to Roane that the Constitution had become "a mere thing of wax in the hands of the judiciary, which they may twist and shape into any form they please."

Criticism of *McCulloch* was soon overtaken in Jefferson's correspondence by a looming national catastrophe, what the former president called "a fire bell in the night." His reference was to one of the monumental American political controversies of the nineteenth century: the terms on which Missouri was to be admitted to the union. In the winter of 1820, Congress was almost equally divided between senators and congressmen from the Southern and Western states, who supported Missouri's admission as a slave state, and those from the North and East, who, with equal vehemence, insisted that slavery not be expanded into the Louisiana Territory, of which Missouri was a part. The Missouri question stirred anew the discontent of states'-rights advocates, who opposed the idea that Congress could impose conditions of admission on an individual state. At its most basic level, the Missouri debate was about the future of slavery, as Judge Roane freely acknowledged. Writing to President James Monroe, Roane said that he would rather see the Southern states secede than be "dammed up in a land of slaves by the Eastern people."

Jefferson was as appalled by the Missouri controversy raging in Congress as was Roane, but he did not descend to Roane's proslavery, secessionist rant. In fact, Jefferson favored a gradual emancipation of slaves, but he did not think the issue of slavery could or should be resolved by Congress. The Missouri question filled him with terror for different reasons. "I consider it at once the knell of the Union," he told John Holmes, a Massachusetts congressman, and he blamed Federalist politics for the impending debacle. Jefferson believed that the Federalists were engaged in a cynical, transparent ploy to use the Missouri controversy to resuscitate their party's failing fortunes. That their arguments, if successful, would divide the nation irreparably along geographical lines did not, as Jefferson saw it, concern them. (Jefferson's warning of "the knell of the Union" underscored his own commitment to a strong United States, though his concept of union was very different from John Marshall's.)

Speaker of the House Henry Clay managed to fight through the partisan rhetoric and convictions on both sides of the Missouri issue to offer a compromise. Missouri was to enter the union as a slave state, but, to maintain balance between slave and free states, Maine was to be admitted as a free state. As part of the Missouri Compromise, slavery would thereafter be prohibited in the Louisiana Territory north of Missouri's southern boundary. Clay's compromise became law, despite the unanimous opposition of the nineteen-member Virginia delegation in the House of Representatives.

The Richmond Junto's response to the Missouri Compromise was ferocious. "We scarcely ever recollect to have tasted a bitterer cup," wrote the *Enquirer*'s editor, Thomas Ritchie. "A Constitution warped from its legitimate bearings, an immense region closed forever against Southern and Western people—such is the 'sorry sight' which rises to our view." And once again Marshall's *McCulloch* opinion was featured in the *Enquirer*'s pages, portrayed as the judicial hammer that promised to pound the Southern states into further submission. Later that year, the *Enquirer* published John Taylor's *Construction Construed and Constitutions Vindicated*, a turgid states'-rights manifesto that included a justification for the secession of the Southern states. Taylor devoted five of sixteen chapters to attacking *McCulloch*. "The charter [of the Bank of the United States] has been justified on principles so bold and alarming," Taylor wrote, "that no man who loves the Constitution can fold his arms in apathy." According to Taylor, *McCulloch* granted Congress unlimited license to legislate so that it would eventually "rear a progeny of unconstitutional bastards which were not begotten by the people."

Ritchie sent Jefferson a copy of Taylor's manifesto, which the former president received with gratitude. "The judiciary of the United States is the subtle corps of sappers and miners constantly working under ground to undermine the foundations of our confederated fabric," Jefferson told Ritchie. He remained mystified as to how the chief justice could persuade the five Republicans on the Court to tear down what he considered the impenetrable boundaries between federal and state sovereignties. "An opinion is huddled up in conclave, perhaps by a majority of one, delivered as if unanimous," Jefferson wrote, "and with the silent acquiescence of lazy or timid associates, by a crafty chief judge, who sophisticates the law to his mind by the turn of his own reasoning." To Archibald Thweat, he complained: "The judiciary branch is the instrument which, working like gravity, without intermission, is to press us at last into one consolidated mass."

While Jefferson fretted about what he saw as the destruction wrought by the Marshall Court, a new constitutional challenge to state sovereignty was headed to the justices for oral argument. The case involved the sale of a lottery ticket by two brothers, Philip and Mendes Cohen, who were managers of the Norfolk branch of Cohens Lottery and Exchange Office of Baltimore. The Cohen family had profited handsomely from the lottery phenomenon in early-nineteenth-century America, when many states, as well as the District of Columbia, recognized that Americans' zeal to get rich quick could greatly enlarge their public coffers.

The lawsuit was precipitated by the conflict between an act of Congress authorizing a lottery for the District of Columbia that would help defray the costs for a new city hall, and a law passed by the adjacent state of Virginia defending its lottery turf by making it a crime for anyone to sell out-of-state lottery tickets. The Cohen brothers were arrested in Norfolk in June 1820, for violating the state law by selling a District of Columbia lottery ticket. The decision of the Norfolk municipal court convicting the brothers under the state law and fining them $100 was directly appealed to the U.S. Supreme Court, because there was no judicial procedure for appealing a municipal-court decision to a higher Virginia court.

If considered outside its historical context, the appeal of a lowly municipal-court decision dealing with a state gaming statute was hardly fertile ground for great constitutional law. But, like *Martin v. Hunter's Lessee* and *McCulloch v. Maryland,* the case of *Cohens v. Virginia* presented the Marshall Court with another irresistible opportunity to expand the authority of the federal government over the states. The key question to be decided was jurisdictional: whether the Supreme Court could make a final judgment about the validity of a state criminal law that was in direct conflict with legislation passed by Congress. Despite the technical nature of the legal question, politicians on both sides of the issue—states'-rights advocates and proponents of broad federal authority—recognized that they faced another crucial showdown.

Before the justices heard oral argument, the Virginia legislature attempted a preemptive strike by passing resolutions denying the Supreme Court's authority to hear the Cohen case and forbidding the state's attorneys from arguing the merits of the dispute. The *Richmond Enquirer* heartily endorsed the resolutions, declaring that the principles they defended were essential "to the existence and preservation of state-rights."

When the Court convened to hear arguments in *Cohens v. Virginia* on February 18, 1821 (without the ailing Bushrod Washington), Virginia's counsel, Alexander Smythe, confined his argument to the jurisdictional issue. He contended that Virginia, as a sovereign state, could not be forced against its will to submit to the appellate authority of the U.S. Supreme Court. Smythe pleaded his case with passion, issuing a veiled threat of rebellion should the Court decide against the state of Virginia.

The Cohens' attorney, William Pinckney, who had successfully advocated broad federal powers in *McCulloch,* responded with equal fervor. "The judicial control of the Union over state encroachments and usurpations is indispensable to the sovereignty of the Constitution—to its integrity—to its very existence," he insisted. "Take it away and the Union becomes again a false and foolish confidence—a delusion and a mockery!" The Supreme Court's supervisory authority over the states was particularly critical in criminal cases, he argued, because "the sovereignty of the states—state pride—state interests—are here in paramount vigor as inducements to error."

Attorneys on both sides, recognizing that the merits of the Cohen case were far less important to the Court than the jurisdictional issue, devoted much less time to those questions. President James Monroe's attorney general, William Wirt, argued the Cohens' side of the dispute. Contending that the "necessary and proper" clause provided Congress with ample authority to create a lottery for the District of Columbia, Wirt claimed that the Cohens' sale of a D.C. lottery ticket in Norfolk was perfectly legal and could not be prohibited by a state criminal statute. Daniel Webster, who had been appointed by Marshall to make the state's argument because the Virginia legislature had forbidden its own attorneys to do so, countered that the congressionally authorized lottery for the District of Columbia was local in nature, unlike a national bank, and could not be permitted to interfere with the legitimate gaming operations of a sovereign state.

The day after arguments on the merits were completed, Marshall delivered the Court's unanimous opinion. He first presented Virginia's argument on the crucial jurisdictional issue in its most confrontational form: "that the Constitution of the United States has provided no tribunal for the construction of itself, or of the laws or treaties of the nation, but that this power may be exercised in the last resort by the courts of every state in the Union." Surely, the chief justice wrote, that could not have been the intention of the framers, for that would mean that each state "will possess a veto on the will of the whole." Returning to the sweeping constitutional vision of a strong union that he had articulated in *McCulloch,* Marshall summarily rejected Virginia's claim: "A Constitution is framed for ages to come, and is destined to approach immortality as nearly as human institutions can approach it." The framers "must be unwise statesmen indeed if they have not provided it, as far as nature will permit, with the means of self preservation from the perils it may be destined to encounter." For Marshall, the means of effectively binding the union under the Constitution and the federal laws was the Supreme Court of the United States.

Having laid out the broad parameters of the Court's constitutional authority, Marshall proceeded to answer the particular questions at issue. Virginia argued that, as an independent sovereign, it could not be brought before the Court. Marshall asserted that the Court's jurisdiction depended on the issues in a case, not on the contending parties. When the interpretation of a federal law was at issue, as it was in *Cohens,* the Court properly accepted appellate jurisdiction. Marshall conceded that the Eleventh Amendment to the Constitution prohibited the federal courts from hearing cases brought against a state by a citizen of another state. But that amendment was passed for a particular purpose, to protect an individual state from suits by private creditors, the chief justice noted, and it did not give Virginia broad immunity from the Court's jurisdiction. Besides, he added, *Cohens* was not a "prosecution" contemplated by the Eleventh Amendment. The Cohens had not initiated the suit, but had only appealed a criminal-law decision in which they were defendants.

Marshall then offered his most expansive vision of the nation:

> In war we are one people. In making peace, we are one people. In all commercial regulations, we are one and the same people. In many other respects, the American people are one, and the government which is alone capable of controlling and managing their interest in all these respects, is the government of the Union. It is their government, and in that character they have no other. America has chosen to be, in many respects, and for many purposes, a nation; and for all these purposes, her government is complete; to all these objects, it is competent. The people have declared, that in the exercise of all powers given for these objects, it is supreme. It can, then, in effecting these objects, legitimately control all individuals or governments within the American territory. The constitution and laws of a state, so far as they are repugnant to the Constitution and laws of the United States, are absolutely void. These states are constituent parts of the United States. They are members of one great empire—for some purposes sovereign, for some purposes subordinate.

With that stirring declaration of an indivisible union, Marshall rejected Virginia's claim of immunity from the Supreme Court's jurisdiction.

Marshall's *Cohens* opinion served as a necessary complement to the Court's decision in *Martin v. Hunter's Lessee.* Together, they settled the issue of the Supreme Court's appellate judicial authority over criminal as well as civil decisions of state courts on matters involving federal law.

Having established the Supreme Court's jurisdiction in *Cohens,* Marshall was content, as he had been in *Marbury v. Madison,* to give his critics a victory on the merits. In *Marbury,* Marshall had ruled that Jefferson's secretary of state, James Madison, did not have to deliver Marbury's commission. In *Cohens,* Marshall accepted Webster's argument on behalf of the state of Virginia that the District of Columbia's lottery, authorized by congressional statute, was not intended to serve a national purpose, but only to further the local interests of the district.

The Court concluded it was a proper exercise of the sovereign power of Virginia to forbid the sale of D.C. lottery tickets within its boundaries, as it had done in its criminal statute.

Shortly after Marshall announced his decision in *Cohens,* Jefferson reiterated his concern about the Marshall Court in a letter to Spencer Roane. "The great object of my fear is the federal judiciary," he wrote. "Let the eye of vigilance never be closed." He need not have worried about the judge's vigilance. Roane was soon planning a published attack on Marshall's *Cohens* opinion, and he wrote former president James Madison to enlist his assistance in the enterprise. Madison declined to be drawn into the fierce political controversy. Unlike Jefferson or Roane, Madison had never held tenaciously to a rigid states'-rights ideology. When Roane argued that Virginia could deny the Court's jurisdiction in *Cohens,* Madison disagreed, taking the chief justice's position on the critical constitutional question. "On the abstract question whether the federal or the state decisions ought to prevail," he wrote Roane, "the sounder policy would be to yield to the claims of the former."

Undeterred, Roane wrote a series of essays for the *Richmond Enquirer* under the pseudonym Algernon Sidney in which he assailed Marshall's *Cohens* opinion as "a most monstrous and unexampled decision." The only explanation for the Court's perverse ruling, Roane wrote, was the justices' "love of power which all history informs us infects and corrupts those who possess it." The Marshall Court was at the "zenith of despotic power," Roane charged, singling out the Republican justices for particular attack. Roane accused them of being in lockstep with the "ultra-federal leader who is at the head of their court," and corrupted by their federal salaries to support the government that, in Jefferson's phrase, "feeds them."

Marshall reacted angrily, writing Story that the *Cohens* opinion had been attacked "with a degree of virulence superior even to that which was employed in the bank question." Two weeks later, after more of Roane's assaults on the Court had been published, Marshall wrote Story, "For coarseness and malignity Algernon Sidney surpasses all writers who have ever made pretensions to any decency of character." Marshall knew that Judge Roane was the author of the essays. The chief justice held out no hope that his Court opinion would be defended in Virginia's Republican-controlled press. As a result, Marshall lamented, Roane "will be supposed to be the champion of states' rights instead of being what he really is, the champion of dismemberment."

Story was convinced that Jefferson, not Roane, was the inspiration for the fusillade of published criticism of the Court. He told Marshall that he had seen a letter of Jefferson's displayed in a Boston bookstore next to a book entitled *The Republican,* written by a Pittsfield, Massachusetts, author named William Jarvis. Story said that in Jefferson's letter, which was written in praise of Jarvis's book, the former president had denied that the Court was the final authority on constitutional questions. Jefferson's "obvious design," Story wrote, was "to prostrate the judicial authority and annihilate all public reverence for its dignity." Jefferson's views "fill me alternately with indignation and melancholy," Story said. "Can he wish yet to have influence enough to destroy the government of his country?"

Jefferson's letter to Jarvis was not the insurrectionist document that Story claimed. To be sure, Jefferson refused to accord the justices the respect that Marshall and Story considered their due. "Our judges are as honest as other men, and not more so," Jefferson wrote Jarvis. "They have, with others, the same passions for party, for power, and the privilege of their corps." This caustic description of judges aside, Jefferson's letter only reiterated his long-held view that the judiciary, like the other branches of the federal government, should be accountable to the people. Jefferson believed that Marshall's grand pronouncements on the Court's role as the final arbiter of the Constitution thoroughly distorted the framers' intentions. Under Jefferson's reading of the Constitution, the Court could no more tell the president or Congress what was constitutional than the president or Congress could dictate the Constitution's meaning to the Court. Each branch was responsible, independently, for upholding the Constitution. If any erred egregiously, the people, through their federal and state representatives, could correct the error by constitutional amendment.

Story's suggestion that Jefferson's views, if widely shared, could destroy the nation struck Marshall as accurate and stimulated the chief justice to respond with his most sweeping denunciation of the nation's third president. "What you say of Mr. Jefferson's letter rather grieves than surprises me," Marshall wrote Story. "It grieves me because his influence is still so great that many, very many will adopt his opinions, however unsound they may be." Marshall claimed to understand the darkest recesses of Jefferson's mind: "He is among the most ambitious & I suspect among the most unforgiving of men. His great power is over the mass of the people, & this power is chiefly acquired by professions of democracy. Every check on the wild impulse of the moment is a check on his own power, & he is unfriendly to the source from which it flows. He looks, of course, with ill will at an independent judiciary."

Jefferson, meanwhile, had sent Roane a "cooked up" extract endorsing John Taylor's book expounding the most extreme states'-rights philosophy. In an open letter of praise for Taylor's work, Jefferson congratulated the author in extravagant terms, and took the occasion to emphasize that the federal and state governments represented independent sovereignties. "It is a fatal heresy to suppose that either our state governments are superior to the federal, or the federal to the states," he wrote. When there were disagreements between two equal sovereigns—the federal government and the states—it was best that a third, neutral party mediate the dispute, he concluded. No longer should the Marshall Court have the final constitutional word, as it had in *Martin, McCulloch,* and *Cohens.* Jefferson recommended that in the future a special convention of the people resolve the controversy.

Strong opposition to the *Cohens* decision was largely confined to the states'-rights citadel of Virginia. Charleston, South Carolina's *Southern Patriot,* for example, called the decision an illustration "of the true theory and intention of the Constitution." Although Jefferson's letter endorsing Taylor's states'-rights manifesto was published widely, it did not appear to have any tangible effect. The former president continued to search for ways to curb the Marshall Court. The best remedy, Jefferson wrote Governor James Pleasants of Virginia, was to amend the Constitution so that the justices would serve six-year terms, renewable by the president and both houses of Congress. But nothing came of Jefferson's suggestion.

In the year following the *Cohens* decision, Spencer Roane died and the Richmond Junto's published attacks on the Marshall Court ceased. And the Court's landmark decisions in *Cohens v. Virginia, McCulloch v. Maryland,* and *Martin v. Hunter's Lessee* settled uneasily into the fabric of

American constitutional law. In fact, sectionalism and the ominous debate over slavery would only intensify opposition from states'-rights advocates to Marshall's concept of union.

"Old men, I find, do not get over sprains and hurts quite as quickly as young ones," Marshall wrote to his wife, Polly, reporting an injury he sustained on the evening of February 19, 1824. The chief justice, sixty-nine years old, had stumbled over a cellar door after he returned to his lodgings from a dinner at President Monroe's official residence. He dislocated his shoulder, suffered a concussion, and was unconscious for fifteen minutes. "Although I feel no pain when perfectly still, yet I cannot get up and move about without difficulty & cannot put on my coat." But he reassured her that his doctors "say I mend a great deal faster than they expected." He was comforted daily by callers, including the president himself, as well as the wives of Monroe's Cabinet secretaries, who "have brought me more jelly than I can eat."

Hopes for Marshall's quick recuperation extended far beyond the chief justice's immediate circle of family, friends, and Washington acquaintances. His injury occurred shortly after the justices heard arguments in *Gibbons v. Ogden,* one of the most important cases of the entire Marshall Court era. That case, which again pitted states'-rights advocates against those championing broad federal authority, raised fundamental issues about Congress's authority to regulate commerce among the states (with repercussions that are still being debated by the justices of the Rehnquist Court in the twenty-first century).

The origin of the controversy in *Gibbons v. Ogden* dated back to 1808, the year when the New York legislature granted Robert Fulton and Robert Livingston the exclusive right to operate steamboats in New York waters, in order to encourage the development of steamboat technology. Fulton and Livingston had pioneered steam navigation, and their thirty-year monopoly was intended to allow them to exploit their invention commercially. But Connecticut and New Jersey lawmakers bristled at the New York monopoly. They retaliated by passing laws allowing their own state to grant steamboat monopolies and authorizing the seizure of vessels licensed in New York. The ill-will fomented by the competing state-imposed steamboat monopolies became so deep-seated, said U.S. Attorney General William Wirt when he argued *Gibbons* for the federal government, that the three mid-Atlantic states were "on the eve of civil war."

Once business partners, Thomas Gibbons and Aaron Ogden became courtroom adversaries after they offered competing ferry services between Elizabethtown, New Jersey, and New York City. As Gibbons was well aware, Ogden had been licensed by Fulton and Livingston to operate his ferry service under the terms of New York's steamboat monopoly. But Gibbons claimed higher legal authority for his service, that of the federal government, under a coasting statute passed by Congress in 1793. When Gibbons, in open defiance of New York's monopoly law, continued to operate his steamboat service, Ogden obtained an injunction from the New York courts ordering Gibbons to shut down his business. Gibbons appealed the injunction to the U.S. Supreme Court, and on February 4, 1824, the justices heard the first of five days of arguments in the case.

Virtually every important case argued before the Marshall Court produced a galaxy of the nation's finest lawyers, and *Gibbons v. Ogden* was no exception. Daniel Webster, representing Gibbons (with Attorney General William Wirt), proved to be the most influential advocate. He was determined to force the Court to confront the broadest possible constitutional argument in favor of the federal government.

New York's steamboat-monopoly law was null and void, Webster asserted, because Congress alone had the authority to regulate commerce on the navigable waters of the United States. Webster described Congress's authority to regulate commerce in the most expansive terms. It was full and complete, he said, embracing not only the buying and selling of goods, but also navigation. It included all commercial transactions between states. And it was exclusive, leaving no room for state regulation.

After Webster and the other attorneys completed their arguments in *Gibbons,* Marshall sustained his injury, sending tremors of anxiety through the press that was following "the great Steamboat Case" closely. Could Marshall possibly write an opinion for the Court, or would he, as rumored, assign the important judicial task to his colleague Justice Story? On March 3, only two weeks after he lay unconscious from his fall, Marshall entered the thronged courtroom, his arm still in a sling. He was weak and moved slowly to his chair. His voice was low and unsteady as he began to read his opinion for a unanimous Court.

The opinion belied the debilitated physical condition of its author. It was a muscular pronouncement of broad federal power. Marshall described Congress's authority to regulate commerce "with a breadth never yet exceeded," Justice Robert Jackson observed 118 years later. The chief justice borrowed some of Daniel Webster's arguments, even his very words, to assert that the framers intended for Congress to have full, unobstructed authority to regulate the nation's commercial relations. But then, as in so many of Marshall's other opinions, the chief justice decisively departed from an influential lawyer's arguments to make the opinion his own. He admitted that Webster's argument that Congress possessed the exclusive authority to regulate commerce was tempting, but said he did not have to make a final judgment on it in this case. Instead, he said that the case turned crucially on the conflict between New York's steamboat-monopoly law and the congressional coasting statute. The New York law could not stand, because the Constitution made the federal law supreme.

In the last paragraph of his opinion, Marshall issued a pointed warning to outspoken states'-rights advocates like Jefferson and John Taylor. He conceded that "ingenious minds" could, by the narrowest possible interpretation of the Constitution, drastically reduce the powers of the federal government. But to indulge in that "refined and metaphysical reasoning," Marshall wrote, would "explain away the Constitution of our country and leave it a magnificent structure to look at, but totally unfit for use."

The *Gibbons* decision was especially discouraging to Jefferson. Not only had Chief Justice Marshall announced another stunning nationalistic decision, but Jefferson's best hope for an independent voice on the Court, Republican Justice William Johnson, wrote a concurring opinion that went even further than the chief justice in describing Congress's broad powers to regulate interstate commerce. Johnson concluded that Congress's authority was exclusive, as Webster had argued.

Marshall's opinion in *Gibbons v. Ogden* put to rest for all time any notion that the nation could return to the Balkanized commercial relations among the states that had existed under the unsuccessful Articles of Confederation. The effect of the Court's decision was immediate. Only a year after New York's steamboat monopoly was broken up by the Court, the number of steamboats plying their commercial trade in New York's waters had increased from six to forty-three. *Gibbons* effectively made New York City the commercial center of the nation, opening up the Hudson River and Long Island Sound to a brisk, unfettered commercial traffic. Marshall's decision would later become the basis for extending Congress's interstate regulations to newer modes of transportation, beginning with railroads, and to new forms of commerce, including nuclear power, again demonstrating Marshall's genius for glimpsing the nation's future.

Epilogue

IN 1821, when Jefferson was seventy-seven years old, he sat for the famous American portrait painter Thomas Sully. As befitted an American icon, he struck the pose of a quiet visionary. His hazel eyes looked steadily outward, his mouth was fixed in determined repose. The hair was lustrous, brown hues flecked with red and outlined by reddish-blond locks curled around his ears and over his neck. His white collar was framed by a scarlet vest that was almost fully covered by a dark fur-trimmed overcoat. Like Houdon's likeness of Jefferson, sculpted decades earlier, Sully's portrait projected the image of greatness in the style of the idealized Roman emperors of the ancient world.

Jefferson, in his old age, was far removed from Sully's portrait. His health was precarious and his appearance was fragile. His hair was completely gray and his complexion blotchy, a result of recurring digestive and intestinal disorders. The handsome overcoat in Sully's painting was rarely seen. More typically, Jefferson wore a plain gray waistcoat and loose-fitting pantaloons tucked carelessly into his riding boots.

The year when Sully painted Jefferson's portrait, the former president fell from a step and broke his left arm. Though he had gradually reduced his physical activity over the years since his retirement from the presidency, even after the accident he refused to give up his afternoon ride on his trusted horse, Old Eagle. The horse was led to the back terrace of Monticello, where the master mounted by grabbing the reins with one hand and painfully swinging his body onto the saddle. The daily horseback ride gave Jefferson the fleeting feeling of robust health and independence, but, like Sully's portrait, it was mostly illusion. Jefferson was sick in body and spirit, sometimes wishing aloud that he had not outlived most of his distinguished contemporaries of the American Revolution. "Man, like the fruit he eats, has his period of ripeness," he wrote his former secretary of war, Henry Dearborn. "Like that, too, if he continues longer hanging to the stem, it is but an useless and unsightly appendage."

Jefferson's finances had gone from bad to desperate. He had sold his magnificent sixty-five-hundred-volume book collection to Congress for the undervalued sum of $24,000. When he ran out of parcels of land to sell to preserve his ownership of Monticello, he began to put his slaves on the auction block. A crushing financial blow was delivered after Jefferson, already deeply in debt, signed two $10,000 notes taken out by his neighbor Wilson Cary Nicholas. Soon afterward, the financial Panic of 1819 hit Virginia with devastating force. Both the state and national banks squeezed debtors like Nicholas and Jefferson, neither of whom could honor his obligations. Jefferson's signature on Nicholas's defaulted notes alone cost him $1,300 a year in interest, an amount that pushed him close to bankruptcy. In 1821, three Virginia banks turned Jefferson down for loans.

Despite the financial turmoil at Monticello, there were still reasons for Jefferson to savor his old age. His daily regimen remained essentially intact as he approached eighty. He rose with the sun, bathed his feet in cold water to ward off colds, and spent his mornings pruning the flowers in his garden and answering his correspondence. After his afternoon horseback ride, he dined with friends and dignitaries who made the pilgrimage to his mountain retreat. And he delighted in entertaining and advising his swarm of grandchildren who resided at the estate. Before retiring for the night, Jefferson indulged one of his great pleasures, reading, usually perusing classic works of Greek and Roman history and philosophy.

Jefferson insisted on responding to every person who wrote him, no matter the writer's status or subject matter. In the best of times it had been a chore, but now it was an increasing burden: in retirement, he received more than a thousand letters a year. But there were exceptions to the drudgery, most notably when he put pen to paper to write his old political nemesis John Adams. "You and I ought not to die, before we have explained ourselves to each other," Adams had written Jefferson. And that suggestion, put forward gingerly by the nation's second president, stimulated a correspondence between the two founding fathers over the last fourteen years of their lives that represents the most brilliant exchange of letters between public men in American history. They traded opinions on words (Jefferson advocated the introduction of commonly used American words like "belittle" into the language), books (both admired and reread Thucydides and Tacitus), and political ideology. Neither man abandoned his conviction that *his* party and *his* presidency embodied the true spirit of the American Revolution.

Jefferson had always perceived the battle between Republicans and Federalists as a moral struggle between good and evil, and he did not doubt who was on the side of the angels. In the early 1820s, the Federalists were no longer a viable opposition party, but the threat they had represented to the republic, in Jefferson's eyes, persisted. Although he no longer called his political enemies "monarchists," preferring instead the appellation "consolidationists," the meaning was the same: the Federalists still endangered what he saw as the true principles of republican government by upsetting the necessary equilibrium between the federal and state governments.

In Jefferson's last years, John Marshall, above all other opposition leaders, retained the power to undermine the former president's republican principles. The Marshall Court's decisions appalled Jefferson, and the specter of Marshall manipulating his Republican colleagues on the Court continued to infuriate and bewilder him. There was no worse danger to the republic, Jefferson had warned his first appointee to the Court, Associate Justice William Johnson, than "the consolidation of our government by the noiseless, and, therefore, unalarming instrumentality of the Supreme Court." But nothing, it seemed, could deter the chief justice.[*]

---

[*]In 1824, for example, Marshall wrote the Court's opinion not only in *Gibbons v. Ogden,* but also in *Osborn v. Bank of the United States,* in which the chief justice again rejected a state's claim that it could tax the national bank and that it was immune from federal jurisdiction under the Eleventh Amendment.

Not long before he died on July 4, 1826, Jefferson considered which of his many public accomplishments should be inscribed on his tombstone. Understandably, he ruled out any reference to his battles with John Marshall during or after his presidency. In his struggles with the chief justice, Jefferson had come off second best, as his repeated denunciations of Marshall's opinions attested. At the time of the *Marbury* decision, Jefferson did not appear overly concerned about the implications of Marshall's opinion. But upon reflection, and after Marshall began to speak for a unanimous Court in one nationalist decision after another, Jefferson recognized that the chief justice presented a formidable, and seemingly invincible, enemy. Jefferson's states'-rights philosophy was subjected to one humiliation after another in the decisions of the Marshall Court.

Jefferson's insistence during his retirement years that the federal government and the states represented two independent and equal sovereigns claimed the support of the most radical Republicans. Moderates like Madison and Monroe, though Jefferson's longtime allies, understood the need for a strong federal government. Madison, in particular, left no doubt that he believed that, in a clash between federal and state authority under the Constitution, the states must defer to the supremacy of the federal government.

Jefferson's states'-rights philosophy found new life in later generations, but the uses to which it was put probably would have appalled the nation's third president. Jefferson was, after all, committed to a *United* States, though his prescription for securing a strong union was radically different from Marshall's. But in the decade after Jefferson's death, John C. Calhoun developed a strain of his states'-rights philosophy to justify the secession of Southern states from the union. And in the next century, segregationist governors from the South, such as Arkansas's Orval Faubus, trumpeted states' rights to justify their defiance of U.S. Supreme Court desegregation decrees. In response to Faubus's recalcitrance, a unanimous decision by the Warren Court in 1958, citing with approval Marshall's *Marbury* opinion, declared that the Court was the final arbiter of the Constitution.

Most recently, a five-member conservative majority of the Rehnquist Court has introduced its own expansive version of states' rights. Led by Chief Justice William H. Rehnquist, this narrow majority has rewritten modern constitutional doctrine to narrow the scope of Congress's authority under the commerce clause. But whereas Jefferson's states'-rights philosophy was developed in 1798, in part, to protect individual liberties from incursions by the federal government, the Rehnquist Court conservatives have expressed no such intent. In fact, the results of the Rehnquist Court majority's decisions have often been to cut off governmental protection of individuals, as it did in declaring unconstitutional the federal Violence Against Women Act. The Rehnquist Court conservatives, moreover, are highly selective in the application of their states'-rights philosophy, as dramatically demonstrated in their decision in *Bush v. Gore,* which halted a Florida Supreme Court mandated recount of votes and effectively handed the 2000 presidential election to George W. Bush. One can only imagine Jefferson's reaction had Chief Justice Marshall and his Federalist colleagues delivered a Court opinion that decided the 1800 presidential election in favor of John Adams or Jefferson's Republican colleague Aaron Burr.

In assessing his legacy, Jefferson did not mention his aggressive strategy in 1798 (in collaboration with Madison) that effectively drew the public's attention to the oppressive Alien and Sedition Acts and helped lead to his election as president. He also excluded reference to his successful, and essentially moderate, policies during his first presidential term, which made his reelection a foregone conclusion. He did not even call attention to his part in consummating negotiations for the Louisiana Purchase.

In the end, Jefferson reduced his most notable public achievements to three. First was his authorship of the Declaration of Independence. Second was his drafting of the Virginia Statute of Religious Freedom. The third memorable accomplishment was a work-in-progress during his last years, the founding of the University of Virginia. In retrospect, Jefferson's choices were wise. He recognized then, as have generations of Americans since, that these deeds would serve as important symbols for the nation's values. His concept of a great public university at Charlottesville underscored his belief in the capacity of every citizen to improve through knowledge and education. And his drafts of the Declaration of Independence and the Statute for Religious Freedom were not only brilliantly crafted documents, but also transcending literary monuments to representative democracy and individual liberties.

In the spring of 1826, Harvard Professor Jared Sparks traveled to Richmond to confer with the world's foremost authority on George Washington, Chief Justice Marshall. Sparks, who was editing Washington's papers, approached Marshall's home through a broken wooden gate and asked an old woman who answered the front door where he could find the master of the house. She pointed to a small brick building in one corner of the yard. When Sparks knocked on the door, he remembered, "it was opened by a tall, venerable-looking man, dressed with extreme plainness, and having an air of affability in his manners." The chief justice welcomed Sparks, and for the next hour, the two men discussed Washington's letters and other scholarly matters of mutual interest. At the end of the session, Sparks later wrote, "I retired much pleased with the urbanity and kindly manners of the Chief Justice." He concluded, "There is a consistency in all things about him; his house, grounds, office [and] himself bear marks of a primitive simplicity and plainness rarely to be seen combined."

By his own melancholy admission, Marshall crossed over from the "right side of seventy" the year of Sparks's visit, and he spoke increasingly of the aging process. During the Court's 1826 term, he wrote Polly from Washington that his tired body was content to sit by a warm fire wrapped in a wool cloak. "A person as old as I am feels that his home is his place of most comfort and his old wife the companion in the world in whose society he is most happy." In his declining years, he allowed his mind to wander nostalgically to his youthful courtship of Polly. He fondly remembered her as a teenage beauty at balls in Yorktown and Williamsburg, her rejection of his initial advances, and, after her cousin had sent Marshall a lock of Polly's hair, his renewed amorous pursuit.

While the Court was in session, Marshall assured Polly, his daily regimen remained unchanged. He arose early, walked three miles before 7 A.M., then settled down to a day of study of the cases to be argued before the Court. His day usually ended with a hearty dinner and a bottle of Madeira shared with his judicial colleagues before he retired for a solid night's sleep. Marshall conceded that his dronelike life in Washington was occasionally relieved by a social engagement or two, often at the invitation of President John Quincy Adams.

Like Jefferson, Marshall was plagued in his old age by incessant financial worries. But whereas Jefferson was consumed by his own debts, Marshall fought to keep his wayward sons afloat. The reckless spending habits of the chief justice's son John was a source of particular concern. "I am very much pressed in consequence of my son John's extravagance," the chief justice wrote a banker who had transferred funds from Marshall's account to cover John's latest debt. A second Marshall son, James, appeared to be no more responsible than his brother, John. "I am surprised as well as grieved at the magnitude of your debts," the chief justice wrote James. "I should be glad to hear that John also was paying off debts instead of spending his money at Baltimore and other places of, what he thinks, amusement."

But just as Jefferson's correspondence with John Adams helped lighten the physical and financial burdens of old age, Marshall's exchange of letters with Justice Story (when the Court was not in session) served as an invigorating tonic for the chief justice. Sometimes, the two men simply thanked each other for small gifts (a quintal of cod from Story in Massachusetts; a small cask of Virginia hams from Marshall). When he heard that Story had listed his favorite female authors in a speech to the Phi Beta Kappa Society, Marshall could not resist a gentle ribbing. "I was a little mortified," Marshall wrote Story, "to find that you had not admitted the name of Miss [Jane] Austen into your list of favorites." Marshall then argued his case for Austen's inclusion: "Her flights are not lofty, she does not soar on eagle's wings, but she is pleasing, interesting, equable, and yet amusing." With mock sternness, he concluded, "I count on your making some apology for this omission."

More often than not, the Marshall-Story correspondence was a serious exchange of compatible opinions (unlike the Jefferson-Adams letters) about politics and the future of the republic. Marshall feared the rise to national power of Andrew Jackson and deplored the attacks by Jackson's rabid supporters on President John Quincy Adams and his secretary of state, Henry Clay. Much to Marshall's chagrin, his preference for the reelection of John Quincy Adams in 1828 was published in a Democratic newspaper in Maryland, which quoted the chief justice as saying "Should Jackson be elected, I should look upon the government as virtually dissolved." Marshall quickly issued a statement denying the quote, but he admitted that he favored the reelection of Adams.

By 1830, the secessionist movement led by John C. Calhoun of South Carolina (now Jackson's vice president) was gaining momentum in the South. Increasingly concerned about the movement, Marshall was both surprised and pleased that President Jackson made a public toast to the union, glowering in Calhoun's direction. The chief justice wrote Story that he was also gratified to read an article in the *North American Review* by former President Madison clarifying the meaning of his Virginia Resolution of 1798 and unequivocally supporting federal supremacy. "Mr. Madison is himself again," wrote an approving chief justice. "He avows the opinions of his best days and must be pardoned for his oblique insinuations that some of the opinions of our Court are not approved. Contrast this delicate hint with the language Mr. Jefferson has applied to us."

Marshall never altered his negative opinion of Jefferson. He reacted scornfully to Jefferson's letters published posthumously by his grandson, in which Jefferson advocated popular sovereignty, condemned the policies of the Federalists, and made "repeated unwarrantable aspersions on myself." Marshall wrote Henry Lee that he had long questioned the wisdom of Jefferson's policies and principles, dating back to Jefferson's term as Washington's secretary of state. "I have never believed firmly in his infallibility," Marshall noted. "I have never thought him a particularly wise, sound, and practical statesman." And Jefferson had done nothing since his years in Washington's Cabinet to make Marshall change his "mode of thinking."

The last years of Marshall's life were no happier than Jefferson's. His health deteriorated, and his spirits did not recover from the death of his beloved Polly in 1831. He continued to be pessimistic about the survival of the union, for the secessionist movement refused to die. At the Court, the astonishing unanimity of the justices, which Marshall had skillfully nurtured over the years, had vanished; three or four justices regularly wrote separate opinions. And the Court majority began to shift the constitutional balance from the federal government to the states (a development that accelerated under the leadership of Marshall's successor, Chief Justice Roger Taney). At the same time, the Court's prestige appeared to be declining. One of Marshall's most powerful decisions, taking the state of Georgia to task for ignoring the terms of a federal treaty with the Cherokee Indians, was openly defied by the state and criticized by President Jackson.

"My worn out frame cannot, I believe, be repaired," Marshall wrote court reporter Richard Peters, Jr., on the last day of April 1835. "Could I find the mill which would grind old men and restore youth, I might indulge the hope of recovering my former vigor and taste for the enjoyments of life. But as that is impossible, I must be content with patching myself up and dragging on as well as I can." He died in office less than three months later.

Marshall was, by nature, a modest man, and he seemed genuinely uncomfortable in contemplating his place in American history. This discomfort was apparent when Justice Story in 1827 asked Marshall to provide an autobiographical sketch. "The events of my life are too unimportant and have too little interest for any person not of my immediate family to render them worth communicating or preserving," Marshall wrote Story. He nonetheless overcame his reluctance and sent Story a lean, but revealing, narrative on his life before his appointment to the office of chief justice. Besides providing a factual account of the first forty-five years of his life, Marshall reiterated his conviction that a strong federal government was essential to an enduring union.

On his tombstone, Marshall chose to have recorded only the dates of his birth, of his marriage to Polly, and of his death. It was left to others to enumerate his achievements. After Marshall died, Justice Story wrote a poetic tribute to Marshall, "the great, the good, the wise." Even political leaders with different philosophies praised Marshall. His judicial opinions, said President Andrew Jackson, "gave him a rank among the greatest men of his age."

Marshall's legacy did not depend on eulogies. His circuit-court opinion in *U.S. v. Burr* was later cited as precedent for the U.S. Supreme Court's position that no one, not even the president, is above the law. It has been a constitutional truism that resonated most dramatically 167 years after the Burr trial in *U.S. v. Nixon,* when Chief Justice Warren

Burger, writing for a unanimous Court, rejected President Richard Nixon's claim of executive privilege, insisting that he must turn over the Watergate tapes to the special prosecutor. Less than two weeks later, Nixon released the tapes. And three days later, he resigned the presidency.

Marshall's indispensable contributions to the nation are, moreover, found throughout the early volumes of the *United States Reports,* the official volumes of Supreme Court decisions. They begin with his opinion in *Marbury v. Madison,* in which the chief justice established the independence of the federal judiciary, and include Marshall's later judicial pronouncements, which translated his commitment to a strong federal government into constitutional law, from *McCulloch v. Maryland* to *Gibbons v. Ogden.*

He was the fourth leader of the Supreme Court, but, because of his foundational Court opinions, he is known to this day as "the great Chief Justice."

Source Notes

The bibliography on Jefferson and Marshall is immense and too great to reproduce here. I have tried to limit the source notes to primary source materials and the basic secondary works that I have used. I have relied primarily on the writings of Jefferson found in three major published works: Julian P. Boyd, et al., eds., *The Papers of Thomas Jefferson,* in 28 volumes; Paul L. Ford, ed., *The Works of Thomas Jefferson,* in twelve volumes; and A. Lipscomb and A. Bergh, eds., *The Writings of Thomas Jefferson,* in twenty volumes. I have also used materials from the Jefferson collections at the Alderman Library at the University of Virginia, Charlottesville, the Massachusetts Historical Society in Boston, and the Library of Congress. *The Papers of John Marshall* are published in ten volumes. I have also studied the Marshall letters at the College of William and Mary, Williamsburg, Virginia, where Charles F. Hobson is editing the final volumes of the Marshall papers for publication. The major biographical work on Jefferson is Dumas Malone's six-volume series, *Jefferson and His Time.* I also found Merrill Peterson's *Thomas Jefferson and the New Nation* (1970) especially useful. The standard biographical study on Marshall is Albert J. Beveridge's four-volume work, *The Life of John Marshall;* an excellent and more objective Marshall biography is Jean Edward Smith's *John Marshall: Definer of a Nation* (1996).

The source notes are, for the most part, self-explanatory. I have used acronyms to identify frequently cited sources. Thus, a citation from page

179 of volume nine of *The Papers of John Marshall* becomes JMP9p179. U.S. Supreme Court decisions and law-review articles follow legal methods of citation: *Marbury v. Madison,* 1 Cranch 137 (1803), means that the Supreme Court decided the case in 1803 and that the opinion begins at page 137 of the first volume of decisions reported by William Cranch. Later Supreme Court decisions are simply reported by the official volume number of the U.S. Reports—e.g., *U.S. v. Nixon* is cited as 418 U.S. 683 (1974). A law-review article cited as 100 *Yale L.J.* 229 (1990) means that the article was published in 1990 and can be found at page 229 of volume one hundred of the *Yale Law Journal.*

Abbreviations Used

AB–Albert J. Beveridge, *The Life of John Marshall*
DM–Dumas Malone, *Jefferson and His Time*
JES–Jean Edward Smith, *John Marshall: Definer of a Nation*
JMP–*Papers of John Marshall,* Charles F. Hobson, et al., eds.
MP–Merrill Peterson, *Thomas Jefferson and the New Nation*
TJPLC–Thomas Jefferson Papers, Library of Congress
TJPAL–Thomas Jefferson Papers, Alderman Library, University of
　Virginia
TJPMHS–Thomas Jefferson Papers, Massachusetts Historical Society,
　Boston
TJPJB–*Papers of Thomas Jefferson,* Julian P. Boyd, et al., eds.
TJWPF–*Works of Thomas Jefferson,* Paul L. Ford, editor
TJWL&B–*Writings of Thomas Jefferson,* A. Lipscomb and A. Berg, eds.

Page

9　"He [Jefferson] is among . . ." John Marshall to Joseph Story, Aug.
　13, 1821, JMP9p179.
9　"The great object . . ." Thomas Jefferson (TJ) to Spencer Roane,
　March 9, 1821, TJWPF12p201.

Prologue

15 "usurper, plunderer . . ." Declaration of Independence, TJPJB1 pp429–32.

15 "waged cruel . . ." Ibid., p. 426; Jefferson's reference was to the slave trade, which he blamed on George III.

15 Jefferson recalled with bitterness, TJPJB9p364.

16 modern historians, Willard S. Randall, *Thomas Jefferson: A Life* (1993), pp. 412, 413; C. R. Richardson, "The Fragile Memory: Thomas Jefferson at the Court of George III," *Eighteenth Century Life,* vol. 6 (1981), pp. 1–16.

16 meeting with Lord Carmarthen, TJPJB9p364.

18 "That nation . . ." TJ to John Page, May 4, 1786, ibid., p. 446.

18 "wretched" Ibid., p. 445.

23 Henry urged, Jonathan Eliot, ed., *The Debates in the Several State Conventions on the Adoption of the Federal Constitution,* vol. 3 (1907), pp. 41–43.

24 "America as . . ." John Marshall, *An Autobiographical Sketch,* John S. Adams, ed. (1937), pp. 9, 10.

25 "a well regulated democracy . . ." JMP1pp256–70.

25 "highest veneration . . ." Eliot, ed., *Debates,* p. 578.

30 "would swallow up . . ." TJPJB9p278.

31 "If the end . . ." H. Syrett, ed., *Papers of Alexander Hamilton,* vol. 8 (1965), p. 107.

32 "the heats . . ." TJ to Martha Jefferson Randolph, March 22, 1792, TJPJB23p326.

33 "A womanish . . ." AH to E. Carrington, Syrett, *Hamilton Papers,* vol. 11, p. 439.

33 "to occupy themselves . . ." TJ memoranda of conversations with the President, 1792, TJPJB23p186.

34 "nothing more than . . ." TJ to Edward Rutledge, Nov. 30, 1795, TJPJB28p542.

35 ". . . the mask of Republicanism . . ." TJ to Madison, Nov. 26, 1795, TJWPF8p197.

37 "war message" See TJ to John Dawson, March 21, 1798, TJPJB10p99.

37 "men who were Samsons..." TJ to PM, April 24, 1796,
    TJWPF8p235.

1: "Swindling Propositions"

39 "the spitting beast" James Morton Smith, ed., *The Republic of Letters:
    The Correspondence Between Thomas Jefferson and James Madison,
    1776–1826,* vol. 2 (1995), p. 997.
40 TJ's reaction to House action, Feb. 15, 1798, ibid.
40 "If the dispositions..." TJ to Horatio Gates, Feb. 21, 1798,
    TJWPF8p371.
40 "plunder us..." Madison to TJ, Feb. 12, 1798, Smith, *Republic of Let-
    ters,* vol. 2, p. 1018.
41 "insane," "the war party" TJ to Madison, March 21, 1798,
    TJWPF8p386.
42 "The communications..." TJ to JE, April 11, 1798, TJPAL.
42 "swindling propositions" Ibid.
42 "similar propositions..." Ibid.
42 "the country..." TJ to JE, May 6, 1798, TJPAL.
43 "They have no idea..." TJ to MJE, June 6, 1798, TJPAL.
43 "It is even whispered..." TJ to JP, June 6, 1798, TJPAL.
43 "The journey..." Marshall to CCP, April 15, 1798, JMP3p463.
44 "the greatest God-send..." TJ, "Anas," TJWPF1p355.
44 "the Hon. J. MARSHALL..." *New York Commercial Advertiser,* June 18,
    1798.
45 "No doubt..." TJ to Madison, June 21, 1798, TJWPF8p439.
46 "You know..." TJ to EP, Jan. 29, 1799, TJWPF9p27.
46 "What an occasion..." *Aurora,* June 21, 1798.
46 "Th: Jefferson..." JMP3p471.
47 "J. Marshall..." Ibid., p. 472.
47 "not with real..." Marshall to TP, ibid., p. 485.
48 "unawed by power..." Ibid., p. 468.
48 "receives your matured approbation..." Ibid., p. 471.
48 "Millions for defense..." AB2p348.
48 "The negotiations..." Ibid., p. 351.

2: "The Reign of Witches"

49 "to put our vessel . . ." TJ to JM, Jan. 1, 1797, TJWPF8p262.

50 "His Highness . . ." Richard N. Rosenfeld, *American Aurora* (1997), p. 3.

50 "We are wonderfully . . ." James Morton Smith, *Freedom's Fetters: The Alien and Sedition Laws and American Civil Liberties* (1956), p. 9.

50 "a spirit of party . . ." DM3p375.

51 "worthy of . . ." MPp604.

51 "They have brought . . ." TJ to JM, June 7, 1798, TJWPF8p434.

51 "being driven . . ." Smith, *Freedom's Fetters,* p. 142.

52 "May he . . ." MPp606.

52 "from a legal . . ." TJ to P. Fitzhugh, June 4, 1797, TJWPF8p302.

53 "wild Irishman" Smith, *Freedom's Fetters,* p. 224.

54 "to the seditious . . ." Ibid., p. 229.

55 "screen from scrutiny . . ." Ibid., p. 250.

55 ". . . vicious industry . . ." Ibid., p. 267.

56 "viewed by . . ." Marshall to TP, Aug. 11, 1798, JMP3p485.

57 For President Jefferson's attitude toward seditious libel, see Leonard W. Levy, *Jefferson and Civil Liberties: The Darker Side* (1963).

57 "To preserve . . ." TJ to W. Mumford, June 18, 1799, TJPLC.

58 On TJ-Madison collaboration on Kentucky and Virginia Resolutions, see Adrienne Koch, *Jefferson and Madison: The Great Collaboration* (1950); Adrienne Koch and Harry Ammon, "The Virginia and Kentucky Resolutions: An Episode in Jefferson's and Madison's Defense of Civil Liberties," *William and Mary Quarterly,* vol. 5 (1948); DM3pp395–409.

59 "where powers are assumed . . ." Draft of Kentucky Resolutions, TJPLC.

60 "In every free . . ." TJ to JT, June 1, 1798, TJWPF8p431.

61 "I think . . ." TJ to Madison, Nov. 17, 1798, ibid., p. 457.

3: A Sense of Duty

64 "I have been . . ." Marshall to PM, Aug. 18, 1798, JMP3p363.

64 "a haughty . . ." Ibid., p. 482.

65   "Before this reaches you . . ." Marshall to GW, March 8, 1798, ibid., p. 399.

65   "the eyes of the blindest . . ." GW to TP, April 16, 1798, Worthington C. Ford, ed., *The Writings of George Washington,* vol. 13 (1889), p. 495.

66   "there seems . . ." James Morton Smith, *Freedom's Fetters,* p. 285.

66   "the domineering spirit . . ." AB2p357.

67   "a considerable riot . . ." Ibid., p. 354.

67   On Marshall's visit to GW, see James K. Paulding, *A Life of Washington,* vol. 2, (1835), pp. 191, 192; see also AB2pp374–79; JES pp240–42.

67   "considerations which are . . ." Marshall to TP, Sept. 9, 1798, JMP3p508.

68   "He [Washington] had . . ." John Marshall, *An Autobiographical Sketch,* pp. 28, 29.

69   "dancing around bonfires" James T. Callender, *The Prospect Before Us* (1800), pp. 126, 127.

69   For *Gazette* questions and Marshall's responses, see JMP3pp502, 503.

71   "John Marshall . . ." AB2p390.

71   "mysterious and unpardonable . . ." Ibid., p. 391.

71   "If General Marshall . . ." Ibid., p. 392.

72   "Notwithstanding . . ." Ibid., p. 396.

72   "a punishment . . ." Marshall to TP, Oct. 15, 1798, JMP3p516.

72   Clopton was called "anarchist . . ." AB2p397.

72   rumor by "Buckskin" *Virginia Gazette,* Oct. 9, 1798.

72   Pickering proposed prosecution, JMP3p497.

73   "The real French party . . ." Marshall to TP, Oct. 22, 1798, p. 520.

73   "For my own part . . ." TJ to STM, Oct. 11, 1798, TJWPF8p450.

74   "the very best . . ." TJ to JT, Nov. 26, 1798, TJWPF8p481.

74   "in case of . . ." Adrienne Koch, *Jefferson and Madison,* p. 190.

74   "to concur with . . ." Ibid., p. 191.

74   "never saw . . ." AB2p400.

74   For the Federalists' defense, see ibid., pp. 402–6.

75   Beveridge wrote that Marshall was author, Ibid., p. 402.

75   Later scholars suggested Lee, see JMP3pp499, 500; JESp601n.

75   "to a very pernicious . . ." GW to Marshall, Dec. 30, 1798, JMP3p531.

75 " 'Tis certainly . . ." Marshall to GW, Jan. 8, 1799, JMP4p3.

76 "with great . . ." TJ to EG, Jan. 26, 1799, TJWPF9p15.

78 "I must hope . . ." Marshall to EG, Nov. 12, 1798, JMP3p521.

78 Marshall's deposition, Nov. 12, 1798, ibid., p. 521.

79 "an absolute . . ." Marshall to GW, Jan. 8, 1799, JMP4p4.

80 Henry endorsement of Marshall, AB2p412; JES248.

81 For TJ's opinion of PH, see MPp43; TJ to T. Coxe, May 21, 1799, TJ to EP, April 22, 1799, both in TJWPF9p68.

81*n* "Still . . ." TJ to T. Coxe, May 21, 1799, TJWPF9p70.

81 "Marshall's romance" TJWPF9p65.

81 "The fate of my election . . ." Marshall to James Marshall, April 3, 1799, JMP4p10.

81 On the Richmond election day, see AB2pp413–15; JESpp249, 250.

83 "With infinite pleasure . . ." GW to Marshall, May 5, 1799, JMP4p13.

83 "marks a taint . . ." TJ to AS, May 14, 1799, TJWPF9p67.

83 "certain federalists . . ." TJ to T. Coxe, May 21, 1799, ibid., p. 69.

84 "The consequence . . ." Marshall to George Washington, May 16, 1799, JMP4p15.

84 "There never . . ." AB2p419.

4: Defending the President

85 "The army and navy . . ." TJ to TMR, Jan. 17, 1799, TJPMHS.

86 "a mere old woman . . ." Page Smith, *John Adams,* vol. 2 (1962), p. 1000.

87 "Surprise . . ." AB2p424.

87 "graveled . . ." TJ to Madison, Feb. 19, 1799, TJWPF9p53.

87 "grudgingly . . ." TJ to Monroe, Feb. 19, 1799, ibid., p. 56.

88 "It appears to me . . ." Marshall to TP, Aug. 25, 1799, JMP4p22.

88 Marshall's response to JA's address, JMP4p39.

90 "Our Washington . . ." Ibid., p. 46.

90 "I can tell you . . ." Marshall to James Marshall, Dec. 16, 1799, JMP4p44.

91 "If they are deterred . . ." Ibid.

91 "I hope . . ." Marshall to JA, Dec. 29, 1799, JMP4p50.

92   "dexterous maneuver" TJ to Edward Livingston, April 30, 1800, TJWPF9p132.

92   On the Robbins case, see 10 *Annals of Congress,* 6th Cong. 1st Sess. (1800); JMP4pp82–109; for the modern research on the case, see Larry D. Cress, "The Jonathan Robbins Incident: Extradition and Separation of Powers in the Adams Administration," 111 *Essex Institute Historical Collection* 99 (1975); Ruth Wedgwood, "The Revolutionary Martyrdom of Jonathan Robbins," 100 *Yale L. J.* 229 (1990).

95   "BRITISH . . ." *Aurora,* Aug. 12, 1799.

95   "extreme impropriety" *Aurora,* Oct. 9, 1799.

95   Jefferson congratulated Pinckney, TJ to CP, Oct. 29, 1799, TJWPF9p87.

96   "unjust, impolitic . . ." 10 *Annals,* 6th Cong., 1st Sess., p. 511.

96   Marshall's rebuttal argument, Ibid., pp. 596–618; see also JMP4 pp82–109.

97   "The case really was . . ." Marshall to RG, March 16, 1800, JMP4p114.

98   "one of the most . . ." Joseph Story, "Eulogy to John Marshall," in John F. Dillon, ed., *John Marshall: Life, Character and Judicial Service,* vol. 3 (1903), pp. 357, 358.

99   For reports of Gallatin's silence, see AB2p473; JESp262.

99   Recent research, Cress, "Robbins Incident"; Wedgwood, "Revolutionary Martyrdom."

99   "Had Thomas Nash . . ." JMP4p109.

101 "perverseness . . ." Ralph A. Brown, *The Presidency of John Adams* (1975), p. 176.

101 "his enemies . . ." Ibid.

103 "The office . . ." John Marshall, *An Autobiographical Sketch,* pp. 28, 29.

5: Prelude to a Revolution

104 "began to enter into . . ." TJ to Madison, Feb. 26, 1799, TJWPF9p61.

104 "the X.Y.Z. delusion" TJ to John Taylor, Nov. 26, 1798, TJWPF8p480.

104 "Firmness . . ." TJ to Madison, Jan. 30, 1799, TJWPF9p31.

105 "express in affectionate . . ." TJ to WCN, Sept. 5, 1799, ibid., p. 80.

106 Republican prospects, TJ to CP, Oct. 29, 1799, ibid., p. 86.

106 "monarchising" TJ to Elbridge Gerry, Jan. 26, 1799, ibid., p. 17.

107 "You have seen . . ." TJ to WB, Feb. 2, 1800, TJPAL.

107 "necessity to rally . . ." Ibid.

107 "our Bonaparte" TJ to Thomas Mann Randolph, Feb. 2, 1800, TJWPF9p111.

107 "Of the sacredness . . ." TJ to JB, Jan. 29, 1800, ibid., p. 106.

108 "scribblers"; "Chief Juggler" James Morton Smith, *Freedom's Fetters,* p. 277. On the Alien and Sedition Act prosecutions in general, see ibid.; Leonard W. Levy, *Legacy of Suppression: Freedom of Speech and Press in Early American History* (1960); Francis Wharton, *State Trials During the Administrations of Washington and Adams* (1849).

109 "monstrous attempt . . ." *Aurora,* March 17, 1800.

110 "in excuse . . ." 10 *Annals,* 6th Cong., 1st Sess., p. 117.

110 Marshall's observations, Marshall to James Marshall, April 4, 1800, JMP4p121.

110 "a [daily] falsehood . . ." Ibid.

111 "libels and satires . . ." JA to T. Pickering, Aug. 13, 1799, C. Adams, ed., *Works of John Adams,* vol. 9 (1856), p. 13.

111 "hardly in the infancy . . ." Smith, *Freedom Fetters,* p. 314.

112 "must prove . . ." Ibid., p. 325.

113 "sufficient general slander . . ." *Gazette of the United States,* April 24, 1798.

113 "the paymaster . . ." James T. Callender, *The Prospect Before Us,* pp. 126, 127.

113 "The reign . . ." Wharton, *State Trials,* pp. 688–90.

114 "Such papers . . ." TJ to JC, Oct. 6, 1799, TJWPF9p84.

114 "now firing . . ." JTC to TJ, March 14, 1800, TJPLC.

114 "An attempt . . ." J. Monroe to TJ, May 25, 1800, ibid.

114 "indignation . . ." Smith, *Freedom Fetters,* p. 343.

114 "that we shall not . . ." Ibid., p. 345.

114 "substantially defended" TJ to Monroe, May 26, 1800, TJWPF9p136.

115 "fact falsely . . ." Smith, *Freedom Fetters,* p. 347.

115 "a professed aristocrat" Ibid., p. 352.

115 "because it [the verdict] . . ." *Richmond Examiner,* June 6, 1800.

116 Marshall's later comments, see chap. 9, p. 212.

117   For TJ's view of his support for Callender, see DM3p332; for a contrary view, see Joseph J. Ellis, *Founding Brothers* (2000), pp. 208, 209, David McCullough, *John Adams* (2001), p. 584.

117   Marshall's disdain for Callender, Marshall to St. George Tucker, Nov. 18, 1800, JMP6p15.

6: "The Fangs of Jefferson"

118   "Were we to both . . ." MPp632.

118   "Besides my . . ." TJ to Monroe, March 26, 1800, TJPAL.

119   TJ and Madison discussed issues, TJ to Madison, Nov. 26, 1800, Smith, *Republic of Letters,* vol. 2, p. 1121.

119   For TJ's election predictions, see TJ to Madison, March 8, 1800, ibid., p. 1129.

121   "the overthrow . . ." AH to JJ, May 7, 1800, Syrett, *Hamilton Papers,* vol. 24, p. 465.

122   "the fangs of Jefferson" AH to T. Sedgwick, May 4, 1800, ibid., p. 453.

123   "economical government . . ." TJ to GG, Aug. 13, 1800, TJWPF9 p139.

123   "Shall I continue . . ." *Gazette of the United States,* Sept. 10, 1800.

123   "Can serious and reflecting men . . ." Willard S. Randall, *Thomas Jefferson,* p. 542.

123   "It has been so impossible . . ." TJ to Monroe, May 26, 1800, TJWPF9p136.

123   "the rational Christian . . ." TJ to BR, Sept. 23, 1800, ibid., p. 148.

124   "imprudent and brazened . . ." Brown, *John Adams,* p. 181.

125   For TJ's view of peace settlement, see TJ to Madison, Sept. 17, 1800, TJWPF9p144.

125   For Marshall's view, see Marshall to JA, Sept. 17, 1800, JMP4p279.

125   "converted themselves . . ." Marshall to RK, Sept. 20, 1800, ibid., p. 283.

126   "a firm, inviolable . . ." JESp275.

126   "disgusting egotism . . ." DM3p488.

126   "I wish . . ." Marshall to St. George Tucker, Nov. 18, 1800, JMP6p15.

127   "I believe . . ." Marshall to CCP, Nov. 20, 1800, ibid., p. 17.

127 "On your legislature . . ." Marshall to CCP, Nov. 22, 1800, ibid., p. 18.

127 "The election . . ." CP to TJ, Dec. 2, 1800, TJPLC.

129 "I understand . . ." TJ to AB, Dec. 15, 1800, TJWPF9p155.

129 "the operation . . ." TJ to Madison, Dec. 19, 1800, ibid., p. 158.

129 "the Feds appear . . ." TJ to Madison, Dec. 26, 1800, ibid., p. 161.

130 "I consider it . . ." Marshall to EC, Dec. 28, 1800, JMP6p45.

130 "undue foreign attachments . . ." Marshall to AH, Jan. 1, 1801, ibid., p. 46.

130 "Jefferson is . . ." AH to OW, Dec. 16, 1800, Syrett, *Hamilton Papers,* vol. 25, p. 257.

130 "Disgrace abroad . . ." AH to J. Bayard, Dec. 27, 1800, ibid., p. 277.

130 "To Mr. Jefferson . . ." Marshall to AH, Jan. 1, 1801, JMP6p46.

132 "utterly disclaim . . ." DM3p497.

132 "My personal friends . . ." AB to TJ, Dec. 23, 1800, TJPLC.

132 "The Federalists . . ." TJ to MJE, Jan. 4, 1801, TJWPF9p166.

133 "All the old patriots . . ." JA to E. Gerry, Dec. 30, 1800, Adams, *Adams Works,* vol. 9, pp. 577–78.

134 "Who shall . . ." John Marshall, *An Autobiographical Sketch,* p. 30.

134 "I had never before . . ." Ibid.

134 "of moderate disposition" TJ to Thomas Mann Randolph, Jan. 29, 1801, TJPMHS.

135 "there is such a mixture . . ." TJ to MJR, Jan. 26, 1801, ibid.

135 "At present . . ." Ibid.

135 "to exclude Jefferson . . ." DM3p504.

136 "Many attempts . . ." TJ to Monroe, Feb. 15, 1801, TJWPF9p179.

136 "the gales of monarchy . . ." TJ to JT, Feb. 15, 1801, TJPMHS.

136 "even if . . ." Ibid.

137 "I propose . . ." TJ to Marshall, March 2, 1801, JMP6p86.

137 "I shall . . ." Marshall to TJ, March 2, 1801, ibid., p. 87.

7: "The Least Dangerous" Branch

138 "meanly furnished . . ." George L. Haskins, *History of the Supreme Court of the United States,* vol. 2, pt. 1, *Foundations of Power: John Marshall, 1801–1815* (1981), p. 82.

140 "Of the importance . . ." Marshall to CCP, March 4, 1801, JMP6p89.

140 "So far as . . ." Marshall to RK, Feb. 26, 1801, ibid., p. 82.

140 "The democrats . . ." Marshall to CCP, March 4, 1801, p. 89.

140 "it is not difficult . . ." Ibid.

141 "animated by . . ." *Columbian Centinel,* March 4, 1801.

142 "The changes of . . ." DM4p17.

142 For TJ's inaugural address, see Adrienne Koch and William Peden, eds., *The Life and Selected Writings of Thomas Jefferson* (1944), pp. 321–25.

142 On TJ's meaning of "republicans and federalists," see TJ to Henry Knox, March 27, 1801, TJWPF9p236; TJ to John Dickinson, July 23, 1801, ibid., p. 281.

144 "It [the inaugural address] is . . ." Marshall to CCP, March 4, 1801, JMP6p89.

145 "The storm through which . . ." TJ to JD, March 6, 1801, TJWPF9p201.

145 "It is pleasant . . ." TJ to JW, March 21, 1801, TJPAL.

145 "The storm is over . . ." TJ to SA, March 29, 1801, TJWPF9p239.

145 "led hoodwinked . . ." TJ to JD, March 6, 1801, ibid., p. 201.

145 "subversion" TJ to JW, March 21, 1801, TJPAL.

147 "Mr. A crowded in . . ." TJ to Henry Knox, TJWPF9p237.

147 "It can never be . . ." WGB to TJ, March 16, 1801, TJPLC.

148 "legal oppression" TJ to John Eppes, March 27, 1801, TJPAL.

148 "have retreated . . ." Charles Warren, *The Supreme Court of the United States History,* vol. 1, *1789–1835* (1922), p. 193.

149*n* "The public . . ." TJ to GJ, March 27, 1801, TJWPF9p238.

150 Marshall's mortification, Marshall to James Marshall, March 18, 1801, JMP6p90.

150 "a friend of impartial justice . . ." Warren, *Supreme Court History,* vol. 1, p. 196.

150 "We can no longer . . ." TJ to JP, March 21, 1801, TJWPF9p218.

151 repeal of the Judiciary Act, TJ to Archibald Stuart, April 8, 1801, TJWPF9p247.

152*n* "silent acquiescence" see G. Edward White, *History of the Supreme Court of the United States,* vols. 3 & 4, *The Marshall Court and Cultural Change, 1815–35* (1988), pp. 184–91.

153 "bacon-face" Haskins, *History,* vol. 2, pt. 1, p. 96.

153 "busy, restless incendiary . . ." Ibid., p. 91.

154 prize case *Talbot v. Seeman,* 1 Cranch 1 (1801); for background on case, see Haskins, *History,* vol. 2, pt. 1, pp. 482–85; JESpp291–95; Warren, *Supreme Court History,* vol. 1, p. 199.

156 Congress alone possessed, Marshall overstated Congress's war powers. Under Article II of the Constitution, the president is commander-in-chief, a power that Jefferson himself was using at the time of *Talbot,* in authorizing the navy's defense of American commerce against attacks by Barbary pirates in North Africa.

157 "the least dangerous" *The Federalist,* introduction by E. Earle (1937) p. 504.

158 TJ's first State of the Union, Koch and Peden, *Jefferson's Life and Writings,* at p. 325.

159 *U.S. v. Schooner Peggy* 1 Cranch 103 (1801); for background on case, see Haskins, *History,* vol. 2, pt. 1, p. 162; JESpp296–98; Warren, *Supreme Court History,* vol. 1, p. 198.

160 "executive usurpation" Warren, *Supreme Court History,* vol. 1, p. 199.

161 "midnight judges" see chap. 8.

163 "have retired . . ." TJ to JD, Dec. 18, 1801, TJPLC.

163 "lopping off . . ." TJ to BR, Dec. 20, 1801, TJWPF9p345.

163 "the President's measure" Richard E. Ellis, *The Jeffersonian Crisis: Courts and Politics in the Young Republic* (1971), p. 45.

164 "There is no doubt . . ." Ibid.

165 "The fight over repeal . . ." Ibid., p. 46.

167 "restore our judiciary . . ." TJ to M. Volney, April 20, 1802, TJPLC.

167 "determined at all events . . ." Ellis, *Jeffersonian Crisis,* p. 57.

168 "Are the gentlemen . . ." Haskins, *History,* vol. 2, pt. 1, p. 168.

168 "essential defects . . ." Marshall to OW, April 5, 1802, JMP6p104.

168 "Our future duties . . ." Marshall to WP, April 6, 1802, ibid., p. 105. Marshall later had second thoughts about the new duties, but still said he would abide by the wishes of his colleagues; see Marshall to WP, April 19, 1802, ibid., p. 108.

169 letter to Bayard, Marshall to JB, April 12, 1802, ibid., p. 106.

169 face-to-face meetings with Bayard, JESp306.

169 "I am neither surprised . . ." Ibid., p. 307.

169 "I believe . . ." Ellis, *Jeffersonian Crisis,* p. 61.

170 "This is a subject . . ." Marshall to WP, April 19, 1802, JMP6p108; see also Marshall to WP, May 3, 1802, ibid., p. 117.

170 "The judiciary . . ." Haskins, *History,* vol. 2, pt. 1, p. 166.

171 *Stuart v. Laird* 1 Cranch 299 (1803); for background on case, see Ellis, *Jeffersonian Crisis,* pp. 63–65; Haskins, *History,* vol. 2, pt. 1, pp. 180, 181.

172 "There is so much . . ." Marshall to CCP, Nov. 21, 1802, JMP6p125.

8: Mr. Marbury's Missing Commission

173 For background on the Marbury case, see AB3pp101–56; Robert L. Clinton, *Marbury v. Madison and Judicial Review* (1989); Donald O. Dewey, *Marshall Versus Jefferson: the Political Background of Marbury v. Madison* (1970); George L. Haskins, *History of the Supreme Court of the United States,* vol. 2, pt. 1, *Foundations of Power: John Marshall, 1801–1815,* pp. 182–204; Charles F. Hobson, *The Great Chief Justice and the Rule of Law* (1996), pp. 47–71; JMP6pp160–87; JESpp309–26; Kathryn Turner, "The Midnight Judges," 109 *U. of Pa. L. R.* 494 (1961); Warren, *The Supreme Court of the United States History,* vol. 1, *1789–1835,* pp. 231–68.

174 John Marshall conceded, Marshall to James Marshall, March 18, 1801, JMP6p90.

175 "stone by stone" Haskins, vol. 2, pt. 1, p. 166.

176 "What think you . . ." Warren, *Supreme Court History,* vol. 1, p. 204.

176 "An attempt . . ." Ibid.

177 On the Pickering impeachment, see chap. 9.

177 "audacious attempt . . ." Dewey, *Marshall v. Jefferson,* p. 98.

178 For Lee's argument, see *Marbury,* 1 Cranch 137 (1803) at p. 138.

179 "did not remember certainly . . ." Ibid., p. 143.

179 "delicately situated" Ibid., p. 144.

180 "a fact which . . ." Ibid.

183 Marshall's opinion, 1 Cranch 137 (1803) at p. 154.

183 "peculiar delicacy . . ." Ibid.

183 "do the laws . . ." Ibid.

184 "He acts . . ." Ibid., p. 158.

184 "The very essence . . ." Ibid., 163.

184 "It is scarcely . . ." Ibid., p. 170.

185 "where specific duty . . ." Ibid., p. 167.

186 "The question . . ." Ibid., p. 176.

186 "It is emphatically . . ." Ibid., p. 177.

189 "The opinion . . ." TJ to AA, Sept. 11, 1804, TJWL&B10p88.

189 "This practice . . ." TJ to William Johnson, June 12, 1823, in T. J. Randolph, ed., *Memoirs, Correspondence and Private Papers of Thomas Jefferson*, vol. 4 (1829), pp. 377–82.

9: A "Bungling Way" to Remove Judges

192 "in silence" TJ to Levi Lincoln, Aug. 30, 1803, TJWL&B10p417.

192 "with as little debate . . ." TJ to W. C. Nicholas, Sept. 7, 1803, TJWPF10p10.

192 "No remedy . . ." WGB to TJ, Richard E. Ellis, *The Jeffersonian Crisis*, p. 21.

192 "My opinion . . ." TJ to GC, Dec. 31, 1803, TJPAL.

193 "the transmontane Goliath . . ." Ellis, *Jeffersonian Crisis*, p. 164.

193 For background on Pickering impeachment, see 8 *Annals of Congress*, 1st Sess., (1804); Ellis, *Jeffersonian Crisis*, pp. 69–75; George L. Haskins, *History of the Supreme Court of the United States*, vol. 2, pt. 1, *Foundations of Power*, pp. 211–14, 234–38; Lynn W. Turner, "The Impeachment of John Pickering," *American Historical Review*, April 1949.

194 "to the House . . ." Ellis, *Jeffersonian Crisis*, p. 71.

195 "This business . . ." Ibid., p. 72.

195 "If the facts . . ." Turner, "Impeachment," p. 493.

196 "Tomorrow . . ." Ibid., p. 503.

198 "have lent their influence . . ." TJ to CG, July 7, 1802, TJPLC.

198 "into a mobocracy . . ." Ellis, *Jeffersonian Crisis*, p. 80.

199 "Ought the seditious . . ." TJ to JN, May 13, 1803, TJPLC.

200 "Change the scene . . ." Ellis, *Jeffersonian Crisis*, p. 81.

200 For background on the Chase impeachment trial, see AB3 pp157–222; Raoul Berger, *Impeachment: The Constitutional Problems* (1973); Ellis, *Jeffersonian Crisis*, pp. 76–107; Haskins, *History*, vol. 2,

pt. 1, pp. 215–45; William H. Rehnquist, *Grand Inquests: The Historic Impeachments of Justice Samuel Chase and President Andrew Johnson* (1992); Warren, *Supreme Court History,* vol. 1, pp. 273–97.

201   For Chase's articles of impeachment, see *Annals of Congress* (8th Cong., 1st sess.)pp1237–40.

204   "Our Courts are filled . . ." *Evening Post,* Jan. 20, 1804.

204   "Admitting . . ." Marshall to SC, Jan. 23, 1805, JMP6p347.

205   "I think . . ." Ibid.

208   "a dangerous man . . ." Rehnquist, *Grand Inquests,* p. 19.

208   "it was the practice . . ." *New York Evening Post,* Feb. 6, 1805.

209   For the Chase trial, see *Annals,* 8th Cong., 2nd sess. (1805).

210   "the government . . ." Ibid., pp. 160, 161.

210   "No, Sir . . ." Ibid.

211   "monstrous pretension . . ." Ibid., p. 163.

211   "Nay . . ." Ibid., p. 251.

212   "If counsel . . ." Ibid., p. 264.

212   "Do you recollect . . ." Ibid., p. 266.

212   "I will . . ." Ibid.

212   "really discovered . . ." AB3p196.

213   Hopkinson argument, *Annals,* pp. 354–94.

214   "the unprincipled . . ." TJ to George Hay, June 19, 1807, TJWPF10p403.

214   "I see . . ." Rehnquist, *Grand Inquests,* p. 101.

215   "Our property . . ." *Annals,* p. 483.

215   Randolph's summation, Ibid., pp. 641–62.

215   "to say whether . . ." Ibid., p. 662.

216   "the Sergeant-at-Arms . . ." Ibid., p. 664.

216   For the Senate roll call, see ibid., pp. 664–69.

217   "It appears . . ." Ibid., p. 669.

218   "We did so . . ." Rehnquist, *Grand Inquests,* p. 110.

218   "a mere scarecrow" TJ to Thomas Ritchie, Dec. 25, 1820, TJWPF12p177.

219   "delivered a short . . ." Ellis, *Jeffersonian Crisis,* p. 105.

10: Treason Against the United States

220 For the background on the Burr conspiracy, see Thomas P. Abernethy, *The Burr Conspiracy* (1958); AB3pp274–342; James A. Cabell, *The Trial of Aaron Burr* (1900); Matthew L. Davis, *Memoirs of Aaron Burr with Miscellaneous Selections from his Correspondence,* vol. 2 (1837); George L. Haskins, *History of the Supreme Court of the United States,* vol. 2, pt. 1, *Foundations of Power,* pp. 246–311; Mary-Jo Kline, ed., *Political Correspondence and Public Papers of Aaron Burr,* vol. 2 (1983); Milton Lomask, *Aaron Burr: The Conspiracy and Years of Exile, 1805–1836* (1982); Walter F. McCaleb, *The Aaron Burr Conspiracy and A New Light on Aaron Burr* (1966); DM5pp215–370; David Robertson, *Reports of the Trials of Col. Aaron Burr,* 2 vols. (1808); JESpp348–74; Charles Warren, *The Supreme Court of the United States History,* vol. 1, *1789–1835,* pp. 301–15; JMP7pp3–165.

221 "gross irregularities . . ." Lomask, *Aaron Burr,* p. 15.

222 "How long . . ." Ibid., p. 75.

222 Anonymous letters, see DM5p234.

223 "The people . . ." Kline, ed., *Political Correspondence,* vol. 2, p. 986.

224 "drive the enemy . . ." Lomask, *Aaron Burr,* p. 158.

225 "to the main design . . ." Ibid., p. 168.

225 "strictly watched . . ." DM5p244.

225 "sundry persons" TJ proclamation, Nov. 27, 1806, TJWPF10p301.

226 "the criminal attempts . . ." TJ annual address, Dec. 12, 1806, TJWPF10pp311–12.

227 "projected enterprise . . ." TJ to JW, Jan. 3, 1807, ibid., p. 333.

227 For TJ's congressional address of Jan. 22, 1807, see TJWPF10 pp348–50.

228 "It not infrequently . . ." Warren, *Supreme Court History,* vol. 1, p. 305.

229 For Marshall's *Bollman* opinion, see 4 Cranch 75 (1807).

229 "It is the revision . . ." Ibid., p. 101.

230 "If war be . . ." Ibid., p. 126.

230 "engaged in . . ." Ibid., p. 135.

230 "institute fresh . . ." Ibid., p. 137.

231 "this once illustrious . . ." Lomask, *Aaron Burr,* p. 217.

232   Burr trial, *U.S. v. Burr,* 25 F. Cas. 1 (1807).

232   "I am absolutely . . ." Cabell, *Trial,* p. 9.

232   "to take . . ." Robertson, *Reports,* vol. 1, p. 4.

233   "innocent . . ." Ibid., p. 5.

233   "Alarms . . ." 25 Fed. Cas. p. 11.

234   "I do not . . ." Ibid., p. 12.

234   "War can . . ." Ibid., p. 13.

234   "The fact to be . . ." Ibid., p. 15.

235   "This insurrection . . ." TJ to JC, March 18, 1807, TJPAL.

235   A week later, TJ to GM, March 26, 1807, TJPMHS.

235   "The fact is . . ." TJ to JB, April 2, 1807, TJWPF10p382.

235   "As if an express . . ." TJ to WBG, April 20, 1807, ibid., pp. 383, 385.

236   "That there should be . . ." Ibid.

237   "to provide that . . ." TJ to GH, May 26, 1807, ibid., p. 395.

237   "as far above . . ." Ibid.

238   "This is a peculiar case . . ." Robertson, *Reports,* vol. 1, p. 128.

239   "perpetual philippics . . ." Ibid., p. 144.

239   "blood hounds . . ." Ibid., p. 145.

239   "in the heat of debate . . ." Ibid., p. 148.

239   "Shall we move . . ." TJ to GH, June 19, 1807, TJWPL&B11p228.

240   "as secretly as possible" TJ to CR, June 19, 1807, TJPMHS.

241   "that this demand . . ." 25 F. Cas. 34 (1807).

242   "that the purposes . . ." TJ to GH, June 12, 1807, TJWPF10p398.

242   "is written . . ." TJ note, n.d., ibid., pp. 406–07.

242   "divert the public attention . . ." Ibid.

243   "no exception . . ." TJ to GH, June 20, 1807, TJWPF10p404.

243   "could bandy him . . ." Ibid.

244   "strutted . . ." Lomask, *Aaron Burr,* p. 251.

244   "Your letter . . ." Kline, ed., *Political Correspondence,* p. 986.

245   "Aaron Burr . . ." Lomask, *Aaron Burr,* p. 254.

246   "How far . . ." Marshall to WC, June 29, 1807, JMP7p60.

246   "If these newspaper statements . . ." 25 F. Cas. 81 (1807).

246   "I have no objection . . ." Robertson, *Reports,* vol. 1, p. 378.

247   For Hay's opening speech, see ibid., pp. 433–51.

247   "much censured . . ." Ibid., p. 450.

248   "Would you begin . . ." Ibid., p. 454.

249 "they did not mean . . ." Ibid., p. 516.

250 "extrajudicial" Ibid., p. 555.

250 "the right and duty" Ibid., p. 584.

251 "The question . . ." Robertson, *Reports,* vol. 2, p. 64.

251 "Sir . . ." Ibid., p. 98.

252 "will o' the wisp treason . . ." Ibid., p. 337.

252 For Marshall's opinion, see 25 F. Cas. 159 (1807).

252 "must appear . . ." Ibid., p. 165.

253 "that the advising . . ." Ibid., p. 176.

253 "That this court . . ." Ibid., p. 179.

253 "general evil disposition" Robertson, *Reports,* vol. 1, p. 472.

254 "We of the jury . . ." Ibid., vol. 2, p. 550.

254 "There is but one . . ." GH to TJ, Aug. 11, 1807, TJPLC.

255 "The event . . ." TJ to GH, Sept. 4, 1807, ibid.

255 "If he is convicted . . ." TJ to GH, Sept. 4, 1807, TJWL&Bp360.

255 "As I do not . . ." TJ to GH, Sept. 7, 1807, ibid., p. 365.

256 "If defeated . . ." Ibid.

257 "My confidence . . ." GH to TJ, Oct. 15, 1807, TJPLC.

259 "fatigued & occupied . . ." Marshall to Richard Peters, Nov. 23, 1807, JMP7p165.

11: Final Battles

260 For background on riverbed (known as the *batture*) controversy, see George Dargo, *Jefferson's Louisiana: Politics and the Clash of Legal Traditions* (1975); W. B. Hatcher, *Edward Livingston* (1940); DM6pp55–73; JMP7pp276–88; TJWL&B18pp1–132.

261 "legal claimants . . ." DM6p57.

261 "a mere nullity" Ibid., p. 59.

262 "in my shops . . ." TJ to T. Kosciuszko, Feb. 26, 1810, TJWL&B 12p369.

262 "a general tavern" TJ to J. Monroe, Feb. 21, 1823, TJWPF12p276.

263 "not depending . . ." TJ to Madison, Oct. 15, 1810, TJWPF11p151.

264 "The subject . . ." GH to TJ, July 15, 1810, TJPLC.

264 For Marshall's opinion in *Livingston v. Jefferson,* see JMP7p282.

265 "are entitled . . ." Ibid., p. 284.

266   "pseudo-republican . . ." TJ to Henry Dearborn, July 16, 1810, TJWPF11p143.

267   "I love his laugh . . ." JS to S. Fay, Feb. 25, 1808, W. Story, ed., *Life and Letters of Joseph Story,* vol. 1 (1851), p. 167.

268   For background on *Martin v. Hunter's Lessee,* see George L. Haskins, *History of the Supreme Court of the United States,* vol. 2, pt. 1, *Foundations of Power,* pp. 357–65; JMP8pp108–26; G. Edward White, *History of the Supreme Court of the United States,* vols. 3 & 4, *The Marshall Court and Cultural Change, 1815–1835,* pp. 165–74.

268   "instructed . . ." Haskins, *History,* vol. 2, pt. 1, p. 362.

269   "No calamity . . ." *Hunter v. Martin,* 18 Va. 25 (1815).

269   On Marshall's intrusion, see White, *History,* vols. 3 & 4, pp. 167–73.

270   Story opinion in *Martin v. Hunter's Lessee,* 1 Wheat. 304 (1816).

271   "If there were . . ." Ibid., p. 348.

271   For background on *McCulloch v. Maryland,* see AB4pp282–327; John A. Garraty, ed., *Quarrels That Have Shaped the Constitution* (1962), pp. 37–56; JMP8pp254–80; JESpp440–46; Charles Warren, *The Supreme Court of the United States History,* vol. 1, 1789–1835, pp. 499–540; White, *History,* vols. 3 & 4, pp. 541–57.

274   Marshall opinion in *McCulloch v. Maryland,* 4 Wheat. 316 (1819).

274   "the various crises . . ." Ibid., p. 407.

275   "Let the end . . ." Ibid., p. 421.

275   "they may tax . . ." Ibid., p. 432.

276   "Our opinion . . ." Marshall to JS, March 24, 1819, JMP8p280.

276   "We shall be . . ." Marshall to BW, March 27, 1819, ibid., p. 281.

276   For background on essays about *McCulloch,* see Gerald Gunther, ed., *John Marshall's Defense of McCulloch v. Maryland* (1969); JMP8 pp282–87.

276   For "Amphictyon" essays, see Gunther, ed., *Marshall's Defense,* pp. 52–77.

276   "never could . . ." Ibid., p. 58.

277   For Marshall's essays, see JMP8pp287–309.

277   "not very unlike . . ." Marshall to JS, May 27, 1819, ibid., p. 314.

277   "some other essays . . ." Marshall to Bushrod Washington, May 6, 1819, JMP8p311.

277   For Roane's essays, see Gunther, ed., *Marshall's Defense,* pp. 106–54.

278   "a general letter . . ." Ibid., p. 110.

278 "I find myself . . ." Marshall to BW, June 17, 1819, JMP8p317.

278 For Marshall's new essays, see ibid., pp. 318–63.

278 "all of which . . ." JMP8p351.

278 "Let 'Hampden' . . ." Ibid., p. 363.

279 "with great approbation . . ." TJ to SR, Sept. 6, 1819, TJWPF12p135.

279 "a fire bell . . ." TJ to John Holmes, April 22, 1820, ibid., p. 158.

279 "dammed up . . ." JESp454.

279 "I consider it . . ." TJ to JH, April 22, 1820, TJWPF12p158.

280 "We scarcely . . ." *Richmond Enquirer,* March 7, 1820.

280 "The charter . . ." John Taylor, *Construction Construed and Constitutions Vindicated* (1820), p. ii.

280 "The judiciary of . . ." TJ to TR, Dec. 25, 1820, TJWPF12p177.

281 "The judiciary branch . . ." TJ to AT, Jan. 19, 1821, ibid., p. 196.

281 For background on *Cohens v. Virginia,* see AB4pp342–67; JMP9 pp106–47; JESpp456–62; Warren, *Supreme Court History,* vol. 1, pp. 541–64; White, *History,* vols. 3 & 4, pp. 504–24.

282 "to the existence . . ." *Richmond Enquirer,* March 23, 1821.

282 "The judicial control . . ." 6 Wheat. 264 (1821) at p. 371.

283 For Marshall's opinion, see ibid. at p. 375.

283 "that the Constitution . . ." Ibid., p. 377.

283 "A Constitution . . ." Ibid., p. 387.

284 "In war . . ." Ibid., pp. 413–14.

285 "The great object . . ." TJ to SR, March 9, 1821, TJWPF12p201.

285 "On the abstract . . ." Madison to SR, June 29, 1821, W. Rives and P. Ferdall, eds., *Letters and Other Writings of James Madison,* vol. 3 (1867), p. 222.

285 "a most monstrous . . ." *Richmond Enquirer,* May 25, 1821.

285 "feeds them" TJ to SR, March 9, 1821, TJWPF12p202.

285 "with a degree . . ." Marshall to JS, June 15, 1821, JMP9p167.

285 "For coarseness . . ." Ibid.

286 "obvious design . . ." JS to Marshall, June 27, 1821, ibid., p. 177.

286 "Our judges . . ." TJ to WJ, Sept. 28, 1820, TJWPF12p162.

286 "What you say . . ." Marshall to JS, July 13, 1821, JMP9p179.

287 "cooked up" TJ to SR, June 27, 1821, TJWPF12p202.

287 "It is a fatal heresy . . ." Ibid., p. 203.

287 "of the true theory . . ." *Southern Patriot,* March 31, 1821.

287 The best remedy TJ to JP, Dec. 26, 1821, TJWPF12p216.

288 "Old men . . ." Marshall to PM, Feb. 23, 1824, JMP10p5.

288 For background on *Gibbons v. Ogden,* see AB4pp397–450; JMP10pp7–34; JESpp473–80; White, *History,* vol. 1, pp. 568–84.

289 "on the eve . . ." 9 Wheat. 1 (1824) at p. 229.

290 "with a breadth . . ." *Wickard v. Filburn,* 317 U.S.111 (1942).

290 For Marshall's opinion, see 9 Wheat. 1 (1824) at p. 186.

290 "ingenious minds . . ." Ibid., p. 222.

290 For Johnson's concurrence, Ibid.

Epilogue

293 "Man, like the fruit . . ." TJ to HD, Aug. 17, 1821, TJWPF12p205.

294 "You and I . . ." JA to TJ, July 15, 1813, L. Cappon, ed., *Adams-Jefferson Letters,* vol. 2 (1959), p. 358.

294 For the Adams-Jefferson letters, see generally L. Cappon, *Adams-Jefferson Letters,* 2 vols. (1959); see also DM6pp93–106; Joseph J. Ellis, *American Sphinx: The Character of Thomas Jefferson* (1997), ch. 5, pp. 229–290.

294 "the consolidation . . ." TJ to WJ, March 4, 1823, TJWPF12p279.

294*n* For *Osborn v. Bank of the United States,* see 9 Wheat. 738 (1824).

295 For the Warren Court opinion, see *Cooper v. Aaron,* 358 U.S. 1 (1958).

295 On the Rehnquist Court commerce-clause rulings, see, e.g., *U.S. v. Lopez,* 514 U.S. 549 (1995); *U.S. v. Morrison,* 120 S. Ct. 1740 (2000), declaring unconstitutional the federal Violence Against Women Act of 1994.

296 For *Bush v. Gore,* see 531 U.S. 98 (2000).

297 "it was opened . . ." Interview with Jared Sparks, JMP10p283.

297 "right side of seventy" Marshall to Polly Marshall, Feb. 12, 1826, JMP10p273.

297 "A person . . ." Marshall to PM, March 12, 1826, p. 276.

298 "I am very much . . ." Marshall to P. Slaughter, Aug. 22, 1827, John Marshall Papers, Williamsburg, Va.

298 "I am surprised . . ." Marshall to James Marshall (son), undated, ibid.

298 "I was a little . . ." Marshall to JS, Nov. 26, 1826, JMP10p315.

299 "Should Jackson . . ." *Marylander,* March 22, 1828.

299   Marshall quickly issued Marshall to John Pleasants, March 29, 1828, reprinted in *Niles Weekly Register,* April 12, 1828.

299   "Mr. Madison . . ." Marshall to JS, Oct. 15, 1830, John Marshall Papers, Williamsburg, Va.

299   "repeated unwarrantable . . ." Marshall to HL, Oct. 25, 1830, ibid.

300   State of Georgia, *Worcester v. Georgia,* 6 Peters 515 (1832).

300   "My worn out frame . . ." Marshall to RP, April 30, 1835, John Marshall Papers, Williamsburg, Va.

300   "The events . . ." John Marshall, *An Autobiographical Sketch,* p. 3.

300   "the great . . ." AB4p592.

300   "gave him a rank . . ." JESp524.

300   *U.S. v. Nixon* 418 U.S. 683 (1974).

300   "the great . . ." Robert G. McCloskey, *The American Supreme Court* (1960), p. 16.

Acknowledgments

Many people contributed generously to this project. I begin with my agent, Esther Newberg, who offered encouragement throughout the process, from proposal to finished book. My editor at Simon & Schuster, Alice Mayhew, provided enthusiasm for the manuscript (when mine was sometimes waning) and her usual superb editorial skills. Roger Labrie, also at Simon & Schuster, gave consistently helpful editorial suggestions and the gentlest reminders of deadlines.

The staffs at the Alderman Library, University of Virginia, the Library of Congress, and the Massachusetts Historical Society were unfailingly helpful in expediting my research needs. I also want to thank the International Center for Jefferson Studies at Charlottesville for awarding me a travel grant in the summer of 1998, and its director, Douglas L. Wilson, for his support and insights.

At New York Law School, Deans Harry H. Wellington and Richard A. Matasar supported the project not only with kind words but also with summer research grants. My research needs were met expertly by the staff at the New York Law School library, particularly William R. Mills, who responded to my seemingly endless requests for more materials with consistent good cheer and professionalism, and Roy B. Basit, who handled the multitude of calls for interlibrary loans flawlessly. My student research assistants at New York Law School—Jennifer Barnes, Jacqueline Flug, Paul Kemnitzer, and Jennifer Weintraub—saved me many hours of work with their first-rate research. In the final months of the project, the computer skills of my faculty assistant, Cathy Jenkins, proved indispensable.

I was fortunate to have colleagues both at New York Law School and elsewhere who made excellent suggestions for the improvement of the manuscript, though the final version, is, of course, mine alone. At NYLS, I benefited from the editorial suggestions of Richard B. Bernstein, Annette Gordon-Reed, William P. LaPiana, and Edward A. Purcell, as well as the comments from other colleagues at a faculty seminar in which I presented a chapter of the manuscript. I also called upon the expertise of colleagues at other institutions: Charles F. Hobson, David T. Konig, R. Kent Newmyer, Peter S. Onuf, and G. Edward White.

Finally, I want to thank my family for providing encouragement and many helpful suggestions: my children, Sara, Lauren, and David; my son-in-law, Tom Irwin; and my nephew, Roger Simon. And, most of all, I want to thank my wife, Marcia, who, besides being a terrific editor, is a wonderful soulmate.

Index

About the Author

JAMES F. SIMON received a B.A. from Yale College and a law degree from the Yale Law School. He has served as correspondent and contributing editor of *Time* magazine, specializing in legal affairs. He is the author of several critically acclaimed judicial histories, including *The Antagonists: Felix Frankfurter, Hugo Black and Civil Liberties in Modern America* and *The Center Holds: The Power Struggle Inside the Rehnquist Court,* which was a *New York Times* Notable Book. Simon has been a Visiting Lecturer in American Studies at Yale University and a Harvard Fellow in Law and the Humanities at Harvard University. He is the Martin Professor of Law and Dean Emeritus at New York Law School.